COOKING BY THE GARDEN CALENDAR

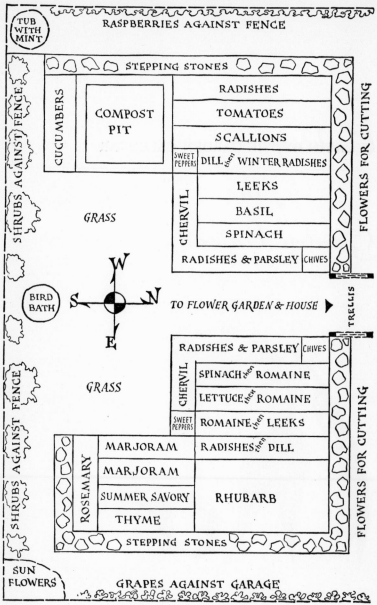

THE AUTHOR'S GARDEN

Cooking
by the
Garden Calendar

by RUTH A. MATSON

Illustrations by Margot Tomes

The American Garden Guild and

Doubleday & Company, Inc., Garden City, N.Y., 1955

LIBRARY OF CONGRESS CATALOG CARD NUMBER 55-5570

FOREWORD

This book is written for gardeners who like to eat and for eaters who like to garden. These fortunate folk take lively interest in good cooking, which makes good eating possible. Good eating in its turn spurs them to new achievements in their separate but allied arts. They have a further special bond in common: the proud produce of the garden patch, the orchard, and the herb corner. Cooks and gardeners are artists who supplement each other. Cooks can inspire gardeners to try something new that will make for imaginative cooking; gardeners can raise crops that are a challenge to the craft of the cook. When the two get together in the interests of good eating, both cookery and gardening are enriched and made zestful, and the dinner table is a happy gathering place.

That's the way of this book. As one who loves to garden, likes to cook, and is blessed with a hearty liking for good food, I write for gardening cooks and shall roam from kitchen to garden and back again, hoping to quicken their interest and awaken ideas rather than presuming to instruct in either cooking or gardening. There will be some hundred or so recipes not found in most standard cookbooks, and some garden directions. In general, however, I go on the assumption that both cook and gardener know their business and need only a hint to see the possibilities. I leave to others the esoterica of the hothouse and *la haute cuisine*, and dedicate myself to the interests of the down-to-earth, casual, even lazy connoisseur whose appreciation, like mine, is grounded in good appetite.

Because the seasons and the weather have a compelling influence on both cooking and gardening, I have organized my ideas from the point of view of "cooking by the garden calendar."

We start with February for a reason. January is too early for the gardener in us; it's in February we feel the first stirring of garden fever. More especially, February is a good month for soup, and a dozen excellent and unusual soups can be brewed from last year's surplus in cellar, storage pit, or freezer. These give a good take-off for thinking about garden planning for the coming spring.

Each chapter explores topics appropriate to the particular month. These groupings have been easy to select, for every month in the year brings something to entice the cook or put her on her mettle, whether it be the delights of asparagus in June or the problem of surplus frozen beans at the tired end of winter. For the sake of order, like crops have in general been kept together; we revel in the summer fruits, for example, in September even if some happen to ripen in August. Also for the sake of order, I stay pretty close to the climatic situation of the Northeast, with which I am most familiar, counting on knowledgeable gardening cooks of other parts of the country to apply their own seasonal variations in planting times, peak yields, and harvesting.

Within this general pattern there is considerable flexibility, even looseness. Not all soups are discussed in February—would you want Iced Broccoli Soup in a month of bitter cold? Carrots, strawberries, other fruits and vegetables appear and reappear, as seasonal variations in enjoying them may dictate. It's better so. If one read at one sitting everything there is to say about beets, emotional indigestion would be inevitable, and who would ever try Polish Beets? Which reminds me to add that for ease in following all of this the recipes for items printed in capital letters may be located by consulting the index.

Since this book draws on my own experience and interests, it omits much that others might consider important. Margarine, for one, which to my mind should be left to the preference of the individual cook, rather than endlessly repeating: "butter or margarine." Pressure cookers, for another. Anyone who reads this book will be aware that I haven't had much experience with pressure cookers but have experimented extensively with electric blenders. They'll see, too, at a glance that I'm an enthusiast for sour cream and for liqueurs with fruit.

I hope they'll see that this book has been fun to write, that I have found myself practically drooling over all the ideas for good eating that have come my way over the years. Friends and acquaintances have had a hand in this book, sharing recipes, combinations they've found good, garden and kitchen practices that save time and effort. It is with profound thanks to them that I close this note of introduction.

And so to February, a good month for soups.

R. A. M.

Cleveland, Ohio, 1954

CONTENTS

Foreword 5

I FEBRUARY: Soup's On 11
Adventuring with soups. The hospitable tureen. Notable soups of Europe. American classic. Magic with cans.

II MARCH: Too Late for Winter, Too Early for Spring 36
Those surplus vegetables. Herbs to the rescue. Carrots come out of the cellar. The Italians know their vegetables.

III APRIL: Fresh Variable Greens 52
A delicate hand with salads. Four and twenty greens. Soup from the babbling brook. Take one, they're for free. Month of the maple moon.

IV MAY: The Garden Comes to Life 71
Rhubarb, delight of the gardening cook. First crop of the season. The herbs grow green. Five most versatile herbs. The Big Ten. Herbs in the salad garden.

V JUNE: Eat 'Em Young 97
First mess of peas. Be fair to carrots. And be fair to spinach. Stretching the harvest of greens. Strawberry festival.

VI JULY: Start Picking 114
The fruit we sometimes forget. Raspberries—not for the birds. Blueberry season. Small fruits in the garden. A little of this and a little of that. Down with bean slicers.

VII AUGUST: The Problem of Plenty 132
Take a couple of cucumbers. The white heart of cauliflower. Scallop, Cymling or Pattypan. A lavish hand with vegetables. Queen of the crop.

VIII SEPTEMBER: Reveling in Fruit 157
Back yard orchard. Bite into a peach. Mix your own drinks. Fine kettle of fruit. Edible mushrooms only.

IX OCTOBER: They Needn't Be Dull 174
Those "winter keepers." Queen of the cabbages. The bread and butter vegetables, potatoes and onions. What about winter storage? Tail end of the garden.

X NOVEMBER: Fruits That Like Frost 199
Quince on a spree. An apple a day keeps the cook busy. The slow-ripening pear. Nutcracker suite. Cleanup for winter.

XI DECEMBER: Holiday Cooking from the
Garden's Bounty 218

Gifts for the gardening cook. Hearty fare from the casserole. If you didn't dry them, buy them. How good it smells! Night raid on the cranberry.

XII JANUARY: Parade of Winter Fruits 233

Oranges, frozen or flaming. Experimenting with fruit and liqueurs. Ambrosial pineapple. The strawberries we froze last summer. I can dream, can't I?

Bibliography 248

Index 249

CHAPTER I
February

SOUP'S ON

If you are cooking by the garden calendar, February is a good month to adventure with soup. It's winter, you can't do much in the garden. It's too early to start seeds indoors. A bowl of hot soup is a welcome sight, a stimulus not only to appetite but to dreams of growing garden specialties that will make for more and better soups. Can you, for example, chop a leek out of the frozen earth for hot Vichyssoise? If not, now is the time to jot down leeks on the seed order. Did you pot up some sweet basil to winter over as a house plant to furnish, among other virtues, a garnish for tomato soup? If not, it's a thought for next September.

Soup is what you make it any time of the year, and year round the gardening cook has a head start on making a fine thing of it. Most gardeners are secretly adventurers, and soup is fun to experiment with. Basic materials are at hand, or can be, in garden, storage bin, canning shelves, or deep freeze. The soup kettle is a lenient taskmaster, adapting itself to many ingredients, making few demands on the time of the busy gardener. Start the pot simmering before you go out to dig, and there's lunch ready when you come in. Bring out the tureen of a winter evening, and you can linger over the garden catalogues without supper spoiling.

A well-made soup does more than satisfy hunger, although it does that supremely well. A rich and hearty homemade soup served steaming from the hospitable tureen satisfies the creativity of the cook and suits the temper of the gardener; good soup gives the same sense of comfortable nourishment one feels in working the soil. It is an invitation to enjoy leisure after a hard day's work; it sets the stage for conviviality and relaxation.

Reputations have been built on a repertory of good soups, and a repertory is easy to develop. A few basic ideas, a little imagination, and a liking for tasting as you go along are all that's needed. That last is important: good soups are built on judicious seasoning, and the kettle that has not been dipped into from time to time usually betrays this neglect.

Soup can be simple. Take a potato and an onion from the cellar bin, a chunk of butter and some milk, and what have you? A soup so homely, so easy to make, that its virtue at first glance seems almost too humble: a minor miracle, a sound soup, hearty for winter appetites, a versatile soup that may be varied to suit one's taste and one's supply shelf.

Try it for a quick lunch with dark rye bread, or French bread cut in chunks, and bring out Cheddar cheese and apples and red grapes for dessert.

HOT POTATO SOUP

> 1 large potato
> 1 large onion
> 1 tablespoon butter
> 1 (or more) teaspoon salt
> ½ teaspoon fresh ground pepper
> 2 cups rich milk

Peel the potato and the onion, and slice them into a saucepan. Barely cover with cold water. Add a generous tablespoon of butter and the salt and pepper, then let them cook tender—about 10 to 15 minutes. Mash the vegetables to pulp with a potato masher (you may purée them through a sieve, but our household likes the grainy texture achieved by rough mashing). Add the milk; heat to boiling; serve at once.

> *Time required: 20 minutes*
> *Quantity produced: 1 quart*

As for the versatility: add a leek for a subtly sweetish flavor, or celery minced fine, or a fleck of thyme or dill or marjoram. A teaspoonful of caraway seeds may be simmered in Hot Potato Soup in true German tradition. Don't forget that leftover mashed potatoes are a perfectly acceptable substitute for the original potato. You can even make a good quick chowder by adding a can of minced clams to the basic recipe. With this, thyme, by all means.

Or you may turn to the famous potato soups of France for inspiration. The simplest is that of the French peasant, a more frugal version of the recipe given above, made with water instead of milk, with perhaps a handful of sorrel chopped into it—and always with dried bread afloat in the tureen. The bourgeois favorite, *potage Parmentier*, calls for less onion, more potato, consommé instead of milk or water, with a good pinch of chervil for dash. *La haute cuisine* produces Crème Vichyssoise (just as good hot in winter as chilled in summer—well, almost), rich with chicken stock and cream and speckled with chives.

CRÈME VICHYSSOISE

> 1 cup chopped onions
> 2 chopped leeks (the white part only)
> ¼ cup melted butter
> 2 cups raw diced potatoes
> 1 quart chicken stock
> Salt and white pepper
> 1 cup light cream
> 2 tablespoons chopped chives

Sauté the chopped onions and leeks in melted butter until they yellow—about 20 minutes. Add the potatoes; pour in the chicken stock. Add salt to taste, depending upon how salty the stock is, and also ¼ teaspoon white pepper. Cook until the potatoes are soft (10 to 15 minutes), then put through a fine sieve, food mill, or blender while hot. If the Vichyssoise is to be served hot, return the soup to the stove after sieving it, heat to boiling, remove from the fire, and add cream. Heat again, but do not boil. Pour into the hot tureen and sprinkle the chives on top. For cold Vichyssoise, chill the soup thoroughly before adding the cream.

> *Time required: 60 minutes, exclusive of chilling*
> *Quantity produced: about 2 quarts*

It's a good idea to add the cream only to the portion likely to be eaten at one time. The cream in Vichyssoise may sour quickly even if the soup is kept on ice; minus the cream, it will keep for days in the refrigerator, or it can be frozen.

Unless I've potted my own in October, I always find myself buying two pots of chives at this time of year. The first I try to pick up as soon as they appear in market, in order to select one with young growth, two inches high or less. In time, even with the severe cutting chives are subjected to in our household, it peters out and browns off, and another has to be bought to fill the gap until the garden chives come up. I've tried repotting the bulblets in a bigger pot, with more soil around the roots, and this does help prolong the life of the chives, but not enough. I'm now resigned to considering that first pot expendable.

The flavor of the leek is what gives Vichyssoise its subtlety, but this recipe makes an excellent soup using just the onions. One friend of mine varies her Vichyssoise with a combination of clam juice and chicken broth, an experiment I'd endorse except that I'm a purist about Vichyssoise.

Until I started raising my own leeks, it always seemed that when I had a craving for Vichyssoise, particularly on hot days in June or July, leeks were nowhere to be found in market. This frustration had a happy outcome: not only did I start growing my own crop, but also I found I could freeze the leek base for Vichyssoise. This is done in much the same way as celery: the leek is sliced, sautéed in butter for 5 minutes, then poured, butter and all, into a small container, to be chilled and frozen. Thus one can have a ready supply of leeks for Vichyssoise, complete with the measure of butter in which to sauté the onion. Chopped leeks, blanched for 5 minutes in boiling water with a little butter, may be frozen into ice cubes to be stored in the freezer, ready for soups or stews.

Small gardens force one to be ingenious. This year, in order to have two rows of leeks where one grew before, I'll plant my packets in drills three inches apart and shall thin the rows so that the maturing bulbs will be staggered. Each leek will have its minimum three-inch spread, and the two rows can be treated as one in hilling up the leeks for blanching. It ought to work!

Lacking enough room for all the leeks you want, try growing some in the perennial border. Pick a spot toward the back and mark it well lest you mistake the sprouting bulbs for blades of grass and weed them out. Let some go to flower—they make an interesting arrangement—and leave some in the ground for winter use.

Few casual gardeners seem to trouble with leeks, which are no trouble, really; perhaps they are put off by the association with onion. Actually the leek is mild, sweetish, and bland, with a pleasant aroma. French cooks are never without a generous supply; they use leeks in soups, ragouts, salads, or they prepare them like asparagus as a vegetable. Leeks that have been simmered in soup can be lifted out, chilled, and served as hors d'oeuvre with vinegar dressing. They add subtlety to split pea soup and to a purée of vegetables for cream soup. They are somewhat difficult to clean, since soil clings among the tight-furled leaves. If they are to be used cut up, it helps to split them lengthwise first, and scrub out any dirt with a little brush. Seedling leeks may appear in salad seasonably in June, when thinning time is at hand; now, in February, our month of soups, it's soup we're concentrating on.

Minestra benefits from a leek or two, although if you're without leeks, don't think you need to be without Minestra. With the high prices of even soup meat, a really excellent soup made without stock is a jewel. Such is Minestra, the Italian peasant's version of vegetable soup, thick, hearty, delicious—and rich without benefit of even the smell of a soupbone. This soup has such stature with Italians that it bears only the generic name "Minestra," meaning "the soup." Minestra in itself can make a full meal, with bread and butter and fruit for the children's lunch, or with Italian bread sticks and cheese and a glass of wine for the grownups. It has the added virtue of being extremely cheap and easy to make, and most home gardeners can turn to their own cellars for the chief ingredients.

MINESTRA

> 4 carrots
> 4 potatoes
> 4 stalks of celery with leaves
> a 2-inch wedge of cabbage
> 1 onion
> 1 leek (optional)
> 1 clove of garlic
> 1 small bunch of parsley
> 2 teaspoons salt
> 1 can kidney beans
> 2 tomatoes (or ½ can)
> 1 teaspoon minced basil (optional)
> 1 tablespoon olive oil
> ½ teaspoon pepper
> Grated Parmesan or Romano cheese

Wash and prepare the vegetables: carrots, potatoes, cabbage, and garlic go into the pot whole; the onion, parsley, leek, and celery should be coarsely chopped. Put these with the salt into 2 quarts of cold water; bring to a boil and simmer for 1 hour. Now take a wire potato masher and mash up the whole vegetables. Add the beans, tomatoes cut up but unpeeled, the basil, olive oil, and pepper. Give the soup at least another hour's simmering and turn it into the tureen. With each bowl pass a dish of grated mild cheese, and let each diner take his own generous sprinkling.

Time required: 2½ hours in all
Quantity produced: about 2½ quarts

Minestra is well worth making in large quantity. It tastes almost better heated up the second day and can be varied with tidbits from the larder. A handful of spinach, a cupful of peas or string beans, broccoli or cauliflower, or a small turnip or zucchini may be boiled in it or added to it. Rice or barley, spaghetti or noodles may be added to make it even heartier. You may try it with a pinch of rosemary or marjoram. And a frankfurter, sliced very thin, or some shredded ham gives further variation. I've sometimes made the last of a Minestra stretch from two servings to four by adding a can of chicken soup with rice.

The Italians have tricks with the soup pot which have an earthy simplicity we would do well to acquaint ourselves with. Garlic croutons (and why don't more home gardeners grow garlic? "Mother" bulbs, complete with growing instructions for separating and planting the clovelets, can be had from seedsmen or nurseries), made by browning bread cubes in butter into which a clove of garlic has been grated, are delicious in clear soup. Tomato juice, celery salt, and minced basil, with a clove or two, simmered with meat stock make a provocative thin soup, served with the characteristic sprinkling of cheese.

THE HOSPITABLE TUREEN There is a tangy herb soup that makes a zestful preamble to a winter dinner or a warming late snack for chill nights. (Watch out for it with highballs, however; it kills the taste of whiskey!)

HERB AND CELERY SOUP

> 1 tablespoon olive oil
> 1 teaspoon minced chives
> 1 cup finely minced celery
> 1 tablespoon minced parsley
> 4 cups beef or chicken broth
> 1 teaspoon fresh or ¼ teaspoon dried chervil
> ½ teaspoon fresh or ⅛ teaspoon dried tarragon
> ⅛ teaspoon nutmeg
> Salt, pepper
> ½ cup white wine
> Dry bread, toasted
> Romano or Parmesan cheese

Sauté in the olive oil very gently for 5 minutes the chives, celery, and parsley. Add the broth, chervil, tarragon, and nutmeg, and let all simmer until the celery is tender—about 20 minutes. Add salt unless the broth was highly seasoned, also a grind of pepper. At serving time, add the wine and reheat to boiling point. Put slices of toast in each bowl, sprinkle with cheese, then pour on the hot soup.

> Time required: 35 minutes
> Quantity produced: 1 quart

Another party soup, a bland, smooth, pale green concoction which will certainly fool many people at the first sip by its faintly herbal flavor, is Avocado Cream Soup. This takes a matter of 10 minutes to prepare if you have a blender. If not, the avocado must be sieved into the hot stock and given a turn with a rotary egg beater after the cream has been added. Proponents of this soup claim that half clam and half chicken broth turn Avocado Cream Soup into an epicure's delight. The soup is good served cold, too.

AVOCADO CREAM SOUP

> 2 cups chicken stock
> 1 cup cream
> 1 large, ripe avocado
> 2 tablespoons sherry
> ¼ avocado for garnish

Set the stock to heat in a saucepan while you put the cream in the blender and add to it the avocado scooped out with a spoon. Blend it only 15 seconds; prolonged blending seems to take flavor from delicate foods like avocado. Pour the avocado cream into the hot stock (I save a little stock to dilute the cream left in the bottom of the blender, so that none of the blend is wasted). Reheat just to boiling, add the sherry, and serve with thin slices of avocado for garnish.

> *Time required: 10 minutes*
> *Quantity produced: 1 quart*

A flair for homemade soup makes possible entertaining with distinction. The fat-bellied tureen is the nucleus, its steaming contents a meal in itself. With salad, interesting breadstuffs, and fruit and cheese for dessert, the stage is set for informal companionability. Conversation doesn't lag when a good soup is the center of attraction; such meals inspire good talk as well as good appetite. In winter, Sunday suppers or after-theater parties where guests can carry their bowls to the fireside; in summer, supper on the terrace or a back-yard picnic: soup adapts itself to any season, any spot.

Winter or summer, the discriminating hostess can ring many changes in her menu without monotony and without abandoning the basic pattern. Minestra (you can boil baby meatballs in it for extra heartiness), bread sticks and pizza, with a tossed salad featuring curly endive, spinach leaves, and slivers of green pepper, Bel Paese and Gorgonzola cheese, with a big bowl of green, red, and black grapes—such a supper is good, hot weather or cold. For a summer supper in the garden, Vichyssoise, smooth and cold, with herb biscuits or brioches, a salad of cooked vegetables marinated with shredded ham and chicken, strawberries to dip in powdered sugar. Or cold clear Russian Bortsch, with cucumber sandwiches, wedges of Cheddar cheese, and a dessert of peaches, with almonds to crack. For winter, there's Polish Bortsch, Lentil Soup, black bean soup, Fish Chowder, onion soup. The possibilities are challenging.

So too with breads: garlic bread, pumpernickel, corn muffins, popovers, rye crisp, sea toast, Holland rusks. And salads: tossed salad with all its variations, Caesar salad, tomato aspic, string bean salad, mixed vegetable salad.

Apart from the pleasure entertaining with soup gives to the guests, there's pleasure for the hostess in its making. Soup is relaxing to make; a few minutes' preparation early in the morning, and one can go about the business of the day, secure in the knowledge that the soup can safely be left to its own devices for long periods and that the necessary additions and tastings can be attended to pretty much on one's own time. There's a sensuous satisfaction, too, in its quiet simmering and rich aroma, which gathers strength as the soup nears perfection. Indeed, soup-making can put the hostess in a party mood. Perhaps that is one reason why I seldom find myself making soup in a pressure cooker as some prefer: I miss the genial and leisurely atmosphere which pervades the kitchen when a good soup is brewing on the back burner.

Europe offers us a long line of noble soups to inspire our culinary artistry and our gardening energy and to reward our thrift in storing and preserving our surplus harvest. Bortsch, for example, Russian or Polish, for the beets in the root cellar (if we're lucky enough to have one in these days of steam heat). Polish Bortsch is enough of an undertaking to make it worth while to do up a big batch so that some can be frozen.

POLISH BORTSCH

> 10 small beets
> 1 cup mild vinegar
> 1½ pounds soup beef, meat and bones
> 3 teaspoons salt
> 1 big onion

1 leek
1 carrot
1 stalk celery
4 sprigs parsley
2 tablespoons butter
1 tablespoon flour
6 peppercorns
2 bay leaves
¼ pound smoked pork sausage (optional)
1 cup sour cream

Save out 1 beet; scrape the rest and chip them into the vinegar mixed with 1 cup of cold water to soak for 3 hours. Meanwhile cover the soup meat with 3 quarts of cold water and bring to a boil, skimming as needed. Add 2 teaspoons of the salt and simmer for 3 hours. Slice and dice the onion, leek, carrot, celery, and mince the parsley. Fry all these in the butter in another soup pot. When they are lightly browned, stir in the flour, lift the beets from the vinegar, and add them to the brew along with the peppercorns, bay leaf, and a teaspoon of salt. Cover with broth from the stewing meat and simmer until the vegetables are tender—about 20 minutes. Now the soup is ready to assemble: strain the remaining broth into the vegetables; add the soup meat, sliced thick, and the sausage, sliced thin. Scrape and grate the tenth beet, raw, into the soup to color it; add a tablespoon of the vinegar and taste for more salt or vinegar. Boil up the soup for 10 minutes, then serve, garnishing each bowl with a good tablespoon of sour cream.

Time required: 4½ hours, on and off
Quantity produced: 4 quarts

Also for the surplus beets is Russian Bortsch, epitome of beet soups. This translucent, ruby-colored soup, always served flanked by a dish of sour cream to be spooned into the soup bowl, is superb, winter or summer, hot or cold. For a February after-the-concert supper party: Bortsch steaming in the tureen, with the glistening sour cream beside it, and platters of cheese and breads to go with it. In summer, chilled, with floating cucumber slices or, surprising and surprisingly good, served cold with a side dish of hot boiled potatoes, which you mash into the soup and smother with sour cream. Russian Bortsch is easy to prepare and, like Polish Bortsch, is worth making in large batches, since in the refrigerator it will keep for 3 weeks or more, and it also freezes well.

RUSSIAN BORTSCH

> 3 pounds beets
> 1 large onion
> 1 tablespoon salt
> 6–8 tablespoons sugar
> 6 tablespoons lemon juice
> 4 eggs
> 1 cup sour cream

Pare the beets, peel the onion, and slice them thin into a large kettle. Add 5 quarts of water. Boil for 10 minutes, then simmer for 1½ hours. Strain out the liquid (discarding beets and onion), and add the salt, sugar, and lemon juice. At this point tasting is in order. Start with less than the amount of salt, sugar, and lemon juice recommended, and keep tasting as you add each, until you achieve a flavor just right for your palate. Now beat the eggs in a large bowl, and into them pour the hot soup very slowly to prevent curdling.

The Bortsch is now ready to be reheated to serve hot. If cold Bortsch is your dish, remember that Bortsch must be cooled gradually before refrigerating. Set the kettle in a large pan of cold water, and as the water warms, change it until the soup is cool. Then pop it into the refrigerator. Serve with sour cream as garnish.

> Time required: 2½ hours
> Quantity produced: about 5 quarts

Sister soup to Polish Bortsch is Hungarian Chicken Pot. This is really a soup stew, a hearty meal in itself. It boasts 10 vegetables and 8 herbs in the making, which endears it to gardening cooks. To enjoy it properly, it should be ladled from the tureen into big shallow soup bowls, and a "bone plate" should be at hand, for part of the delight of it is to pull off with fork and spoon (of course fingers are better if allowed) the tidbits of chicken from the bones of the wings with which the soup is made. I make Hungarian Chicken Pot in my big 2-gallon soup kettle for buffet suppers for 12 or 14; what is left goes into the freezer for another day. Don't be alarmed by the list of ingredients; what would be irksome to prepare is recommended in cans.

HUNGARIAN CHICKEN POT

> 4 pounds backs and necks of chicken
> 4 pounds chicken wings
> 2 pounds chicken giblets
> 2 big onions
> 2 cloves garlic
> 3 stalks celery with tops
> ¼ cup parsley sprigs
> ½ cup Scotch barley
> 1 cup chopped celery
> 1 can kidney beans
> 1 can tomatoes
> ¼ pound spinach, broken raw
> 1 bay leaf
> 8 peppercorns
> 4 cloves
> 6 allspice
> ½ teaspoon dried marjoram
> ½ teaspoon dried chervil
> 1 package frozen peas
> 1 can tiny boiled onions
> 1 can tiny boiled potatoes
> Salt, pepper, paprika

Put in a big pot the chicken backs, necks, wing tips, and giblets. Peel the onions and garlic and throw them in whole, also the celery stalks and parsley. Cover with 6 quarts of water; add 2 tablespoons of salt. Let this brew come to a boil, then simmer for 1½ hours.

Drain the stock into another big pot and cool the chicken enough to handle comfortably. All bits of chicken from necks and backs go back into the soup; also the giblets, after trimming and cubing. The onion and celery, if retrieved, can be mashed and added. The bones can be disposed of.

Assemble the vegetables and spices for the second stage of cooking: barley, celery, kidney beans, tomatoes, and spinach go in now, along with the bay leaf, peppercorns, cloves, allspice, marjoram, and chervil. Let the soup boil up, and then simmer for another hour. At this time put in the chicken wings dusted with paprika and cook for 1 hour more.

Last stage is to toss in the peas, onions, and potatoes, drained of juice, for a final 10 minutes of cooking. Churn the soup around as you ladle it into the tureen, to distribute all the delectable tidbits fairly.

> *Time required: 4½ hours, over all; attention required*
> *intermittently*
> *Quantity produced: 2 gallons*

It always gives me a catch of surprise to find how often very good cooks shy away from making French Onion Soup, as if it were a specialty mysterious and difficult to achieve. This superb soup, perfect for crackling winter days and nights, is in fact of ABC simplicity. French peasants toss a simple version together in a few minutes: a couple of onions browned in a spoonful of fat, boiled up with water, and ladled out upon dry stale bread sprinkled with cheese. No fuss about brewing a basic stock, choosing a special cheese and melting it under the broiler.

I sometimes suspect that these rituals which have come to surround onion soup derive partly from the fact that it is so good there must be some trick to it, and partly from the pretentious efforts of some hostesses to make a cult of this honest and humble potage.

French Onion Soup deserves better than that. It deserves to be at the spoon's tip of every discerning housewife, for family supping, for company dining, for a hearty preamble to a light lunch, for midnight snacks. Remember it come April and October, for a bowl of onion soup with bread and cheese, eaten on the back steps between bouts with the engrossing garden chores of spring and fall, is a thing of revitalizing cheer.

Let's begin by dissipating some of the popular misconceptions about it: any kind of onion will serve, with ordinary yellow onions holding perhaps a slight edge because of their pungent flavor; any kind of stock or broth may be used, beef, veal, chicken, homemade, canned, or bouillon cube (a rich home-brewed beef stock, if at hand, is to be preferred). Any mild dry cheese will do, Gruyère, Swiss, or Parmesan being the most popular with the French; any kind of light bread is all right, toasted or not, just so it be thoroughly stale. The French, of course, use French bread.

Three practical principles affect the success of your onion soup. You want it a rich dark brown for aesthetic effect: brown the onions thoroughly; some of them should be crisped. You want a soup with body, with odoriferous flavor: let the onions simmer in the stock for 30 minutes. You don't want the bread mushy: use a light bread, good and stale, and once it has been drenched with the boiling soup, get it to the diner as fast as you can. And by the way, onion soup improves with keeping—you may make it the day before.

FRENCH ONION SOUP

> 4 medium-sized onions
> 3 tablespoons butter or drippings
> 4 cups stock or broth
> Salt and pepper
> Thick slices of stale bread
> ½ cup grated mild cheese

Slice the onions into the butter in a heavy saucepan and brown them thoroughly; some can be allowed to fry crisp. Add the stock to the onions and simmer for 30 minutes. See that the stock is properly salted and peppered. The bread should be well dried in the oven or toasted. When ready to serve, lay bread slices in the heated tureen or in individual bowls, sprinkle them generously with grated cheese, and pour on the boiling soup. This will melt the cheese instantly. (More cheese may be passed at table.) Serve immediately.

Time required: 50 minutes
Quantity produced: about 1 quart

The rich brown flecks of onion in onion soup remind me that well-browned onions make a superb flavoring and coloring for any meat soup. They can be browned when you have time, in as little fat as possible. Let them get crisp and crumbly. Then store them in a jar in the refrigerator, ready when needed.

Onions come into their own in winter, as home gardeners who store their own well know. And the cook, knowing her onions, can challenge the home gardener to try, for the sake of good eating, something besides the standard white and yellow globes: for roasting, for French frying, for salads, and for onion rings to scatter on sliced tomatoes, the big sweet Spanish or Bermuda onions; the beautiful and juicy red onion for a touch of color in a tossed green salad; for boiling and creaming, the little white globe onion that keeps its shape after cooking; the miniature white silverskins for pickling; shallots, the little brown onions, for a French touch in soups and stews.

The Danes make a bland and delicate cauliflower soup, an excellent dinner soup because, while thick, it is not too hearty to precede the roast. At this time of year you'll have to rely on the market or the freezer for the chief ingredient.

DANISH CAULIFLOWER SOUP

> 1 large cauliflower (2 frozen packages)
> 2 cups meat stock (veal, beef, or chicken)
> 1 tablespoon butter
> 2 tablespoons flour
> 1 egg yolk
> 1 teaspoon salt

Wash the cauliflower and boil it in 2 cups of salted water until it is just tender; drain it, saving the water, and cut off 6 or 8 of the most perfect flowerets for garnish in the tureen. Now, if you own a blender, all is simple: stock, butter, flour, cauliflower, and salt go in all at once; when blended, stir in the cauliflower water and let all boil up. Without a blender, heat the butter and flour, stir in the stock and cauliflower water, press the cauliflower through a sieve into the soup, and let it come to a boil. Either way, just before serving, remove the soup from the stove and stir in gradually the beaten egg yolk; keep the soup hot, but do not let it boil again. Put the flowerets in the tureen for garnish; pour on the hot soup.

Time required: 30 minutes
Quantity produced: 1 quart

The neighboring Germans make a fine rich winter soup which I commend to devotees of the hospitable tureen. Lentil Soup, which rightly should be as much a stand-by as split pea soup, is far too little known and appreciated on our shores. There is added virtue in reminding ourselves of Lentil Soup in these days of rising food costs, for all that is needed to provide the core of a hearty supper for six is a few cents' worth of lentils, an onion, a carrot and a stalk of celery, and a half dozen frankfurters. Not even a ham bone is required to enhance the flavor, although it won't come amiss if one is at hand. The rest of the meal should conform to the essential simplicity of the soup: chunks of bread and cheese, with raw carrots, green pepper strips and celery, make an ample supper. For Sunday supper parties, Lentil Soup with pumpernickel bread and a tossed salad, followed by a slab of cheesecake, is not only *echt Deutsch* but delicious.

LENTIL SOUP

> 2 cups lentils
> 1 onion, chopped
> 1 stalk of celery, sliced
> 1 whole carrot, scraped
> 1½ tablespoons salt
> 6 frankfurters
> 2 tablespoons vinegar

Do not soak the lentils, but rinse them in a bowl of cold water, picking out any black ones. Put them in a soup kettle with 2 quarts of water and the remaining vegetables. Add the salt; let the soup boil up and then simmer for 2 to 3 hours, or until the lentils mash easily. The onion and celery will have disintegrated; mash the carrot and return it to the pot. Slice the frankfurters and heat them in the soup; add the vinegar; turn it all into the tureen and send it steaming to the table.

Time required: 3 hours
Quantity produced: about 2 quarts

One would think from the recipes thus far presented that only Europeans know how to make a worthy soup. We have some good ones of our own, of course: our chowders, our gumbos, our cream of corn. But for specialty-of-the-house soups that lift the lowliest vegetable to the stature of a gastronomical experience, we find our highest inspiration in the great nationality soups which originated on the farms and in the gardens of the Continent. When we create our own soups on the pattern of these masterpieces of good eating, we feel a kinship with the gardening cooks who originated them, a kind of world fellowship of the tureen.

To round out the repertory of February soups, here are three American specialties: Corn-Curry Soup, New England Black Bean Soup, and Fish Chowder.

Corn-Curry Soup is a delicate and subtle variation upon the theme of cream of corn and can be made in a jiffy in a blender. It's an ideal dish for a soup-and-salad luncheon, and ideal for winter, since it is best made with canned cream-style corn, or frozen kernel corn, preferably of the golden varieties.

New England Black Bean Soup is a classic. Such excellent black bean soup comes in cans that I fear it has made the home brewing of black bean soup almost extinct, but to be a real specialty of the house, it, like split pea and Lentil Soup, should be homemade. The black beans are sometimes hard to find in market. S. S. Pierce & Co. of Boston can of course be relied upon for black beans, and the wholesale house of Seeman Brothers carries them under the

White Rose label. You can inquire about retail outlets in your vicinity.

I had such a hunt to locate black beans in my city of a million that it occurred to me to promote a minor renaissance of this historic favorite by suggesting that gardening cooks raise their own. Alas, the black bean is as elusive horticulturally as it is gastronomically. I have been able to discover that it is the black turtle soup bean and not listed in any one of a score of catalogues I investigated. This bean is a very old variety—introduced in this country as early as 1832—and is grown as a field crop and matures too slowly to be useful in our northern latitudes, even if one had the space and the urge to try. It does have some alluring synonyms: black Spanish, Brazilian running bean, Tampico, Venezuelan.

I doubt if any of the black-seeded wax beans, such as Pencil Pod or Sure Crop Wax, would provide the distinctive flavor and greenish color so characteristic of the true New England Black Bean Soup. So my little excursion into the idea of growing one's own black beans must be abandoned. We'll leave the purveying to Seeman Brothers and S. S. Pierce.

CORN-CURRY SOUP

> 2 cups canned cream-style corn or frozen kernel corn
> ½ cup milk
> ½ teaspoon salt
> ¼ teaspoon fresh-ground pepper
> 1 tablespoon finely minced onion
> ½ teaspoon curry powder
> 1 cup thin cream
> 1 tablespoon butter
> Sprinkling of paprika

Combine corn, milk, salt, pepper, and onion and simmer gently 10 minutes. Press through a strainer, mashing all corn grains. Discard only the skins. Mix curry with 1 teaspoon of the mixture and stir it in; add cream and butter. Before serving, sprinkle with paprika. If you have a blender, all ingredients except the cream

and butter can be blended together and then simmered gently with
the butter, with the cream added gradually at the last.

Time required: about 20 minutes

Quantity produced: 1 quart

NEW ENGLAND BLACK BEAN SOUP

> 1½ cups black beans
> 1 medium onion, chopped
> 2 tablespoons rendered salt pork fat
> 1 ham bone
> 1 carrot
> ½ cup chopped celery
> 4 sprigs parsley
> 1 bay leaf
> 2 cloves
> 2 allspice
> 2 teaspoons salt
> 2 teaspoons flour
> 2 teaspoons butter
> ¼ teaspoon cayenne pepper
> ½ cup sherry

For garnish:
> 2 hard-cooked eggs
> ½ lemon, sliced thin
> 1 tablespoon chopped parsley

Soak the beans overnight in cold water. In the morning sauté the
onion to a light brown in the salt pork fat: do this in the soup
kettle. Drain the beans into the kettle, add the ham bone, and
cover with 6 cups of cold water. Put in also the carrot, celery, parsley, spices, and 2 teaspoons of salt for a start. Bring the soup to
a boil and then simmer for 3 hours, or until the beans are tender
enough to mash. More water may be added if the soup gets too
thick. Remove the ham bone and strain the soup through a food
mill or fine sieve into a clean kettle; thicken it with the flour and
butter rubbed together; add the cayenne pepper and let it come
to a boil. Taste for salt; add the sherry just before serving.

When ready to serve, pour the soup into a heated tureen. On top sprinkle the eggs, coarsely chopped, and float the lemon slices dotted with parsley.

Time required: 3½ hours cooking
Quantity produced: about 2 quarts

Fish Chowder slips into a gardening cookbook because it is one of the most satisfying one-dish meals there is and because it wouldn't be itself without the potatoes, onion, parsley, and herbs that are staples with the ardent gardening cook.

Fish Chowder is one of those concoctions for which everyone has his own hotly defended method of preparation; this one is of New England derivation, evolved along the shores of Connecticut. It stands the test of good eating in any part of the country where fresh, firm, white-fleshed fish is available in market. Avoid rich or oily fish: use cod, haddock, or flounder for choice. Chowder may be made with frozen fillets, but for perfection you should start with a 3- to 4-pound fish and have the fishmonger fillet it, giving you the head, tail, bones, and trimmings for a court bouillon. It gives a little extra trouble, but it's well worth it in the flavor of the finished product. Don't forget that experienced New England chowder addicts tell you that chowder improves with age; you'll do well to make it a day ahead.

FISH CHOWDER

> 3- to 4-pound cod, haddock, or flounder, with trim-
> mings
> 2 onions
> 2 sprigs parsley
> 1 stalk celery
> 6 peppercorns
> ½ bay leaf
> ¼ teaspoon thyme
> Pinch of mace
> ¼ pound salt pork, diced small
> 3 cups diced potatoes

¼ cup chopped celery leaves
1 tablespoon minced parsley
4 cups rich milk
2 tablespoons butter
Salt and pepper

Start with the court bouillon: to 2½ cups salted water add the fish bones, head (omit if squeamish), tail, and trimmings, also a slice of onion, the parsley and celery, and the spices—peppercorns, bay leaf, thyme, mace. Let this simmer for 10 minutes while you fry the salt pork to a golden brown in the bottom of the soup pot. As the pork begins to brown, chop in the remaining onion and let it take color. Meanwhile cube the potatoes and cut the raw fish in cubes to match.

Now drain the fish stock into the kettle with the salt pork and onions, add the potatoes and celery leaves with a teaspoon of salt, and boil all for 10 minutes. Then the fish cubes and minced parsley go in, to simmer for another 10 minutes. The final step is to add the milk and bring the chowder to a boil. Taste it for salt; it will probably need another ½ teaspoon or so. Before serving, add the butter and a grind of pepper.

Time required: 50 minutes
Quantity produced: about 2 quarts

If you keep a can of Norwegian *fiskeboller* on the emergency shelf, a couple of unexpected guests can always be accommodated on chowder night merely by adding the *fiskeboller*, juice and all, to the chowder at the last minute. These shapely little white fish cakes are delicately seasoned and add a new note of flavor to the whole dish.

Pilot biscuits, sea toast (try it buttered and oven-browned), or any unsweetened soda cracker are standard equipment with chowder, but for a dressed-up supper, corn sticks or garlic bread make a good addition. With the "usual"—tossed green salad, cheese and coffee and fruit—you have a feast.

MAGIC WITH CANS   In summer, when chives, a few spinach leaves, a green pepper, a cucumber are to be had for the short trip

them now? Will the family rebel at seeing plain buttered beets or Harvard beets again? Maybe some mushrooms or walnuts with the beans will break the monotony?

One thing is sure: this is the month to sit down with our two selves and let the cook check the enthusiasm of the gardener. An honest look at the family's taste in foods is in order, and it should be done pencil in hand. If, for example, we accept the experts' estimate that a family of four eats 60 quarts of beans a year and we're a below-average bean family, now is the time to aim at a bushel-and-a-half crop instead of a two-bushel crop. This would mean cutting the seed order from two pounds to a pound and a half. With the decision firmly made in March, the temptation to succumb to the charms of the easy-growing snap bean will be easier to resist in the expansive flush of spring-planting fever, when the gardener in us gets the upper hand. If it's beets we tire of, perhaps one ounce of seed instead of two—but don't forget the joys of those first early beet greens.

But that's for the future; the beets we have with us always. Don't underestimate the modest beet, at that; it's a more versatile vegetable than is sometimes supposed. See what happens when you treat it as the Poles do, to sour cream. Whether your beets are canned, frozen, or stored raw, Polish Beets are an answer to the winter wail, "What shall we have for a vegetable today?" Polish Beets are delicious and different; they are rich and smooth and dress up a simple meal; indeed, they are worthy fare for a company dinner.

POLISH BEETS

> 2 cups cooked beets (about 12 smallish ones)
> 2 tablespoons sugar
> 2 tablespoons vinegar
> 1 tablespoon flour
> 2 tablespoons butter
> ½ teaspoon salt
> ¼ teaspoon pepper
> ½ cup sour cream

Grate the beets, or mash them fine with a fork. Put them in a saucepan; sprinkle with the sugar, vinegar, and flour (don't let it lump); add the butter, salt, and pepper and set the mixture to heat thoroughly. Stir in the sour cream, and when all is piping hot (but never boiling), the dish is ready.

Time required: 15 minutes
Quantity produced: 4 servings

Have you tried tiny boiled beets, whole, on toothpicks, to serve as canapés with a dip of sour cream? If not, since it's March, buy a can to try. If you like them this way, you can plan to do some June thinning of the beet row when the little beets are cherry-sized. Use the tops for boiled greens; cook the baby beets whole for 20 to 25 minutes in salted water with a dash of sugar and a slice of onion. When they're done, plunge them in iced water—they won't need their skins slipped off—and pack them in containers to lay away in the freezer against next winter.

The flavor of oranges is another booster for beets. The sweet Orange Sauce can be prepared in the morning, ready for the diced beets in the evening.

BEETS IN ORANGE SAUCE

> 2 tablespoons butter
> 3 tablespoons brown sugar
> 2 tablespoons cornstarch
> 1 cup orange juice
> ¼ cup lemon juice
> 2 tablespoons grated orange peel
> 1 tablespoon grated lemon peel
> ¼ teaspoon salt
> ¼ teaspoon paprika
> 2½ cups diced or julienne beets

Melt the butter in a double boiler and blend smooth with a mixture of the brown sugar and cornstarch. Add the orange and lemon juice; grate in the orange and lemon rind and add the seasonings. Stir constantly until the sauce thickens. Come dinnertime, add the beets and heat thoroughly.

Time required: 20 minutes
Quantity produced: 4 servings

You can give winter beets a springtime flavor by cooking them with lettuce, parsley, and chives. This method is an excellent one to remind you of the delights of the young beets as they will come from the garden; it capitalizes upon native freshness of flavor. If you cook beets this way next July or August, omit the sugar, they will not need it. In winter, however, nearly all vegetables benefit from a dash of sugar in the cooking. For a dozen smallish beets, scraped and sliced raw into thin wafers, use 3 generous tablespoons of butter and ½ teaspoon of sugar. Heat the butter and sugar in a frying pan, letting the sides coat a little. Put in the beets, roll them around in the butter, and quickly cover them with 3 or 4 lettuce leaves dripping with water. Cover the pan and let the beets simmer over low heat for 25 minutes or so. When the beets are just tender, discard the lettuce leaves, salt the beets, and give them a grind or two of pepper. Turn them into a hot serving bowl, pour on the juice, and sprinkle chopped chives and parsley on top.

Beets can be baked in their jackets like potatoes; you can do them along with the roast, since they take a 325° oven. Allow them a good hour, more or less, depending upon size. Scrape off the skins when they're done—you won't scald if you hold them with tongs. Baked beets can be served with sour cream and dill, or with melted butter, lemon juice, and tarragon. Beets can be pared, sliced raw, and baked in a buttered casserole. Sprinkle them with sugar, salt, paprika, onion and lemon juice, dot them with butter, and add a little water. This takes about 45 minutes in a hot oven. You can have mashed beets—it's a good way to make use of leftover beets if Polish Beets don't attract your palate—seasoning them with salt, pepper, butter, a little beef stock, and a teaspoon of lemon juice. Another seasoning for mashed beets involves a sauce made of butter and cornstarch, blended with ½ cup of claret and spiced with nutmeg, clove, and a teaspoon of sugar.

If you're one who likes vinegar on beets, let it be tarragon vinegar for a change. You can make your own tarragon vinegar if you maintain tarragon in the herb corner (winter-protected, we hope, in colder climates): a few sprays tucked in a jar filled with red wine vinegar will do it. If you must have your beets pickled, why not try them with herbs? Slice a few cooked beets into a shallow dish and top them with a layer of sweet onion rings. Sprinkle upon them a bay leaf broken up, a teaspoon of chopped marjoram, a grating of nutmeg, and a few slivers of garlic. Let this salad stand for an hour in a French dressing made with one third red wine, one third vinegar, one third oil, and, of course, salt and pepper. Remove the garlic and pour off most of the liquid before serving.

HERBS TO THE RESCUE At the tag end of winter it's herbs to the rescue with green beans as well as with beets. Dill, for instance. A teaspoon of dill seed and a scallion or slice of onion chopped into a package of frozen green beans as they cook, with butter added generously and a hard-boiled egg sieved into the beans at serving time, spruce up the vegetable. Dill gives the beans a faintly herbal taste which sharpens when one bites the softened seed of dill—a flavorsome accompaniment for the spring roast of lamb. Fresh dill with green beans is even better, a happy thought to recall at the height of the summer crop, when a scallion and a flower head of dill can be pulled to cook with beans fresh from the garden row.

If you sauté a chopped slice of onion, ½ clove of garlic, and ¼ cup of minced celery for 5 minutes in 2 tablespoons of butter, and then add ¼ teaspoon each of minced parsley, dried basil, and rosemary, plus ½ teaspoon of salt, you have a good dressing for 2 cups of cooked beans (take out the garlic, though). If guests arrive unexpectedly, you can turn this dish into an ample succotash by adding a can of whole-kernel corn.

The hot bacon dressing so delicious in wilted lettuce is good on hot green beans, especially if made with brown sugar and tarragon vinegar. Onion rings may be sprinkled on top for additional flourish.

Here are some other ways of varying the surplus of green beans:

GREEN BEANS WITH SOUR CREAM SAUCE

> 1 pound green beans
> 2 teaspoons chopped onion
> 2 tablespoons chopped parsley
> 1 tablespoon butter
> 1 tablespoon flour
> 1 tablespoon vinegar
> 1 tablespoon sugar
> ½ cup sour cream
> ½ teaspoon salt
> ⅛ teaspoon paprika

Cross-cut the beans and cook them in a small amount of salted water until just tender (about 15 minutes). Meanwhile sauté the onion and parsley in the butter, then blend in the flour. Add ½ cup of the water in which the beans cooked, then the vinegar and sugar. Let the flour thicken the sauce, then add the sour cream and stir until thick and smooth. Five minutes before serving, drain the beans into the sauce; heat well and give them a final taste for salt. Sprinkle with paprika.

> *Time required: 35 minutes*
> *Quantity produced: 4 servings*

The next is a good recipe on which to practice the prime pledge of the gardener's kitchen: never overcook vegetables. If properly prepared, the crisp texture of the beans and celery is as pleasurable as the delicacy of their flavoring and gives the dish a springtime freshness of taste.

CALIFORNIA GREEN BEANS

> 4 cups young green beans, fresh or frozen, cross-cut in
>   ½-inch bits
> 2 cups celery cut to match
> 3 tablespoons butter
> ½ teaspoon seasoning salt

Set the beans to boil briskly in salted water for about 15 minutes. Taste one in 13 minutes, in order to gauge total cooking time: they should be just barely tender, still crisp to the bite. When the beans are done, drain off the liquid (save it for Minestra) and keep the beans hot in the saucepan. Meanwhile sauté the celery in the butter for 10 minutes (again, taste for doneness at 8 minutes). The celery should brown a little but remain moist with butter. While it is sautéing, sprinkle it with the seasoning salt— this being a California concoction, Lawry's Seasoning Salt is considered perfection. You may, however, use plain salt, adding ⅛ teaspoon each of garlic powder and basil, plus ¼ teaspoon of paprika. When beans and celery are just done, pour the beans on the celery and stir to absorb all the seasoned butter. When piping hot, remove from the fire and serve at once.

Time required: ½ hour

Quantity produced: 6 servings

This dish is well worth careful timing and last-minute attention, but if you prefer to have a last few minutes in the living room before dinner, you can easily transform California Green Beans into a casserole dish which can be prepared in the morning. The method is the same, except that the cooking time of beans and celery should be cut down by 2 minutes. Sauté the celery right in the casserole and, after adding the separately cooked beans, pour on 2 cups of mushroom soup, homemade or canned, and top the casserole with grated mild cheese. It may then be kept at room temperature until dinnertime. Twenty minutes in a hot oven completes the cooking.

A similar but very rich casserole involves a package of beans from the freezer, ½ can of mushroom soup, and a can of French-fried onions. Lay beans, onions, and again beans in layers in a casserole; pour on the mushroom soup thinned down with ½ can of milk. Make a final top layer of onions; pop it all in a 350° oven to bake for 30 minutes.

For a snug dinner, either now in March or on some summer night, how about this: Greek Lamb and Bean Stew, rice pilaf, garlic bread, ripe olives (if you're lucky, you may know a Greek market where you can get Eastern olives in bulk; you may taste and choose the ones best to your liking. There's a little wizened, nutty-flavored kind, very salty, that goes well with this stew—or on the cocktail tray), a tossed green salad, and a sour red wine? You may suit yourself on dessert; the Greeks would serve fruit and cheese and a honey-and-almond cake called paclavah.

GREEK LAMB AND BEAN STEW

> 2 tablespoons olive oil
> 1½ pounds lean lamb, diced to walnut size
> 3 small onions, chopped
> 1 clove garlic
> 1 cup canned tomatoes, drained of juice
> 1 cup stock
> 1½ teaspoons salt
> ¼ teaspoon fresh-ground pepper
> ½ pound green beans, slit lengthwise
> ¼ teaspoon thyme

Pour the olive oil into a deep skillet and, when hot, brown the lamb chunks, onions, and garlic in it. Add the tomatoes, stock, and the salt and pepper. Let all simmer until the lamb is tender—1½ to 2 hours. Now add the string beans and thyme. When the beans are cooked—say 20 minutes—the stew is ready.

> Time required: 2½ hours intermittently
> Quantity produced: 4 servings

Short-cut cooks will guess that the beans may be fresh or frozen, that 4 fresh tomatoes or a cup of tomato juice with a teaspoon of tomato paste may replace the canned tomatoes, and that a bouillon cube will serve for stock. In true Greek manner, the gravy should not be thickened; properly cooked down, it makes a rich sauce that moistens the lamb and flavors the accompanying pilaf.

CARROTS COME OUT OF THE CELLAR It's little wonder that a surplus of carrots is dismaying to the gardening cook. They suffer under a gastronomical handicap. Carrots ordinarily do not call forth "Ah's" of pleasure when they appear at the family dinner table; they almost never show up for company. The time-honored admonition, "Eat your carrots, they'll make your hair curl!" (modern version, "They're full of vitamins!") suggests that, taste-wise, these innocent roots, so gay and crisp and succulent when raw, are nothing but a chore when cooked.

One reason for this apathy toward cooked carrots is undoubtedly the fact that carrots do not make a "perfect" combination with any one meat or fish. Cabbage with corned beef, apples with pork, onions with steak, peas with lamb: these are naturals. Carrots, as a cooked vegetable, are by comparison a misfit, relegated to soups and stews and sometimes to pot roast. For my money, they're better with the pot roast than in it. They can be baked whole right along with the braising roast. Lay them in a row, alternating with fat scallions, in a shallow baking dish. Stick a clove in each, shake on salt and a dash of sugar, and brush generously with melted butter. They take a moderate oven and 35 to 60 minutes' baking time, depending upon size.

Winter carrots, with their middle-aged spread and sometimes hard hearts, need furbishing up far more than the tender roots of June. They do well ground raw and then baked or stewed; with imaginative flavoring they are almost rejuvenated. Put 6 to 8 carrots, say, through the food grinder with a very small onion. Mix this well in a casserole, adding a couple of tablespoons of melted butter, a pinch of sugar, and salt and pepper, Barely cover with meat stock, and they're ready to cook. When serving, sprinkle them liberally with minced parsley. If you like ginger, dust a little on top. Baked riced carrots are good with corned beef and broccoli.

Cooked carrot chunks glazed in a sauce of butter, honey, paprika, and lemon juice make a good secondary vegetable with roasts of beef or lamb; you can combine carrots cut in strips with creamed onions. Diced carrots in sweet-sour sauce are a pleasant variant with meat loaf; carrots simmered in white wine and stock (with a whiff of onion and garlic) give something different to go with steak or broiled fish. Carrots definitely do not belong with cheese or egg entrées—the color scheme itself is enough to kill the combination.

Sometimes the simplest is the best. Carrots cooked with a bit of sugar, diced small and dressed with a rich cream sauce full of chopped parsley; this I grew up with as a child, and my memory of its goodness doesn't cheat me. But wait for Flemish Carrots in June.

THE CROCUSES ARE UP We've by no means exhausted the new ways to dress up the old staples, but after all, it's March, the crocuses are up, we're planting the peas and starting the indoor seeds, and it's a good time to indulge in a look ahead.

Perhaps this is the year to do some garden experimenting in the interests of good eating. Consider, for an example, Italian cookery, since the Italians know their vegetables.

Besides the common ones that go into Minestra—the tomatoes, carrots, cabbage, beans, and onions—there are several vegetables, less well known in American gardens, that give Italians good, and to us unusual, fare. Leeks and garlic we've mentioned: why not give them a whirl? Comparatively few home gardeners grow their own, and what greater satisfaction, apart from the pleasures of one's own table, is there than being able to supply a fellow addict of Vichyssoise with a leek or two, or to give a discriminating friend a braid of plump garlic cloves for Christmas?

There are broccoli and zucchini, still new to many cooking gardeners, although an increasing number are finding out that broccoli is much easier to grow than cauliflower and that zucchini will thrive like any other squash. Zucchini, cooked in the Italian manner with tomatoes, flavored with basil and served with grated Parmesan cheese, is a delicacy not to be missed. There's eggplant, so delicious from the home garden when eaten half grown; there are more peppers than Ruby King and California Wonder. How about a few early pimentos for your salads and chicken à la king? What about the hot peppers? The yellow Hungarian wax pepper, to put bite in your pickles; the red-hot peppers, Tabasco, cayenne, and chili, which not only spark your pickles and sauces but add color to dinner-table arrangements and can be dried for winter use?

If you like to raise from seed, you must start them indoors six to eight weeks before the frost deadline; for a start on pepper-growing, however, I recommend my lazy method of buying plants after danger of frost is past. Pepper plants of many varieties can be bought from seedsmen and markets, and that way I get kinds that are sturdy in my neighborhood.

CONVERSATION PIECE   If peppers do well for you, the pepper bush in the flower border is a nice idea.

And okra. Superb in Minestra or gumbo, as a vegetable with or without tomato, okra can be canned, frozen, or strung up to dry in slices. It is, moreover, a most decorative plant, with attractive foliage and handsome, mallow-like flowers. In fact, you might like to try a few plants of the dwarf variety in the flower border for a conversation piece: White Velvet, for instance, not only has fine flavor, but pale, greenish-white pods that grow up-pointed like candles on a Christmas tree.

Perhaps okra is not much grown in the North by gardening cooks because it is thought to be a tropical plant. Actually, it is no more tender than tomatoes and cucumbers, and can be raised in any climate where they do well. It doesn't require much care once established, but it does resent transplanting, so pick your spot carefully, with an eye to its decorative value. And don't forget: it's the young and tender pods you want to pluck; the fully mature ones become stringy and flavorless.

ITALIANS KNOW THEIR VEGETABLES   Fennel, which is the Italian finocchio, is not often mentioned in the specialty garden books—nor, for that matter, in many except the encyclopedic cookbooks—yet it is an interesting bulb flavor-wise if you like the taste of anise, and it can be grown more easily than celery. Fennel is a perennial herb, grows four feet tall or more, and needs lots of room in which to spread out.

There are many ways in which the gardening cook may like to

adventure with finocchio. The onion-like bulb and celery-like stalks and dill-like leaves can all be used separately. You can even spice an apple pie with anise by using fennel seeds. Or chop half a cup of the feathery leaf fronds into an omelet (add some chives too), and you have an Italian *omelette aux fines herbes*. Mix a few white stalks of the stem in among the celery, and unsuspecting guests will find their tongues savoring a strong anise or licorice taste. Fennel leaves can go into salad; thyme, parsley, and fennel can be sautéed in butter for a dressing for broiled fish.

The bulb can be cooked in various ways. Perhaps the simplest is to slice it lengthwise, sauté it in butter until brown, then add salt and pepper, cover the skillet, and let it simmer in the pan juices until just tender. Sliced, with the stems cross-cut, finocchio can be steamed tender in a heavy pot in 2 tablespoons of butter with a spoonful or two of water; to serve, dress it with 3 tablespoons of olive oil in which a clove of garlic has been sautéed lightly, and give it a sprinkling of Parmesan cheese. Finocchio cooked by this method can be combined with an equal quantity of tomatoes and sautéed in butter with some chopped onions. Salt, pepper, and a dash of sugar are the seasonings.

FINOCCHIO AU GRATIN

> 6 stalks fennel
> 8 stems chard
> 2 cups cream sauce
> 6 tablespoons coarse bread crumbs
> 4 tablespoons grated Parmesan or Romano cheese
> 2 tablespoons butter
> Salt and pepper

Cut the vegetables in 1-inch pieces and boil for 10 minutes in salted water. Meanwhile, make a rich cream sauce and butter a casserole. When the fennel and chard are cooked, sprinkle half the crumbs in the bottom of the casserole, put in the vegetables, and cover them with the cream sauce. Sprinkle on the remaining crumbs and the grated cheese; dot the dish with butter; give it a grind of pepper. The dish is now ready for 20 minutes' baking in a 375° oven.

Time required: 40 minutes
Quantity produced: 4 servings

AMATEUR OF THE EXOTIC They do say that artichokes can be grown by the home gardener but that it's a rarity and not recommended except as a novelty. There are a few amateurs of the exotic who raise them, more often for ornamental effect, however, than as a food crop. They are not a plant to attempt to grow from seed; the trick is to get suckers from established plants and wait a year for bearing-size growth. Since they can be grown on Long Island, they could be grown in the climate where I live; they'd need to be cut back every year, I am told, and protected from the blast of winter with a basket filled with leaves. In fact, they are grown here in Ohio. I wish I had the time, the space, the rich, moist soil, and the pocketbook for fertilizer that artichokes require, for I'd love to have a try at this, one of my favorite table delicacies.

The Italians like artichokes half grown, about 2 inches in diameter. They split them lengthwise and gouge out the spiky core called choke, simmer them in a little water with a spoonful or two of olive oil, and serve them sprinkled with salt and lemon juice or vinegar. Very good they are, too, but as a gardening cook it would be my ambition to produce a close-packed, outsize, beautiful green globe, from my own garden, to eat on my own table, with melted butter that has been given a drop or two of onion juice and a big squeeze of lemon.

There's an unwritten gastronomical law that reminds us that the artichoke, king of winter vegetables, deserves to be featured as a separate course. Many do serve artichokes as a middle course replacing salad, but my own preference is artichokes first, so that the maximum enjoyment of the delicate flavor may be realized by a palate unjaded. The proper serving of artichokes is a kind of ritual: the plate large enough to accommodate the leaves as they are discarded, without crowding and without overflowing onto the table; the individual pipkin for the melted butter or the hollandaise.

Preparing artichokes for serving has its arts too. The tip of each leaf with its little prickle should be snipped off with scissors before cooking, also the whole tip of the artichoke itself: this is no snipping action, it means a cutting board and pressure from a good sharp knife. This procedure makes for easier handling, since artichoke leaves are eaten in the fingers. It makes for easier handling by the cook also, for after the artichokes are cooked (and well drained upside down) it is easy to press apart the outer leaves, pull out the cone of undeveloped white leaves, and scrape out the choke with a teaspoon. The edible leaves can then be tucked back into shape and sent to table neat and attractive. Prepared in this way, there's no fussing at the table with knife and fork to remove the choke. One may, of course, leave the outer leaves slightly spread out and fill the center, flower-like, with hollandaise.

Stuffed artichokes in the Italian manner, served with olives and garlic bread, are almost a meal in themselves and can be made a whole meal by adding minced chicken or diced ham to the stuffing.

STUFFED ITALIAN ARTICHOKES

> *4 large matched artichokes*
> *3 tablespoons olive oil*
> *2 tablespoons diced salt pork*
> *2 shallots or 1 small onion, minced fine*
> *1 sliver of garlic*
> *½ cup chopped mushrooms*
> *1 tablespoon minced parsley*
> *Salt and pepper*
> *⅛ teaspoon grated nutmeg*
> *1 cup rich broth, preferably veal or chicken*
> *1 tablespoon browned flour*

Snip the tips from the side leaves of the artichokes and slice off the stems to make a level bottom, saving the stems to mince for the stuffing. Parboil the artichokes for 5 minutes in salted water. Meanwhile start the filling. Use a kettle of a size to accommodate the artichokes, one that has a tight-fitting cover. Sauté in the olive oil the salt pork, shallots, garlic, and chopped artichoke stems (peel them if they are fibrous). After 5 minutes, add the mushrooms and parsley (minced chicken or ham, if you are using them, go in at this point), and continue sautéing for another 5 minutes. Half a teaspoon of salt, a grating of pepper, and the nutmeg complete the stuffing.

When parboiled and drained, the artichokes must be dechoked. This is done by gently pushing the leaves apart until the prickly choke is revealed. It may then be scraped out with a spoon. Replace the choke with a good spoonful of stuffing, and press the leaves back in place, slipping some stuffing in among the outer leaves as you do so. Tie the artichokes in shape with string or wrap a band of aluminum foil around their middles.

Now fit them in the kettle, upright and side by side (each must rest on the bottom of the kettle). Pour the broth around them, cover tightly, and let them simmer gently until tender—about 1 hour. Lift out the artichokes and keep them hot while you thicken the liquid in the pot with browned flour. Pour this sauce in and around the artichoke leaves, being careful to avoid the leaf tips, which must be handled at table.

Time required: 1½ hours

Quantity produced: 4 servings

The books say that the globe artichoke is actually an immature flower bud—I wonder what the full-blown flower would look like?

CHAPTER III
April

FRESH VARIABLE GREENS

I don't know why "salad days" should be defined in the dictionary as "days of youth and inexperience." Days of youth, perhaps, yes, for there's something about a good salad that partakes of the fresh, fleeting pertness of youth. But inexperience! That's one thing that doesn't go with salad.

A DELICATE HAND WITH SALAD Those who have a sure touch with the salad bowl approach it thoughtfully and confidently;

they toss off a well-seasoned salad practically without tasting it, as if it were no trick at all. It is no trick; their confidence is born of experience, the fruition of experimentation, of observation, of testing out flavors and combinations. Salad has so many possibilities, and taste is such an important factor in its success, that to the inexperienced it seems much more esoteric than it is, tempting one to fall back upon the traditional head lettuce with Russian dressing or the tomato slice on a mayonnaise-daubed leaf of lettuce, which are good in their place, but elementary.

Many otherwise confident cooks shrink from tossing up a green salad, fearing, perhaps, the lifted eyebrow of some "connoisseur" of salad making. And indeed, cultists among salad makers are so disputatious in their herb-splitting, and cookbooks so detailed in listing every possible combination of ingredients, that tossing a salad is made to seem a job unnecessarily difficult, one only for graduates. Worse, we have been led to strive for the piquant, the unusual, in salad dressing, and so have lost sight of the taste of the greens themselves. That is of course the primary step in the experience of salad making.

How long has it been, for instance, since you've tasted the separate greens as they go into the salad bowl? It's a refresher even for the experienced salad maker to sample a leaf of lettuce and compare the taste and texture with romaine, raw spinach, watercress, curly endive, and escarole. For the one who can do her sampling right in the garden row, it's a delight. Testing it out on the spot generates ideas for sound combinations (watercress or endive, not both, since the bitterish endive submerges the peppery cress), for individualizing the greens. Gardening cooks will remind you of the deliciousness of crisp fresh lettuce perfectly plain, served with only the salt shaker; of watercress sprinkled—not dressed—with lemon juice and oil.

Knowing how to use garlic and chives is the next step in building the confidence of the salad maker. Once the tongue has become accustomed to the faint flavor of garlic in green salad, a salad made without rubbing the bowl with garlic seems flat. A spoonful of chopped chives or a drop or two of onion juice is equally essential. These enhance the taste of the salad, do not overpower the delicacy even of lettuce. With lettuce, garlic, chives, oil, lemon juice, pepper, and salt, you have the makings of the classic tossed salad of the French. It will be a bland, delicately seasoned salad, a good one to start one's experience with, or to go back to from time to time to "correct the palate."

The success of a simple tossed lettuce salad starts long before the dressing is mixed and involves what is to my mind the chore aspect of salad—drying the greens. Washing lettuce is no chore at all; a few sloshings in cold water and a good rinse will do it. But the drying! That's a painstaking process. Crispness is the objective: no drop of moisture must be allowed to cling, lest the dressing be diluted and the salad flabby. Shaking the lettuce in a wire basket isn't good enough; a cloth must be used. And it must be a soft, absorbent cloth, gently applied with a patting motion that will not crush the leaves. Romaine, celery cabbage, leaf and Bibb lettuce are the easiest to dry because they aren't too crinkly. The leaves can be laid out separately on a tea cloth and patted dry with another cloth, then rolled up loosely as they lie, ready for chilling and crisping in the refrigerator. Boston lettuce (which I particularly favor for the simple tossed salad we are considering), escarole, curly endive, spinach have so many curls and crevices that it is desirable to dry each leaf separately by hand; a tight head of iceberg lettuce is the hardest of all, especially because the leaves are difficult to separate without bruising and cracking.

Drying greens for salad is patient work, and irksome if one is hurried. I try to get them prepared well ahead of time, preferably the day before, unless, of course, they're fresh from the garden. If I know I'm going to be pressed for time, I find myself choosing romaine as the quickest to prepare.

There is no recipe for tossed green salad. There is a process, which can be described point by point, giving the principles that underlie the various procedures. It is a highly individualized and creative process, which takes on, in a sense, the personality of the creator. The old adage that a man is known by the company he keeps might be amended to read as truly that a woman is known by the salads she likes to make. For in the end, every salad maker stands alone before her salad bowl, surrounded by her oils and vinegars and lemons, greens and herbs and vegetables; hers are the choices, hers the responsibility. Her likes and dislikes, taste and imagination—and experience—determine the finished product, which can be superlative in any one of a dozen different directions.

This is the reason I find myself impatient of those who make claim that there is only one right way to make this, that, or the other salad. There are many right ways, just so the salad be a delight to eat. I give you one of those ways to consider in making your own choices in adaptation or contradiction.

Given the lettuce, well washed and thoroughly dried, waiting crisp in the refrigerator, a clove of garlic and a tablespoon of chopped chives, a top-grade olive oil and a lemon, the mixing can be started, either in the kitchen or at table. I like to rub the bowl—and it must be far too large a bowl—with both halves of the cut clove of garlic and break in the greens in the kitchen. Then I complete the dressing at table, which to me makes for conviviality.

For this classic lettuce salad my measure of oil is 3 tablespoons to 1 of lemon juice. Vinegars for other types, yes, but for this one, which features the lettuce itself, the lemon juice gives less danger of wilting the salad, and the flavor is enhancing, not contrasting.

Quick but unhurried action is now called for. First the oil, measured into a big wooden spoon and sprinkled over the lettuce; then the lemon juice and salt measured into the spoon, stirred around to dissolve the salt, and sprinkled over the bowl. Next, a few quick grinds of fresh pepper, and last of all the chives. These go in last because they tend to soften up more quickly than the lettuce. Now begins the light and rhythmic tossing, which is more a gentle turning of the lettuce over and over until every leaf is coated and all the seasonings well distributed. With this procedure I've had good luck in that the lettuce stays crisp and the salad doesn't "fall." I commend this salad as a perfect foil for lamb roasted with garlic and rosemary, or a highly spiced ragout. What salad is left over makes a good dish of wilted lettuce next day; all that is needed is a little added lemon juice.

CLASSIC PLUS On the classic tossed salad one can play a variety of tunes. For seasonings, here are some combinations I've liked. The proportion of oil to astringent remains constant, 3 to 1, which is about the right amount for salad for two, using half a head of lettuce. The salt would measure about ½ teaspoon, but one has to taste for perfect seasoning. The amounts of herbs suggested are related to the above proportions. Garlic is of course taken for granted:

> . . . oil and lemon juice, salt, 1 teaspoon chives, 1 teaspoon fresh or ¼ teaspoon dried chervil.
> . . . oil and lemon juice, salt, 1 teaspoon chives, 1 teaspoon fresh or a scant ¼ teaspoon dried tarragon.
> . . . oil and lemon juice with 3 or 4 drops onion juice, salt, 1 teaspoon fresh or ¼ teaspoon dried chervil, ¾ teaspoon fresh or ¼ teaspoon dried tarragon.
> . . . oil and tarragon vinegar, salt, 1 tablespoon chives, 1 tablespoon fresh chopped dill, 1 tablespoon fresh chopped basil.
> . . . oil and red wine vinegar, salt, 1 tablespoon chives, 1 teaspoon fresh or ⅛ teaspoon dried of each of the following: summer savory, thyme, basil.
> . . . oil and red wine vinegar, salt, 1 tablespoon chives, 1 teaspoon each of fresh chopped dill, basil, marjoram, chervil (in using dried herbs, ¼ teaspoon each; summer savory should replace the dill).

Herbs, fresh or dried, should be bruised and crushed a little to bring out the volatile oils which give the essence of flavor. There are many other herbs to try out: fennel, anise, and coriander, for example, among the more unusual.

If you like to toss your salad at table but don't want to fuss with the tray arrayed with all the little pipkins, bowls, shakers, grinders, and jars needed for the dressing, you can mix the dressing in a cruet and have that ready at table for the final tossing. For emergency salad making I usually keep on hand a basic mix of French dressing—just the vinegar, oil, salt, and pepper. If a peeled clove of garlic is dropped into it whole, to stand for 48 hours, there'll be the whiff of garlic in the salad without the necessity of bowl-rubbing. A quick sprinkle of whatever herbs strike my fancy or fit my menu, a good shake of the cruet, and all is ready to go.

FOUR AND TWENTY GREENS The range of ingredients is as wide in selecting the greens for salads as it is in combining the seasonings for the dressing. Besides the variety of lettuces and endives already mentioned, there are watercress, celery and beet leaves, chard, collards, and turnip tops. Corn salad, or fetticus, is often overlooked even by gardening cooks; this hardy little salad herb, with its rosettes of spoon-shaped gray-green leaves, is easy to grow, and for an early spring salad can, because of its mild flavor, do duty for lettuce. At this season of the year, when the young wild greens are sprouting, there are also lamb's-lettuce (wild fetticus), mustard and dandelion greens, sorrel. A few leaves of these last greens, if they are really few, will spark a spring salad with the dash of bitter and sour.

It's fun to compile a salad of mixed greens, using whatever is in season. The salad maker with an eye for color contrast and shading can achieve a salad bowl to tempt the eye as well as the palate. I particularly like the bright dark leaves of spinach, the jade-green sprigs of watercress, and the red-veined beet leaf, or rhubarb chard as contrast to the lovely pale yellow-green of lettuce. Experienced salad makers know that such a mixed salad needs to be based on one predominating green, any one of the lettuces, and that added greens should be a little of this and a little of that. My own principle calls for limiting the varieties to three or four for any one salad.

As the vegetable garden comes along, radishes, scallions, rings of red onions, cucumber slices, slivers of green pepper, shavings of young carrot, flowerets of cauliflower enhance a tossed salad. As in the case of mixed greens, too great a mixture of raw vegetables makes a confused salad, both in appearance and taste. Radishes, scallions, and green pepper make a good combination; so do scallions, red onion rings, and cauliflowerets. One of the most delicious salads of this type I ever enjoyed was that served by a friend who tossed up Boston Lettuce, curly endive, a spinach leaf or two, radish slices, raw cauliflowerets, and raw peeled mushroom slices, crisp and white, with a cellar-coolness to their flavor. Her dressing was seasoned with red wine vinegar, chives, and basil, with of course a good rub of garlic in the bowl.

NEVER A TOMATO IN SALAD   One principle I stoutly defend is that tomato should never, never appear in tossed salad. In this matter I'm one of those cultists I've been at pains to deplore. I'm even thinking of starting a NATIS Club (the Never a Tomato in Salad Club), of which I'll be glad to be treasurer of the tradition. Why dry all those greens by hand if the juice oozing from even the most perfect tomato quarters is to be allowed to dilute the dressing and wilt down the salad? I feel somewhat the same way about cucumber, but violently about tomatoes. Cucumbers at least give no offense if they are sliced lengthwise with the pulp removed. In any case, I am such a lover of cucumbers and tomatoes that I prefer to give them top billing as a salad, each by itself (August will tell the tale), and not subject them to the minor role in a salad that has been created to feature lettuce.

Since it's planting time for lettuce—maybe you're already enjoying leaf lettuce from the cold frame—what varieties are you planning to plant? Salad Bowl, perhaps, and one of the Simpson or New York strains for leaf lettuce; for head lettuce, perhaps Big Boston, White Boston, or maybe the old favorite Mignonette, with its russet-tinged dark leaves? Romaine, I hope; Paris White is a good choice if you haven't tried romaine before.

It's rather surprising that romaine is not too frequently raised by home gardeners. While it forms a loose head in summer, it resists heat better than leaf and head lettuce; it can also be sown in August for a fall crop which heads up well, and can be blanched, as it matures, by tying in the outer leaves.

What about trying out some of the more unusual salad plants if you haven't done much experimentation lately? Fetticus, for a change, or Chinese cabbage, which is so much easier to grow than celery and which can do double duty, on the relish tray as well as in the salad bowl. Its sweet lettuce-like flavor and crisp texture make it the ideal addition to coleslaw if you wish to soften the sharp flavor of the cabbage. Chihli and Michihli are the enticing names of two standard strains.

No one with any garden space at all need be without lettuce and salad greens most of the summer season. A packet of seed will give several two-week-interval sowings in short rows, which are desirable for the gardening cook, since the salad garden should be compact to be handy for gathering the makings of salad. Early leaf lettuce can be interplanted with carrots, beets, and parsnips, or it can be planted in rings around the spots where tomato plants will later be set out. Leaf lettuce makes a neat and attractive edging to the garden path—even for the flower border—and can be followed up with petunia seedlings as the early plants are pulled and eaten. Romaine can be started when the spinach is eaten up; Chinese cabbage can replace early peas and beets.

For the sake of one's shoes, there should be a dry path, and we hope a short one, from the kitchen door to the salad and herb garden. Gardening cooks are not always garbed in jeans and apron, and it is a comfort to be able to run out dry-shod to the garden for some last-minute addition to the salad or soup or stew. In the season of unexpected rains, it is very pleasant to be able to saunter out, dressed for dinner and perhaps accompanied by the guests, to survey the garden glistening in the sun after a shower and to gather the greens which will later be exclaimed over as salad. Such a saunter affords opportunity for cooking-gardening chat, a delightful appetizer to dinner.

HOSTESS, TAKE A BOW As a semicolon to salad, which will crop up again and again as the seasons march around, here is one of the best highly seasoned salads that the imagination of a connoisseur of good eating ever invented: Romaine Salad "Caesar." "Caesar" is in quotes because there are many hotly defended variants of this recently grown-popular tossed salad. The only points of general agreement are that Caesar Salad is Californian in origin, that it contains a raw egg and anchovies, and that one's own favorite method of making it is the best.

This recipe is selected because it is not only excellent but simple, and enables the hostess to make all preparation in advance, leaving only the graceful tossing to be done at table.

Caesar Salad, because of its pungent seasoning, deserves to be a separate course, served with sea toast, crisp Swedish wafers, or toasted saltines. Californians serve it as a first course, a pleasant custom. However, it does well with cold cuts and many roasts and is superb in a "steak-and-salad" dinner, in a menu that might start with cream of oyster or Corn-Curry Soup, continue with the steak, charcoal-broiled, and Caesar Salad, and end happily with fruit and cheese, coffee and brandy.

ROMAINE SALAD "CAESAR"

> 2 heads romaine
> 1 clove garlic
> 6 anchovy fillets
> 3 tablespoons Parmesan cheese
> 1 egg
> 3 tablespoons olive oil
> 1 tablespoon wine vinegar
> 4 slices thin-cut bread
> 2 tablespoons butter

See that the romaine is well washed, scrupulously dried, and thoroughly chilled. Well ahead of time mash a clove of garlic in your largest wooden salad bowl, rubbing the garlic well around the sides. Let the bowl stand thus for a few minutes, then scrape out and discard the garlic pulp. Put in the anchovy fillets and cheese, mashing these to a smooth paste. Meanwhile boil the egg in fast-bubbling water for 1 minute, no more. The white should be slightly coddled, just enough to cut the sticky edge of rawness. Add the egg to the anchovy-cheese mixture, blending well. The dressing is completed by adding the oil and vinegar and working it all smooth.

Prepare croutons by buttering the bread slices on both sides, cubing them, and browning them crisp in the oven.

The Caesar Salad is now ready to assemble at dinnertime. Stir up the dressing, break the romaine into the bowl. Sprinkle the croutons atop, and toss and toss until each leaf is well coated and the croutons have absorbed some of the dressing.

No salt or pepper goes into Caesar Salad. There is piquancy enough without pepper, and the anchovies give ample saltiness.

Time required: 20 minutes
Quantity produced: 4 servings

SOUP FROM THE BABBLING BROOK In April we are spurred on to the planting of the early seeds by the sight of the little wild shoots pushing up along the roadsides, in the meadows, in the woods. And in the brooks, for watercress is luxuriant and tender and ready for its day in the limelight.

Watercress in Paris is a signal of spring. Vendors cry it in the streets with a song that never varies, even with the price of cress:

Voilà les cressons de fontaines!
A la santé du corps,
A deux sous la botte!
A deux sous la botte!

And, building on the delicate peppery zest in its fragile leaves, Parisian housewives concoct that springtime brew, *potage au cresson*. And so well might we. For Watercress Soup gives promise of the succulence to which we look forward, in these early days of spring gardening, from our own crops.

WATERCRESS SOUP

>	2 cups diced potatoes
>	4 bunches watercress (¼ pound)
>	2 tablespoons chopped scallions
>	2 tablespoons chopped parsley
>	1 teaspoon butter
>	½ cup cream
>	Salt and pepper

Put the potatoes and greens, coarsely chopped, stems and all, to boil in 1 quart of boiling water with 1 teaspoon of salt. Cook rapidly until the potatoes are tender—about 15 minutes. Rub through a fine strainer. Heat this purée; add butter and cream and a dash of white pepper. Serve with a sprinkling of chives in the tureen.

Time required: 30 minutes
Quantity produced: about 1 quart

Simplicity itself! If you want a more elaborate soup, try half and half water and chicken stock or clam broth. But *potage au cresson* doesn't really need such dressing up. Serve it, in any case, with melba toast or garlic bread or croissants or brioches.

Many of us think of watercress as an understudy to parsley—as a wispy garnish for the meat platter, as dainty rolled tea sandwiches, or at most as a welcome addition to the salad bowl. Watercress does star in salads and it does well, too, as the only green with tomatoes or cucumber or avocado or grapefruit. A half cupful, minced in French dressing, can give distinction to fruit salad.

There are two special ways, however, in which I particularly relish watercress. Neither is very original, and both depend upon a genuine taste for the slight pungency of watercress plain and undisguised. One way is in great crisp sprigs, utterly fresh and unbruised, to munch on during the cocktail hour. The other way is with shad roe, itself one of the rites of spring. Visualize it for yourself: the roe delicately brown and flanked by broiled tomatoes, with strips of crisp bacon alongside, and quarters of lemon. With this, a bowl of perfect watercress and the salt shaker, French bread, sweet butter, a steaming pot of coffee. Let no one think the watercress a mere garnish for the roe. It makes a unique contribution in texture, color, and flavor, an integral part of a perfect meal.

If you've a brook or spring, it's easy to start watercress from cuttings set in a wire basket to keep them from floating downstream to the neighbors. It can even be grown in a tub in a cool, shady spot in the back yard, as Edna Blair so delightfully describes, with pictures of the various stages of culture, in her book, *The Food Garden*. Watercress can be started from seed as well, but that's a pretty ambitious project for the home gardener, and why take the time for it when the season has come to explore the woods and fields for the succulent shoots of April?

TAKE ONE, THEY'RE FOR FREE Milkweed shoots, for example, which can be eaten like asparagus when the shoots are eight or ten inches long, young enough to snap when bent? Or the ferns, bracken and cinnamon, affectionately called "fiddleheads," spring tidbits which connoisseurs of the wild relish highly and will go to great lengths to seek out? Fiddleheads are of enough epicurean value that they are sometimes to be had, canned, at specialty grocers. Best hunt them out, though, along streams, in open woodlands. Watch for the young greenish shoots when they're about eight inches tall, pushing up their three-forked fiddleheads. Like milkweed shoots, they can be boiled (not more than 3 minutes) and served with hollandaise. The delicate taste of fiddleheads is best savored raw in salad: dress them with lemon juice and olive oil.

Or what about mustard greens, sorrel, lamb's-lettuce, for a dish of greens or a sly note in salad? All these are worth exploring by the adventuresome gardening cook. Some of them, if you really value them gastronomically, as I don't, can be domesticated in the home garden in traditional French manner. Sorrel, mustard greens, upland cress or pepper grass, and even dandelion are listed in standard seed catalogues. But to grow them in the garden is far too tame for amateurs of these pungent, almost medicinal greens.

As the spring mellows, those who fancy dandelion greens have their annual field day. Initiates who cherish this bitter-leaf green know the tricks of collecting it: that one avoids the tough, old clusters but digs single plants, preferably those with a blossom just showing in the center; that a bit of root is not to be scorned; and that it requires about half a peck to satisfy the appetites of four robust dandelion addicts.

ADDICTS ONLY Your true New Englander will collect a fine mess and make a meal of it, even to draining the liquid from the cooking and drinking it off like a tisane. And a meal it is, if you follow the old New England rule and boil the greens with fat salt pork and potatoes.

NEW ENGLAND DANDELION GREENS

4 quarts fresh-plucked dandelion greens
¼ pound fat salt pork
8 small potatoes

There's a technique for washing the greens, which are always in danger of being gritty from spring rains. Remove yellowed or broken outer leaves and all but an occasional bit of root, but don't break the plants apart. Give them three good washings in three baths of lukewarm water, each time sloshing the plants up and down and letting the dirt settle for several minutes before you lift them out. Meanwhile set 1½ quarts of water to heat in a capacious pot. When it has reached a good rolling boil, throw in the greens and add fat salt pork cut into ½-inch cubes. Cover the pot and let all simmer gently for 1½ hours. During the last half hour add the potatoes, peeled but left whole. Don't salt the dish until the end, since the salt pork is usually salty enough for flavor.

To serve, lift the greens with forks, shaking off the liquid, and dispose them in a serving bowl. Lay the potatoes on top, and spoon out the salt pork for garnish. It would be heresy to add vinegar to this dish.

Time required: 2 hours
Quantity produced: 4 good servings

With homemade bread and butter and jam for dessert, this makes an ample supper, but be sure you—and your family—really like the bitter iron flavor of dandelions before you embark upon it. If you aren't sure, it's a good idea to try out these greens more gradually: a few young leaves in a tossed salad, or a few added to beet or turnip tops. You may then go on to wilted dandelion greens as a salad or second vegetable. This method of cooking is more in line with modern thinking that greens need only short cooking with no water added beyond that which clings to the leaves in the washing. For wilted greens, pan-fry bacon squares brown, then lift them out and put the greens in the pot with salt and a little vinegar (⅓ cup to 1 pound of greens) sprinkled among the leaves. Cook gently until they have wilted to half their bulk. Replace the bacon, stir gently, and cook only until the greens are wilted to the bottom of the pan. A grating of onion is sprinkled on top when serving. Or wilt greens with a sliver of garlic and dress them with oil and lemon juice.

What applies to dandelion greens applies also to those other pungent greens of late spring: turnip tops, beet greens, mustard, sorrel, lamb's-lettuce. If you're fond of all these, you may combine them into that monster soup stew with pickled pork, that lavish African-Creole-Indian concoction of New Orleans, Gumbo Z'Herbes.

GUMBO Z'HERBES

½ pound mustard greens
1 bunch watercress
½ head green cabbage
½ head lettuce
½ pound turnip greens
1 bunch radish tops
1 pound beet tops
½ bunch parsley (in the South, roquette)
1 pound spinach
2 onions
1 pound pickled pork, diced
2 slices bacon, diced
2 tablespoons drippings
2 tablespoons flour
Salt and pepper
1 bay leaf
¼ teaspoon marjoram
¼ teaspoon thyme
1 clove
9 whole allspice
½ teaspoon Tabasco sauce

Wash all the greens well, tearing off the coarse stems, and boil together in 2 quarts of water until they are well wilted. Drain off the liquid and save it, then chop the greens fine and add the onions, ground raw. Now brown the pickled pork and bacon in the shortening and, when done, lift it out of the pot and put in the chopped greens and onions. Cook for 10 minutes, stirring frequently. Shake on the flour and blend it in. Return the meat to the pot; pour in the liquid in which the greens were wilted. Season with salt and pepper; your tasting will have to determine how much—start with a teaspoon of salt. Add the herbs, spices, and a dash of Tabasco, and cook for 1 hour. The gumbo should be served with rice.

Time required: 2 hours
Quantity produced: 8 servings

If you've had your fill of greens but still have adventurous energy, maybe you'll like to try dandelion wine as the Slovenes make it. You'll need 2 quarts of dandelion flowers, a pound of sugar, half an orange, and a yeast cake. Pick the flowers (wearing

gloves against stain) early in the morning after a good rain, and select good blooms, not too old. Put the dandelions in a crock, pour 2 quarts of boiling water on them, and let them stand thus for two days in a cool room. You now press the whole mess through a sieve, boil the resulting liquid with a pound of sugar and the grated peel of the orange. Take the pot off the stove and return the liquid to the crock, which shouldn't be too full, as the wine will rise as fermentation goes on. Add the juice of the orange half; drop in a crumbled cake of yeast. The liquid is now allowed to ferment for three days undisturbed. It is then ready to be poured into bottles, three-fourths full, and kept for two months in a cool room or cellar. By then the liquid should be golden clear.

WHAT? NO SUGARBUSH? Hardly anyone can boast a sugarbush in the back yard (if he can, he has a rich investment, with maple sugar at $5.50 a gallon), and even if one does have one sugar maple, they say it's not worth the trouble of sugaring it. However, hardly a gardening cook can bear to let the month of the "maple moon" pass by without pulling out of the file some of the choice recipes using maple syrup. For dessert at dinner, for example, there's Maple Mousse, smooth and seductive. There are many good recipes available, but one of the best is this one, a friend's family recipe, one so dependable over the years that it amounts to a foolproof method. Give it a half hour's concentrated attention in the morning, pop it into the freezing unit of the refrigerator (or pack it in ice and salt), and there's your dessert, ready to enjoy. If your freezing compartment will take a double or triple recipe, you might as well make the extra while you're at it; it can be stored in the deep freeze and brought out for another treat. It should, like ice cream, be defrosted slowly in the refrigerator in the original container.

CHARLOTTE'S MAPLE MOUSSE

> ½ cup maple syrup
> 2 eggs
> 1 cup whipping cream
> ⅛ teaspoon salt

Measure the syrup into a small saucepan and set it to heat gently while you separate the eggs, putting the whites in a bowl in the refrigerator (have the cream there too, in another bowl) and the yolks in the top of a double boiler. Beat the yolks until light, then set the pan over simmering water and gradually add the hot syrup.

This is the only tricky stage. Never let the syrup get too hot or boil, or it will curdle the eggs. When the syrup begins to bead around the edges of the pan, it is hot enough. As you pour it into the eggs, keep stirring vigorously with a spoon, then switch to a rotary egg beater and whip until eggs and syrup blend into a thickening custard. This will take from 7 to 10 minutes: when the custard coats the spoon, remove the pan from the heat and continue beating as the mixture thickens and grows cold. This process can be speeded up by replacing with cold water the hot water in the double boiler.

The rest is simple: whip egg whites with the salt; whip the cream. Mix the two and fold into the maple mixture. Turn out into ice trays, cover with waxed paper, and set in the freezing compartment to solidify. An hour and a half of "quick freeze" just before serving time will give the mousse the proper frozen consistency.

> Time required: ½ hour preparation,
> 1½ hours freezing
> Quantity produced: 8 servings

While we are sampling the first run of the new spring syrup, it's a good time to bring forth some home-canned peaches and make

BRANDYWINE BAKED PEACHES

> 8 home-canned peach halves
> 8 tablespoons maple syrup
> ½ cup cream, whipped stiff
> ¼ teaspoon nutmeg
> ½ cup brandy

Lay the peaches, cut side up, in a shallow ovenproof dish from which they can be served. Pour 1 tablespoon of the maple syrup in the hollow of each. Bake in a moderate oven (375°) for 15 minutes. Meanwhile whip the cream with the nutmeg and keep it cool. When the peaches are cooked through, remove the dish from the oven and pour the brandy, warmed, over the peaches. You may light the liquor and bring it flaming to the table. Serve with the whipped cream as garnish.

Time required: 20 minutes
Quantity produced: 4 servings

Vermonters who at church sociables feast on that traditional combination of maple syrup and snow called "Sugar on Snow" often pass dill pickles to offset the unrelieved sweetness of the maple sugar. This is a serious gastronomical heresy, but the idea is sound. Maple syrup or sugar is of such cloying sweetness that it cries out for contrast. Try serving salted almonds with Sugar on Snow or with Maple Mousse, or Swedish wafers, buttered, salted, and browned in the oven.

ONE FOR THE YOUNG FRY You don't have to be a Vermonter to feast on Sugar on Snow. You don't even have to have snow for it; you can use shaved ice. Vermonters, however, pack fresh white snow in barrels and store them in the icehouse, to be brought out at some strategic moment for a money-raising social. The "sugar" is maple syrup boiled down to the strong-thread stage (234°). This is served from individual heated pitchers and poured on a plateful of snow, which quickly congeals it to a chewy mass which needs a fork in the eating. Coffee and doughnuts—and of course the dill pickles—complete the festival. Those whose appetites give out let the syrup cool in the pitcher, beat it to creamy fudge consistency, and carry it away as candy.

The sweet tooth of syrup can be indulged at breakfast too. It's time for old favorites: griddle cakes, buckwheat cakes, waffles; and maple sugar is good shaved over hot cereal or crushed on waffles. Don't forget fried corn-meal mush, scrapple, and French toast to vary the delights of breakfast. To any of these three add bacon, Canadian bacon, grilled ham, or sausage patties and, with a big bowl of salad, there's supper.

If you've gone overboard on buying up the new run of syrup and sugar, you may find the family waistlines rebelling at using it up too fast. Maple sugar hardens quickly and can't be kept too long, but you can postpone the hardening by cutting the block into one-meal sizes, wrapping them in wax paper and aluminum foil, and storing them in the refrigerator. If they do harden, they will sometimes steam soft if placed in a pan set in water in a very slow oven. But the heated sugar must be used at once. Maple syrup, if you've bought a big supply, is best transferred to pint-size glass freezer jars and stored in the freezer, where it won't freeze because of the high sugar content but will keep until next April or longer. If the syrup was bought in cans, no boiling is necessary before transferring to freezer jars; if it was unprocessed, it must be boiled up for 5 minutes and poured into sterilized hot jars. Use a big kettle and never fill it more than half full of syrup; at that, you'll have to keep an eye on it, lest it foam over.

Light mold on syrup doesn't spoil it; the flecks can be skimmed off and the syrup boiled up and poured into clean jars.

CHAPTER IV

May

THE GARDEN COMES TO LIFE

Rhubarb, now that spring is really here, should be the delight of the gardening cook. There are some, I know, who find no delight in rhubarb, and I'm sorry for them. Rhubarb is sharp and pungent with a fresh spring taste, and you can pluck a couple of handfuls as you drag yourself away from the spring tilth to prepare lunch for the family, and have it cooked and ready when the young fry clamor for dessert.

When you pick the rhubarb, twist the stalks off sidewise. Don't jerk upward, you might injure the crown. Snip the inedible leaves and the tough stem base onto the compost pile as you go by. Then a quick wash of the stalks, a quick clipping into bite-sized pieces, and the rhubarb is ready for an enameled saucepan. With one quarter as much sugar or honey as rhubarb, and a spoonful of water, 10 minutes at most will cook it tender. You can spice it with cinnamon or nutmeg or some chopped candied ginger. A table-spoon of grated orange or lemon rind adds to the flavor, as does a sprinkling of chopped seeded raisins. Or, if you've thought of it ahead of time, use rhubarb and fresh pineapple, half and half.

As a matter of fact, you can have been reveling in fresh rhubarb for weeks now if you dug some for forcing last winter or barreled up a few clumps early this spring. Few gardeners I know avail themselves of this advantage, although gardening books all mention how easy it is to do. A box or small barrel, with both ends knocked out—for a small clump you might even try a cylinder made from a tall potato-chip can—is all that's needed. Set it over the plant's crown and, as the young shoots reach for light, there's your early rhubarb, long and tender of stalk.

BOLD FOLIAGE IN THE FLOWER BORDER   If you like rhubarb and think you haven't room to grow it, take another look. In many countries it is used as an ornamental plant. Perhaps there's a spot in the perennial border that cries out for plants with bold foliage and color; perhaps you have a pool rimmed with iris sibirica and could clump your rhubarb against the iris for contrast in tex-ture. Perhaps a row of rhubarb could be used as dividing line between the perennial border and the cutting garden.

One needn't be too fussy about the variety of rhubarb roots to buy; if you beg a few from a friend—and rhubarb lovers are gen-erous in such matters—you'll probably be getting the old-time favorite, Victoria. Among the newer, improved strains with stalks that make a rich, red sauce are McDonald and Valentine. A couple of clumps for each member of the family are about what's needed to supply both springtime wants for pie and sauce and canned or frozen rhubarb to brighten winter menus.

There are so many ways of enjoying rhubarb. Baked rhubarb, for example, can be a dish for connoisseurs—serve it with old-fashioned crinkle-edged sugar cookies. You will have to experiment with the timing of your own personal oven; mine requires almost an hour at 300° to achieve the translucent red that marks perfection in baked rhubarb. The stalks (1 pound makes 2 cups cooked), cut in 2-inch lengths, are laid in layers with sugar between and sugar on top; 1 cup of sugar to 2 of rhubarb is the usual proportion, but I prefer it more tart: ½ cup of sugar to 2 of rhubarb. You may add a teaspoon of lemon rind and a sprinkling of cinnamon. No water need be added, but I like to let the rhubarb and sugar stand for an hour or two before baking, to make it juicier. Last summer, when I pulled the last mess of late rhubarb, the raspberries were starting, and I tossed the first half dozen on my saucer of baked rhubarb. A delicious discovery!

Rhubarb Sherbet, Rhubarb Jelly, Rhubarb Cobbler—but here are the recipes. Rhubarb Sherbet is not found in many standard cookbooks; it is easy to make and delicious, either alone or with a sauce of crushed strawberries.

RHUBARB SHERBET

> 4 cups cubed rhubarb, fresh or frozen
> 1 cup sugar
> ½ cup white corn syrup
> ½ cup orange juice
> 2 tablespoons lemon juice
> 1 teaspoon grated lemon rind
> 2 egg whites
> ¼ teaspoon salt
> 2 tablespoons sugar

Cook the diced rhubarb in ½ cup of water until tender—5 to 10 minutes—then add the cup of sugar, the syrup, juices, and lemon rind and bring to a boil. Pour the mixture into a freezing tray and let it cool. Then freeze it to a mush—about 1 hour. Turn it into a chilled bowl and whip it until it is light and frothy. Beat the egg whites stiff with the salt and 2 tablespoons of sugar. Fold this into the rhubarb and return it to the freezing tray. Let it solidify, giving it an occasional stir; say, twice.

> *Time required: 6 hours over all, with only intermittent attention*
> *Quantity produced: 6 servings*

A gelatin of rhubarb makes an unusual and delicate dessert, a pretty sight when ringed round with strawberries (don't pull off the hulls!) dipped in powdered sugar and resting on mint leaves.

RHUBARB JELLY

> 1 envelope gelatin
> ¼ cup lemon juice
> ½ cup sugar
> 2 cups stewed, lightly sweetened rhubarb, cold

Cover the gelatin with ¼ cup of cold water and let it swell for 10 minutes. Add the lemon juice, 1 cup of boiling water, and the sugar. Stir well and let the mixture cool, then place it in a bowl in the refrigerator. When the jelly just begins to stiffen, add the cold rhubarb and mix well. Pour into molds which have been chilled with cold water and let them stand in the refrigerator until set.

> Time required: ½ hour of cook's attention
> Quantity produced: 1 quart

RHUBARB COBBLER

> ½ cup sugar
> ¼ cup cornstarch
> 4 cups cooked, sweetened rhubarb
> 1 tablespoon butter
> ½ teaspoon ground cinnamon
> 1½ cups biscuit mix
> 1 tablespoon sugar
> 1 tablespoon grated orange rind
> 3 tablespoons melted butter
> ⅓ cup milk

Mix the sugar and cornstarch, add 2 tablespoons of water, and stir smooth. Put this with the cooked rhubarb and heat all to boiling. Turn it into a sizable casserole, dot with butter, and sprinkle with cinnamon. Make the topping by combining the biscuit mix, sugar, and orange rind and adding the melted butter and milk. Drop this by spoonfuls on the rhubarb, sprinkling the dough with additional sugar for sparkle. Bake in a 400° oven for 30 minutes.

> *Time required: 1 hour*
> *Quantity produced: 6 generous servings*

It is rewarding, once in a while, to count up the various combinations in which rhubarb makes good eating. Run a finger down the index of any standard cookbook, and you'll find a dozen variations: rhubarb with raisins, in pie; with pineapple, in sauce or jam; with raspberries and orange, in a conserve; with figs, in marmalade. The rind of lemon and orange lend a subtle flavor to almost any concoction of rhubarb. Cinnamon and cloves, stewed with rhubarb and sugar, give a fine spiced dish. Strawberries blend felicitously with it. You can make rhubarb punch or rhubarb wine.

But pie! Rhubarb is not lovingly dubbed pie-plant for nothing. And what better on a May evening than Deep-Dish Rhubarb and Strawberry Pie for dessert? Mix your favorite piecrust dough and allow enough to roll it ¼ inch thick. The filling for Rhubarb and Strawberry Pie is so good that it's worth making double, using what is not needed for a fat pie in tarts to be topped with ground and grated almonds or macaroons. And for myself, I like chunks of sharp Cheddar cheese with any fruit pie or tart.

DEEP-DISH RHUBARB AND STRAWBERRY PIE

> 2½ cups fresh rhubarb, diced
> ¾ cup granulated sugar
> 2½ tablespoons minute tapioca
> ½ teaspoon lemon juice
> 1 teaspoon grated lemon rind
> ⅛ teaspoon nutmeg
> ⅛ teaspoon salt
> 2 cups ripe strawberries
> 1 tablespoon butter
> Pastry dough

Combine the rhubarb, sugar, tapioca, lemon juice and rind, nutmeg, and salt. Stir well and let all stand for 15 minutes. Add the strawberries, hulled, washed, and well drained. Pile high in a buttered baking dish and dot with the butter. Be sure to roll pastry dough ¼ inch thick and lay it on top, pinching the edges well over the lip of the dish. Slash the crust in star or V design and bake for 10 minutes in a 425° oven, then for 30 minutes at 350°.

Time required: 1¼ hours
Quantity produced: 4 to 6 servings

Rhubarb Punch makes a welcome cooler for those unseasonably hot afternoons of late spring. It can be made in large batches and kept in the freezer or bottled on ice, ready to mix with ice-cold ginger ale at any time you need a breather from the seeding, the transplanting, the cultivating, or when a friend's call gives you the excuse to sit for a few moments on the terrace. It dresses up prettily with orange or lemon slices and a few strawberries floating in the pitcher and a bunch of lemon mint for adornment.

RHUBARB PUNCH

> 3 cups cut-up rhubarb
> ¾ cups sugar
> 1 cup pineapple juice
> 5 tablespoons lemon juice
> 2 cups ginger ale

Cook the rhubarb and sugar with 3 cups of water for 10 minutes, then press through a strainer and cool it before adding the pineapple juice and lemon juice. Chill thoroughly. Pour into an ice-filled pitcher; add the ginger ale.

If you have an electric blender, this is an even better punch, because none of the rhubarb is lost as in straining. Twirl the rhubarb in the blender after it is cooked, before the lemon and pineapple juice are added.

Time required: 30 minutes
Quantity produced: 2 quarts

Since surplus rhubarb must be taken care of before the stalks toughen in June, now arrives the first canning or freezing event of the new season. Rhubarb freezes unusually well, either stewed, baked, or raw. It should be remembered that it needs no blanching when frozen raw; when you cut up rhubarb for a pie, you can pop a duplicate pie-sized portion into a container or bag for the deep freeze.

THE SEASON IS ALL TOO SHORT A special salute should be given the first real crop of the season. I don't suppose there's a gardening cook alive who owns an established asparagus bed who doesn't gloat over the new shoots when they first push up, count the days until the first mess can be cut, and plan a party menu for the family when that day comes. I know what my menu would be: asparagus as the first course, honored as I would honor an artichoke, followed by broiled lamb chops in a savory rice ring (in my palmy days it would have been a crown roast of lamb with the rice piled in the center), with a tossed salad of lettuce, watercress, basil, and chervil, and for dessert, Deep-Dish Rhubarb and Strawberry Pie, with Cheddar cheese and a spot of brandy with the coffee.

The growing of asparagus is well covered in books about vegetable gardening; there's a concise and appreciative page and a half about it in Dempsey's *Grow Your Own Vegetables*, which includes an admonition I like: "Asparagus is the first crop you will harvest each year, and one of the best of Nature's own spring tonics. If you have never eaten this delicious vegetable cut just before cooking, you have a taste thrill to look forward to that can hardly be matched. . . ." This is a statement I heartily endorse and, if my present tiny garden were just five feet wider, I'd be out buying my rust-resistant Mary Washington roots today. But it isn't, so I'll leave the care and feeding of asparagus to the experts, with only the practical suggestion that, for a start, 10 to 12 roots for each member of the family will produce an ample crop, and that you'll need to mobilize your self-control to let the bed find its strength for three years before you begin feasting. When that time comes, cut the asparagus at the last possible minute and carry along a can of cold water to set the stalks in as you gather them.

As for feasting on asparagus, I am a purist. Fat long spears, nicely matched, cooked just to the point of green tenderness, drained on a napkin, and served with a whole pot of hot melted butter—that's my dish. And asparagus deserves being treated with respect as a separate course, preferably as a first course, so that the palate may be undistracted in enjoyment of its pure goodness.

I'll go along, too, with asparagus *au beurre noir*—butter browned to smoking, with a few drops of lemon juice added before serving—also as a separate course. No other ways of serving asparagus can, to my mind, do justice to the perfection of those first upthrusting spears, heralds of the happy season of garden bounty. Hollandaise? Certainly, if it be made with sweet butter and not too much lemon. Parmesan cheese grated on top, after the Italian manner? With bread crumbs browned in butter, parsley and a hard-boiled egg chopped in at the last minute, as the Poles do? Yes, for a change. But I keep coming back to my first choice, asparagus with melted butter.

A COLLAR OF ALUMINUM FOIL Asparagus is really more tricky to cook well than many cooks realize. Even slight carelessness can ruin the gardener's best effort and condemn the diner to face a watery plate of pallid, limp stalks with broken, mushy tips.

It isn't always overcooking that does it, though that is the most common sin against asparagus. Sometimes it's a failure to consider properly the physical attributes of a particular bunch of asparagus. Long thick stalks do best when wrapped in a collar of aluminum foil and cooked upright, stems deep in boiling water and tips cooking in the steam (use the lower half of a double boiler, with the upper half inverted for a cover). Fifteen minutes at a good boil is usually ample for this process. Long, thin stalks and short tips of any girth do well immersed in boiling water in a thick-walled saucepan.

Thorough draining is of paramount importance. It is impossible to pour off all the water, and even a few adhering drops can spoil the sauce: hence a napkin for draining asparagus. Keeping asparagus warm is another problem: it should not stand over steam or hot water—it will continue cooking and lose color. A very few

minutes in a warm oven is permissible, but it's better to let the
diner wait, not the asparagus.

Once asparagus is properly cooked, it may, if not eaten up on
the spot, enter into many a good dish. It may be served cold as
salad, with mayonnaise either plain or mixed with a few crumbled
leaves of tarragon or a good handful of parsley and chives chopped
fine. It may line a cheese timbale, garnish creamed eggs, or, as
an asparagus loaf, be surrounded with grilled ham, bacon, or
sausage.

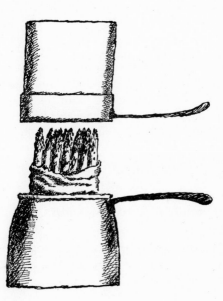

Asparagus Loaf—which is almost a soufflé—has the advantage
that it can be made of the stems alone. From a big bunch of
asparagus you can make Asparagus en Casserole with the tips and
Asparagus Loaf with the stems. The stems, cut in 1-inch lengths,
can be cooked at the same time as the tips, in the water at the
bottom of the double boiler.

ASPARAGUS LOAF

> 1 cup coarse cracker crumbs
> 4 tablespoons butter
> ½ teaspoon grated onion
> 1 tablespoon chopped parsley
> ½ teaspoon salt
> ¼ teaspoon pepper
> 4 cups cooked asparagus
> 2 eggs
> 2 cups hot milk
> 1 cup cream sauce, seasoned with 2 tablespoons
> chopped chives and ½ cup grated mild cheese

Crush well-dried crackers to make coarse crumbs (don't use the fine sifted crumbs that come in cartons) and sauté them lightly for 5 minutes in the butter together with the onion, parsley, salt, and a dash of pepper. Cut the asparagus in 1-inch lengths. Beat the eggs lightly; pour in the hot milk, stirring constantly. Add the crumbs and fold in the asparagus. Bake in a buttered bread tin in a moderate oven (375°) 30 to 40 minutes, or until the loaf is set. Serve with the seasoned cream sauce.

> Time required: 1 hour
> Quantity produced: 6 servings

Asparagus en Casserole may be the heart of a one-dish lunch or supper. Served with corn muffins or crusty French bread and an iced bowl of radishes and scallions from the early garden, it needs only rhubarb pie for dessert to be a perfect springtime meal.

ASPARAGUS EN CASSEROLE

> 1 pound cooked asparagus tips
> 8 thin slices boiled ham
> 2 tablespoons butter
> 2 tablespoons flour
> 1 cup milk
> ½ teaspoon salt
> ⅛ teaspoon fresh-ground pepper

½ cup grated mild cheese
1 tablespoon chopped chives
4 squares toast

Roll 3 or 4 spears of asparagus in each slice of ham, securing the roll with toothpicks or thread. Range these rolls in a shallow casserole. Broil under a hot flame until the ham frizzles slightly, then turn to broil the undersides. Meanwhile, or beforehand, prepare 1 cup of cheese sauce: blend butter and flour, stir the milk in gradually, and when thickened and smooth add salt, pepper, and cheese. Remove the toothpicks or thread and pour the cheese sauce over the asparagus rolls. Sprinkle the chopped chives on top and slip triangles of toast around the edges of the casserole.

Time required: 30 minutes
Quantity produced: 4 servings

THE HERBS GROW GREEN If you have thyme in the garden, now is when it is greening. The chives are high enough to cut, and that second pot transplanted from the kitchen window is beginning to get over its peaked look. I long since uncovered the parsley—every fall we invert a bushel basket stuffed with oak leaves over a corner of the parsley bed, and all winter, even when we have to kick the basket free of ice, we are able to uncover crisp, green sprigs. The herb season is on its way.

I confess to being a casual herb grower. Not that I take herbs lightly, far from it; they are essentials in my scheme of cooking by the garden calendar. But I garden round the fringes of a full-time job and have no space for a proper herb garden. So except for the chives and parsley, and the accident of one forgotten thyme which wintered over with some excelsior from a packing box tucked around it, I treat my herbs as annuals. Every May I squander a dollar on seed, make succession plantings until mid-June, and take what comes up.

It has proved a surprisingly successful method for one who does not harvest herbs for drying in winter. I commend it to those who raise herbs chiefly for immediate good eating—and especially to those who, like myself, have space for herbs only in the salad garden, which needs a yearly turning over. Marjoram, summer savory, even rosemary, which takes so long to germinate, supply me with what our household needs from two four-foot rows. Thyme gets one four-foot row and yields four bumper plants. Parsley, plain and curly, and chervil I plant as a border to the garden path instead of the petunias I used to have before I became space-conscious. Chives punctuate the path corners. Dill, because we use so much in summertime—in salads, in cucumbers, in tomatoes, in beans, in beets—gets four successive sowings of four feet each. Sweet basil, for similar reasons, is in one eight-foot row. These are my "Big Nine," and tarragon, which I use but don't try to grow, makes the "Big Ten."

One advantage of considering all herbs expendable during the summer—except for the one or two potted up for the kitchen window—is that one can be lavish in sporadic cutting and thinning. Thinnings supply me—and several friends—with all the spice needed during the early months of summer. The very first thinnings of dill, parsley, and chervil don't taste like much, but when the dill is three inches high, the thinnings are delicately delicious in tossed salad or on cucumber or tomato slices; and parsley and chervil seedlings, as soon as they have four leaves, can go, root and all, into soups and stews. Savory, basil, thyme, and marjoram have flavor as soon as they sprout; I discovered this in weeding the seedlings, since I had to taste to guess which was herb and which weed.

My back-yard salad-plus-herb garden is a good illustration of what the experts recommend: to concentrate one's energy on what one especially wants, either because it is a family favorite, because it is better home-grown than market-bought, or because it is something one wants a little of, fresh and full-flavored, at odd moments. Spinach, for example. What one has to pay in market for the few leaves for a salad or Minestra! As much as for the whole packet of seed. How much better to be able to pluck them from the garden row; how handy to be able to do this on spur-of-the-moment inspiration, without planning ahead on the grocery order.

JIGSAW-PUZZLE GARDEN It takes some study and experimentation with interplanting and succession planting to achieve a steady supply of salad essentials from June to October, as I learned by trial and error. In my space, and with the lie of the land in relation to sun and shade, I can have two eight-foot rows of leaf lettuce, planted four feet at a time at two-week intervals. As the first four feet are eaten up—we begin to use the thinnings as soon as the little green leaves are two inches across—in goes a sowing of leeks, to be transplanted later into the perennial border. A row of scallions thrives between the lettuce rows. The early sowing of romaine lettuce is in circles around the spots where the tomatoes will be placed; midsummer sowing of romaine for a fall crop replaces the lettuce. Spinach is planted in front of the basil, in the space between it and the parsley; by the time basil and parsley are full grown, the spinach will have been used up. Green peppers can be tucked in the corners between chervil and rosemary.

Cucumbers we plant in two hills beside the compost pit which adjoins the tomato row. They end by sprawling over the compost and climbing the fence. Radishes go everywhere. I plant them along with the parsley, chervil, and lettuce as "row markers," and make succession sowings in any spot that can stand one more green thing growing.

It's all pretty close-packed and would probably scandalize orthodox gardeners, but it is small enough to be practicable for hand weeding and cultivating, which are part of my pleasure in gardening. If it weren't for the regular practice of thinning for the kitchen, and of thinning in such a way that the plants allowed to mature are staggered in their companion rows, it probably wouldn't work.

FIVE MOST VERSATILE HERBS   But we started out with herbs. The side trip into my salad garden suggests that if you do want a few herbs for the kitchen they can be worked in here and there, as space and desire dictate.

There are gradations in herb growing, as there are in using herbs in cooking. If you're new at the game, my suggestion would be to start with the most versatile of the Big Ten: chives, parsley, marjoram, basil, and thyme.

You'd do well to buy a clump of chives or beg one from a friend who is dividing some up, but the rest are easily grown from seed. One packet of each will be more than ample for a start; each packet can supply three sowings for short rows. It was a long time before I believed the directions to "sow thinly." I was afraid the seeds wouldn't come up in nice, evenly spaced rows, but I finally learned that it's easier to sow thinly and transplant into bare spaces than to pull out tiny seedlings that crowd each other into spindly growth.

As the seedlings grow, get acquainted with them. Pull one, crush a leaf and inhale its fragrance, taste it, savor its unique quality. Visualize it in this or that combination: will there be much or little of it needed to impart its mysterious interest to a dish? Then start trying them out. No one can tell another exactly how to use herbs in cooking; it's a matter of taste and imagination. But, like tossing up a salad, a felicitous feeling for herbs is solidly based on experience, and one can listen to what others have found good:

Marjoram—a seedling sprig, enough to make a teaspoonful when bruised and chopped, in that ham loaf, in which you've already put plenty of chopped parsley . . . a sprig in the canned vegetable soup you're heating up for lunch; try the same soup with a seedling basil, to note the difference in flavor, then both together for a perfect blend. Marjoram—a few fresh leaves in the tossed salad, rubbed on a roast of lamb or pork, or in the dumplings with chicken fricassee. If you don't like spinach, see how a teaspoonful of fresh marjoram qualifies the flavor.

I'm hard put to it to decide between marjoram and basil for my top spot in herb cookery. Both go so happily into so many kinds of dishes, singly or together: soups, egg dishes, stews, roasts and sausages, vegetables, salads, and sauces. Marjoram does better in poultry stuffing, basil better with fish. But basil is so incomparable with tomatoes, raw, cooked, or in combination, and fresh so incomparably better than the dried, that for me basil has the edge.

Here, for instance, is my favorite treatment of raw sliced tomatoes. This recipe should really appear in August, the bountiful month for tomatoes, but I use it all year round, and it is particularly appropriate in May, when we'll so soon have the seedling basil to try it with.

BELGIAN TOMATOES

> 1 *Spanish onion*
> 4 *well-ripened tomatoes*
> ¼ *teaspoon sugar*
> ½ *teaspoon salt*
> *Fresh-ground pepper*
> 1 *tablespoon chopped fresh chives*
> 1 *tablespoon chopped fresh basil*
> 1 *tablespoon chopped fresh dill fronds*
> 1 *teaspoon celery seed*

Prepare this dish in a large flat serving platter from which the tomatoes can be served. Slice the onion in thin rings, separate them, and spread them over the bottom of the platter. On these lay the tomatoes, peeled and sliced thickish—between ⅓ and ½ inch thick. Dust the tomatoes very lightly with the sugar and salt, grind a little fresh pepper on each slice, and then sprinkle with the chopped herbs. I use the kitchen scissors for this, crushing the dill and basil slightly in my fingers as I snip off tiny bits, so that each tomato has its fair portion. The platter, covered with well-tucked-under aluminum foil, now goes into the refrigerator, to gain flavor until suppertime.

> *Time required: 15 minutes*
> *Quantity produced: 4 servings*

This recipe can be adapted to baked or broiled tomato halves, which make a wonderful accompaniment for fish (we serve baked tomatoes with creamed finnan haddie for Sunday-morning brunches). Use fine-minced onion instead of the big rings and the chives; sugar, salt and pepper, basil and dill and celery seed remain the same but are sprinkled lightly with fine bread crumbs and dotted with butter. For broiling, chopped raw bacon is better than butter.

Basil is superb in tomato juice, in clear tomato soup, in stewed tomatoes (use also celery leaves, minced onion, and, if you have it, a bit of chopped green pepper). Basil is the making of spaghetti sauce and goes well in Italian meat balls. An excellent sauce for broiled mackerel is made by blending 1 tablespoon each of butter and flour, adding gradually ½ cup each of chicken broth and sherry. Two tablespoons of chopped chives, 1 teaspoon of fresh chopped basil and ½ teaspoon of fresh thyme are the seasonings, with of course salt and pepper to taste.

Basil, too, makes a superb jelly to go with meats, especially with roast lamb, for those of us who are not fanciers of mint jelly or mint sauce. This recipe was originally given me by a fellow enthusiast of basil; it is a rare recipe which I have never seen in any cookbook.

HELEN RULE'S BASIL JELLY

> 1 cup basil leaves
> 1 cup vinegar
> 6½ cups sugar
> 1 8-ounce bottle of pectin
> Green coloring

Mix the basil leaves with the vinegar, sugar, and 1½ cups of water. Bring this mixture to a full rolling boil and boil for 1 minute. Strain off the juice and add to it the pectin and enough green coloring to make a bright green similar to mint jelly. Seal in jelly jars.

> Time required: 30 minutes
> Quantity produced: 9 to 10 glasses

PARSLEY'S GOOD TO EAT   Parsley and chives are generally understood, but sometimes we forget some of the little tricks to feature them. . . . Little balls of cream cheese rolled in minced chives for canapés, in finely minced parsley for fruit salad . . . Or another canapé—toasted parsley strips: work ¼ cup of butter until soft; add 2 tablespoons of grated sharp American cheese, 1 tablespoon of cream, 2 tablespoons of chopped parsley, and 1 teaspoon each of minced green pepper and prepared mustard. This mixture is spread on fingers of bread and broiled golden brown. Rice, tossed well with lots of butter, chopped parsley, and chives, to go with chicken or pork or shrimps . . . Chive butter on toasted rye bread.

The chive butter involves blending ¼ pound of sweet butter with 2 teaspoons of lemon juice and 3 tablespoons of chopped chives. Add 1 teaspoon each of marjoram, thyme, and basil, and you have herb butter de luxe.

Thyme is also pretty well known, especially in fish and clam chowders, soup stocks, stews, and stuffings. A teaspoonful of fresh thyme is wonderful in a spiced tongue, and I like it better than sage for pork stuffing. Thyme can double for marjoram, if need be, and the trio of thyme, marjoram, and basil, in equal proportions, is the making of many a roast, stew, and marinade.

BUILDING UP TO THE BIG TEN If you have zest and space for the rest of the Big Ten, you'll be able to play a symphony of herbs. Dill, sprinkled on almost any fish—it's wonderful on broiled or baked fish when you can pluck and snip a flower head that's just in bud. A teaspoonful of fresh chopped dill in snap beans, in carrots, in beets. Above all, chopped fresh dill on baked potato, with a dollop of sour cream. And with cucumbers, come August.

Summer savory is a delightful herb: try a few seedlings in lentil or split pea soup; snip a few leaves to cut into the early snap beans or broccoli. Savory makes a nice change in dressing for sliced tomatoes, and sometimes I use it with the basil, dill, and celery seed. It gives an interesting touch to cottage cheese mixed with chives and chervil. Chervil, an aromatic parsley, goes into almost everything the French make. Try some in stuffed eggs or in chicken or asparagus soup—even in Vichyssoise. A little chervil made into a maître d'hôtel butter is excellent on broiled filet mignon.

I'd like to say a special word about rosemary. This herb is not much grown in the North because it is known to be a slow-growing perennial whose roots cannot be allowed to freeze. I'm trying to nurse along a tiny bush I brought back from Washington's garden at Mount Vernon. It looks very thrifty, but I wouldn't dare leave it out for its first winter in our cold climate. If it survives the winter potted up in the window garden and strengthens again next summer, I may risk leaving it outdoors for the winter, protected as we do the parsley.

But that's a lot of trouble. Starting a new batch of rosemary every year is no trouble. It never gets really bushy, but it produces enough branches to suffice for summer seasoning. It is one of my favorites among the Big Ten and has been ever since, in Italy, our Gina roasted a leg of young kid rubbed with garlic and rosemary. Rosemary and garlic give a delectable fragrance and flavor to roast lamb treated in the same way. It is delicious in veal stew, in chicken fricassee. A teaspoonful of finely ground rosemary (start with 3 teaspoons and mince to 1 if you're using fresh) in the regular recipe for biscuits is gourmet fare. Rosemary, thyme, and marjoram are the trio I use for chicken and turkey stuffing: my taste is for a mild, bland dressing.

Tarragon, the aggressive little herb with hot, licorice-anise scent, I try to watch myself in using. It has a tendency to overpower other herbs, and even the flavor of the dish as a whole, unless very carefully used. Tarragon stars as the only seasoning besides garlic, salt, and pepper in tossed salad. When I use it in combination with other herbs (as in the Herb and Celery Soup in Chapter I), I use only half as much tarragon as any of the other herbs. If you want to try out the effect of tarragon, try mincing a sprig (or use a pinch, dried) on a portion of broiled chicken; if it suits your palate, you can go on to use it in almost any chicken dish. Try it, too, on broiled fish; tarragon is at its best with chicken and fish.

This trick of trying a little in a single portion is a good one for those who are experimenting with herbs. One sometimes hesitates to risk a new and untried seasoning in a whole dish, which the family may reject after one swallow. It's not quite the same, of course, to try a pinch of savory in the beans already on your plate— the flavor of the herb won't have infused the flavor of the vegetable—but at least you can determine whether the combination of flavors is pleasing to you.

I have on occasion had tasting parties; it's easy with tomato juice, for example. Starting with tomato juice already seasoned with onion and celery, I've ranged pitchers for tasting, each with a couple of sprigs, well bruised to give off flavor, of a different herb: basil, chervil, dill, marjoram, summer savory, tarragon. When the votes are cast, it's apparent how varied are the tastes of half a dozen different individuals. Flavor can be tested on the stove, too. Beans, for instance: green beans cooked not quite tender, then divided into four separate saucepans, to try out dill, savory, basil, and marjoram in the last 5 minutes of cooking.

YOU TAKE THE SAGE Most people, I believe, would include sage and make the basic herb list a Big Eleven—Twelve, with bay. Bay leaf I count in a class by itself, essential for fish or meat stock, stews, spiced tomato juice, pickles and, as such, an herb that's missed if it's not there, but uninteresting to play with. Sage isn't my dish, except in minute quantities in stuffing for pork or in a cheese fondue. I don't even use it in clam chowder—too many times I've had restaurant chowder in which I couldn't taste the clams for the sage. Those who like this easy-to-grow-anywhere herb say I shouldn't by-pass it because of these unhappy memories; experiment, they say, but go easy. And, they add, sage, with its gray-green foliage, is a good color contrast in the herb corner or the rock garden.

FROM ACONITE TO YARROW Beyond these twelve herbs, which most would consider basic to herb cookery, the field is wide open. Fennel we've mentioned. No one would want to be without some of the mints—spearmint, peppermint, apple mint, lemon mint, orange mint—for the tall cool summer drinks. Not for me the mint in peas or carrots, nor the mint sauce for lamb. For my taste, mint is to bury the nose in, not to eat.

There's anise for sauerkraut, cookies, applesauce, sweet pickles; orégano for Mexican and Italian dishes—and orégano gives a piquant flavor to steak if rubbed on the raw meat. Orégano, too, makes a tasty canapé spread: ½ cup of unsalted butter, softened and blended with ½ teaspoon of orégano, 1 tablespoon of chopped parsley, and ½ teaspoon of poppy seeds, to spread on wafer-thin icebox rye bread.

There's caraway, beloved of the Germans, for the spiced beets, the cottage cheese, the cabbage. Caraway, even if you don't like the flavor, is worth growing for its Queen Ann's lacy foliage and flower.

For those who like the flavor of cucumber but can't eat it, there's borage and burnet to put into green salads. The former is delicious in fruit punch, claret cup, or a Tom Collins; the latter makes an excellent cucumber-flavored vinegar.

For the adventurous there are the geraniums—a sprig, uncooked, in the jar of crab-apple jelly; the nasturtiums—young leaves in the salad, flowers floating in the fruit punch. There are potpourris, sachets, tisanes, herb teas. There is no Z among herbs, but you can range from Aconite to Yarrow.

If you want to explore these, plus the drying and mixing of herbs, Rosetta E. Clarkson's classic *Herbs, Their Culture and Uses* is your dish. I commend it to you not only for sound cultural and culinary information, but for ideas about planning herb gardens, formal and informal, with illustrations. How would you like to grow herbs like strawberries in a barrel? Between the spokes of a wagon wheel laid flat, with the hub sunk in the ground? In the neat enclosures of an old house ladder, with the rungs partitioning off the various herbs? This last idea is an excellent one for gardening cooks with limited space, requiring as it does only such a narrow strip of sunny garden.

CAN YOU SWING AN OMELET? One of the great joys of the herb corner is being able to concoct an herb omelet, and the beauty of an herb omelet is that no two need ever be alike. The simplest, with parsley and chives (the *omelette aux fines herbes* of French menus), is a true delicacy. It needs plenty of parsley (at least a tablespoon for each pair of eggs), very little chives (a teaspoon is right for a 4-egg omelet), and it should always be sautéed with the very best butter. The next step in subtlety is to add one more herb to the parsley and chives; it might be basil or tarragon or chervil. The most elaborate herb omelet I ever tasted was compounded with a dozen or more herbs—even lavender went into it —and good it was.

The recipe here given is middle-of-the-road, enhancing, not disguising, the essential egg. The herb flavors play an elusive guessing game with the tongue, as first one, then another takes the lead. The omelet itself is the Mont St. Michel or "swing" version; quick and easy to make, once the knack is learned, tender and light in the eating.

MONT ST. MICHEL OMELET

> 2 tablespoons butter
> 4 eggs
> ½ teaspoon salt
> 1 tablespoon chopped parsley
> 1 teaspoon chopped chives
> ¼ teaspoon each fresh thyme, marjoram, rosemary, summer savory (if dried herbs are used, ⅛ teaspoon each)

Heat the butter in an 8-inch, sloping-sided skillet. Beat the other ingredients in a bowl lightly until egg yolks and whites are blended, but not frothy. Half a minute with an egg beater is ample; too much beating "kills" the eggs, as the French say. When the butter is bubbling but not brown, pour in the eggs. As they begin to cook, give them two or three quick stirs with a fork to let the liquid on top run underneath. Now start swinging the pan round and round over a hot flame. If the omelet sticks, loosen it with a spatula. Keep swinging until the topside is creamy and the underside nicely browned—about 5 minutes. Slide the omelet half out of the pan onto a hot platter; then, with a flip of the pan, fold it over into a half-moon and rush it to table.

> *Time required: 15 minutes*
> *Quantity produced: 2 portions*

This recipe may be doubled for four servings. A swing omelet, however, is at its best when cooked with brisk dispatch, and two 4-egg omelets are preferable to one of 8 eggs—indeed, most delectable of all is the individual omelet of 2 eggs. If your household requires one giant omelet, better stick to the "puffy" or soufflé omelet, which is prepared on a wholly different principle, and all too often prepared to fall.

FROM TROWEL TO SPATULA Fresh fillets of fish baked with herbs are toothsome any day in the year, but they are especially desirable on the docket for May: they have the advantage of easy preparation, enabling the gardening cook to put the lengthening days to profit in the garden and still produce a gourmet's dish for dinner. For a May dinner, one could hardly do better than baked fillets with buttered new potatoes and watercress, followed by asparagus hollandaise, topping the meal off with fruit pie.

Almost any kind of fish fillet can be used, though the less oily fish are best; for my choice it might be young flounder or perhaps perch. Allow 1 or 2 fillets per person, depending on size—about 1¼ pounds in all, for four.

FISH FILLETS WITH HERBS

> 4 portions of fish fillets
> 1 tablespoon olive oil
> Salt and pepper
> ½ teaspoon chervil
> ½ teaspoon tarragon
> 1 tablespoon chopped chives
> 2 tablespoons chopped parsley
> 2 tablespoons butter
> ½ cup dry white wine
> Lemon slices

Oil a shallow ovenproof dish and spread the fillets in it. Sprinkle them with salt, pepper, and the chervil, tarragon, chives, and parsley. Dot butter on top and pour the wine around the fish. You may need more than ½ cup, but the fillets should bathe, not swim, in wine. Bake in a 375° oven for 20 to 25 minutes, and serve in the baking dish, garnished with slices of lemon.

> Time required: ½ hour
> Quantity produced: 4 servings

If you are not fond of the flavor of tarragon, omit it, or try replacing tarragon with basil. Fish fillets may also be sautéed, using the same ingredients: dip the fillets in salted flour, shake them well, and sauté them in butter on one side. When you turn them over, brown them lightly, then sprinkle with the herbs, add the wine, cover, and simmer for 5 minutes or so. A squeeze of lemon added with the wine is a good touch.

One final suggestion for the gardening cook in May: Skillet Chicken with Herbs. You'll have to come in a little earlier than for baked fillets, but at that it takes less than an hour, and while it is cooking, there'll be time to go back and clean up the tools.

SKILLET CHICKEN WITH HERBS

> 2 breasts of chicken, split lengthwise
> ½ cup flour
> Salt and pepper
> ¼ cup butter
> 1 tablespoon chopped chives
> 1 tablespoon chopped parsley
> 1 teaspoon each fresh chopped summer savory,
>   chervil, basil
> ½ teaspoon chopped tarragon (⅛ teaspoon dried)

Shake the chicken breasts in a paper bag with the flour, 1 teaspoon of salt, and ½ teaspoon of pepper, then brown them, skin side down, in the butter in a heavy skillet that has a tight-fitting cover. Turn the breasts over, let them sauté 5 minutes, then sprinkle with the herbs, clap on the cover, lower the heat to simmer, and let the chicken stew in its own juice for 25 minutes. At serving time lift the chicken breasts to a platter. Pour ¼ cup of hot water in the pan, scraping up all the crusty bits, and let it boil up. Pour this sauce over the chicken.

> Time required: 45 minutes
> Quantity produced: 4 servings

RECAP ON HERBS As the season—and the herb plants—develop, there's bountiful cropping to be had. The annual herbs should be pinched out to make them branch, and one can then cull a leaf here or a side shoot there. When they are on the verge of blossoming is the time to harvest them for drying; even if you're not going to dry them, it's a good idea to cut the plants back to six or eight inches to force new growth for more cutting. Rosemary, being a perennial, may be cut back a few inches several times during the growing season.

No book of this kind can be more than sketchy about herbs, their growing and their contribution to good eating, and why should it, when the lore of the herbalist is so well laid forth in so many books on herb culture and cookery? I give you three suggestions for a start: *Herbs, Their Culture and Uses*, by Clarkson, has already been mentioned as a basic reference; *The Home Garden Book of Herbs and Spices*, by Milo Miloradovich, another basic reference volume, includes a section on the quick freezing of herbs; Irma Goodrich Mazza's *Herbs for the Kitchen* contains many a tantalizing recipe. All explore the idiosyncrasies of individual herbs, give detailed directions for harvesting and drying, present charts showing their principle culinary uses, and suggest combinations to enhance dinnertime enjoyment. For complete information, you would do well to consult these or others.

Meanwhile, as a recap to my own meandering through the herb garden, here is a tabulation of the virtues of my Big Ten.

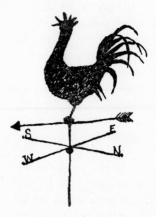

MY BIG TEN

THE BIG FIVE FOR A START

	How many for family of 4?	How tall does it grow?	How much space for each plant?	What tricks for the garden?	What shall we try it in for a start?
PARSLEY (Biennial)	8	12"	6"	Try both curly and plain Makes a good garden border Pot some up for winter. Don't let it go to seed	Anything except dessert Seedlings in soup, stew, chowders
CHIVES (Perennial)	6	12"	12"	Flowers in the rock garden Punctuation for a border Don't bother with seed, beg from a friend	A spoonful in almost anything Vichyssoise Omelets
SWEET BASIL (Annual)	10	24"	10"	Pinch out for bushy plant Pot some up for winter There are dwarf varieties too	Special affinity: tomatoes Good with fish dishes Make your own vinegar
SWEET MARJORAM (Perennial)	10	12"	10"	Treat it as an annual Fragrant in the flower border	As versatile as basil Chicken stuffing Sausage meat
THYME (Perennial)	8	12"	6"	If lazy, treat as annual, otherwise mulch Try one of the prostrate thymes between steppingstones or in rock garden	Also very versatile Chowders Stuffings

ADD FIVE FOR A SYMPHONY IN HERBS

DILL (Annual)	12	30"	10"	Successive sowings so seedlings can be repeatedly used	Specialty with cucumber
				Don't transplant	Potatoes
				Let self-seed for stronger stems	Good with all fish
ROSEMARY (Perennial)	2	20"	10"	Treat as an annual, otherwise don't let roots freeze	Distinguished with lamb
				Mark rows with radishes when you plant seeds	Poultry stuffing
CHERVIL (Annual)	6	15"	5"	Nice for a salad-garden border	Omelet
				Mark rows with radishes	Broiled fish
				It likes part shade	Broiled chicken
SUMMER SAVORY (Annual)	6	18"	6"	Weak-stemmed, don't count on it for looks	String beans
				In bloom, flowers look like pink snow	Split pea or lentil soup
					Sauces of poultry or fish stock
TARRAGON (Perennial)	2	20"	12"	Buy root divisions; it doesn't set seed	Tossed salad
				Will winterkill in heavy, moist soil	Almost any chicken dish
				Graceful when full grown	Broiled fish
					Make your own vinegar

THEN, IF YOU WANT DOUBLE OR NOTHING

Anise	Geranium
Borage	Mint
Burnet	Mustard
Caraway	Nasturtium
Fennel	Sage

CHAPTER V

June

EAT 'EM YOUNG

Luckily, there's a spigot at the corner of the garage nearest the salad garden, so I can indulge myself in the supreme delight of pulling a radish or a carrot or a scallion and munching it while the cool of the moist earth still suffuses it. This is a moment when the pleasures of eating and of growing merge into one splendid ecstasy.

I feel it in myself as I've seen it on the faces of like-minded lovers of the good earth, watching the gleam of satisfaction as some ardent gardener gazes on the straight, well-weeded rows of young growth. He bends unhurriedly to pull a Cherry Belle, turns it to contemplate its glorious scarlet from every angle, brushes off the clinging earth—absently wiping his hand on the side of his jeans—and at last bites into the crisp root. At this moment his face is rapt. It has the glow of contentment with all the weeks of preparation and nurture, contentment with the future which will bring countless other such moments.

Non-gardeners may wonder what's so special about a radish that could be bought fresh and crisp in market without all the trouble of fertilizing, digging, planting, and weeding. Let them watch the face of one who gardens at this moment, and they must surely understand that this is the pay-off on an investment of faith and love.

This joy in fruition leads us who feel it to want to taste to the full the innate deliciousness of what we grow. In June we abandon —for a while, at least—all our herbs and sauces and taste-titivators. We want our vegetables, our fruits, our greens unadorned. June isn't the time we dip our radishes in sour cream or softened sweet butter (butter does cut the radish sharpness, though); it's the time we glory in the bowl of Crimson Giants, White Icicles, Black Spanish Globes, and sprinkle only enough salt to heighten the three degrees of pungency.

June isn't the time we cook our scallions and serve them with hollandaise, like asparagus; it's the time we put them in the relish bowl, with the watercress and radishes and the carrots so young they don't need to be cut into carrot sticks. June is the time for little boiled buttered onions, for the new peas in their own sauce.

FIRST MESS OF PEAS One of the happiest recollections of my childhood is the first mess of peas. They were a ritual. We always had them for lunch, peas and more peas, with great pitchers of milk and fresh-baked homemade bread with strawberry jam— it's still an excellent menu. The whole family picked the peas and then assembled on the front porch to share the shucking. It was a rite performed mostly in silence, so that we could enjoy the sound of pods popping and peas rattling into the bowls between our knees, and the soft plop of the shells as they fell on the newspapers spread at our feet. Mother never made the mistake of cooking the peas 35 minutes, which was standard time in those days, but she did commit the heresy of boiling them in a big potful of water. It didn't, to my memory, detract from the flavor, but we know now that the less water the better; and, best of all, none at all.

If you've never tried waterless cooking of new young vegetables, this is the season of the year to try it out. It's a method that would be old stuff to the housewives of France, who have always known that vegetables suffer from being inundated with water in the cooking, but has only recently begun to receive the respect it deserves here in America. It's a method that brings out the best of native flavor in almost any vegetable, snap and lima beans, asparagus tips, cauliflower, broccoli, zucchini, summer squash. It has the added virtue of bringing back the original sweetness of frozen vegetables or of those bought in market in the lean garden months. Only the time of cooking varies from vegetable to vegetable, and one must work out one's own specific times on one's own stove. The time I give for peas was worked out on a gas stove and would be only roughly right for electricity or kerosene.

Shell 2 pounds of peas, saving the pods for Pea-Pod Soup, which we'll come to presently. Put a thin slice of butter in the bottom of a heavy saucepan, then line the pan with dripping just-washed outside leaves of lettuce. In this nest put the peas, also freshly washed and lightly drained. Add a few pods for additional flavor; cut up 3 or 4 scallions on top of the peas. Dot with 1 tablespoon of butter and top with another lettuce leaf. Clap on a tight cover and set the pan over a high flame just long enough to heat the pan thoroughly. When you can hear the butter bubble, turn the flame low and let the peas simmer for 15 minutes, no more.

Now fish out the lettuce and the pea pods, salt the peas lightly (about ½ teaspoon), and feast yourself upon the most delicious dish of peas you've ever eaten. They are a delight to the eye as well, since they aren't overcooked and keep their brilliant green, shiny with buttery sauce.

The French might use button onions instead of scallions and would undoubtedly throw in a pinch of thyme, but I prefer the full

flavor of the peas themselves. Don't let's ever put mint in peas!
If you must have herbs with them, you might like to try a pinch
of thyme or sweet basil or a spoonful of fine-minced celery.
Chopped chives and parsley, of course, are never amiss with peas.

Italians cook peas in much the same manner as do the French,
only with olive oil instead of butter. One excellent Italian recipe
is Piselli all' Italiano, a dish good enough to be featured as a
separate course. Or you may serve it in a ring of rice, to set off a
roast of lamb or veal or a dinner of baked salmon or tongue.

PISELLI ALL' ITALIANO

> 1 tablespoon minced parsley
> 1 small whole onion
> 1 sliver of garlic
> 1 tablespoon olive oil
> 3 thin slices boiled ham
> 2 pounds freshly shelled peas (plus a few pods)
> ½ teaspoon salt
> 1 tablespoon butter

Put parsley, onion, and garlic (stuck with a toothpick for easy re-
moval) in the oil to sauté lightly for 2 minutes while you chop
up the ham, fat and lean together. Add the ham to the pan, stirring
frequently until it shrinks, about 5 minutes. Fish out the garlic.
Now add the peas, stir them round to soak up the oily sauce, then
add 2 tablespoons of water, or chicken stock if you have it at hand.
Throw in a few pods for flavor; add salt and butter. Cover the pan;
let the peas simmer until tender, about 15 minutes. Before serving,
transfer the onion to the soup kettle. All the juice should absorb
in the cooking; if not, either serve the peas in the juice or, if you
are using a rice ring, thicken the juice with a bit of flour. By no
means drain it off, it's too good to lose!

> Time required: 30 minutes
> Quantity produced: 4 servings

A French version featuring mushrooms with peas is not unlike
Piselli all' Italiano in method. Both work upon the European prin-

ciple of sauce first, then the main ingredient. Peas Continental is a concoction I prefer to make in winter with frozen or canned peas, but perhaps your crop is so bumper that you're looking for ways to vary the monotony—if June peas ever become monotonous!—or the leftovers.

PEAS CONTINENTAL

> 1 cup sliced fresh mushrooms
> 1 tablespoon minced onion
> 2 tablespoons butter
> ¼ teaspoon salt
> ⅛ teaspoon pepper
> ¼ teaspoon nutmeg
> ½ teaspoon fresh or ⅛ teaspoon dried marjoram
> 2 tablespoons sherry (optional)
> 3 cups drained, cooked peas

Sauté the mushrooms and onion until tender in the butter in a heavy skillet—allow 5 to 10 minutes. Add the seasonings, the sherry, and, last, the cooked peas, well drained. Heat thoroughly and serve.

> Time required: 15 minutes
> Quantity produced: 4 servings

Another good use for a few leftover peas is to combine them with tiny new boiled potatoes in a cream sauce made of liquid from the potatoes and the peas as well as milk. Half a teaspoon of fresh chopped basil is a welcome addition, with chopped parsley and paprika for garnish.

But what about the pods from all these peas? Must they all go on the compost heap, those succulent, meaty shells? Not according to Belgian farmers, who make a soup of pea pods that tastes more of peas than do peas themselves. You may dress up Pea-Pod Soup with croutons fried in butter and a sprinkling of chopped chives. With bacon sandwiches, stuffed eggs, and crackers and cheese, it makes a fine, hearty supper, good for June or any other month of plump pea pods.

PEA-POD SOUP

Group I

       2 quarts pea pods, washed and stemmed
       ½ head lettuce (outside leaves will do, or thinnings
         from the row)
       1 small onion
       6 sprigs parsley
       1 tablespoon butter
       1 teaspoon salt

Group II

       1 tablespoon butter
       2 tablespoons flour
       1 cup thin cream

Assemble the ingredients of Group I with 3 cups of water in a capacious pot. Set it to boil briskly until the pulp scrapes easily from the pods. This takes about ½ hour or, in a pressure cooker, 10 minutes after the pressure has been built up. (I have made this soup both ways, but while pressure-cooking has manifest advantages, I have been unable, with this soup, to get as fine a flavor and color as with the old iron pot.) Strain the soup through a sieve, pounding with a pestle until all the green succulence is forced through, leaving only the paper-like shells of the pods. Sieving is easier than using a food mill, which lets the pods stick and clog.

Now take Group II. Blend butter and flour over a low flame and use this roux to thicken the thin purée. Let it boil up, then add the cream (more, if you can spare it). Heat the soup well, but don't let it boil again. Taste it for salt before you serve it.

Time required: 1¼ hours over all
Quantity produced: 1 quart

If your household likes this soup as much as ours does, you'll want to take advantage of the good pea-pod season by making large quantities of the Group I purée for immediate freezing and later feasting.

Pea-Pod Soup may be a gastronomical novelty to many cooks, as sugar peas are to far too many gardeners nowadays. These edible-podded peas used to be very popular as a gardening and culinary specialty, valued for their delicious flavor and high nutritive quality. Their sweetness is indicated by their catalogue names: Mammoth Melting Sugar (the tall variety which needs supports) and Dwarf Gray Sugar (a two-footer). I imagine that one reason why sugar peas have fallen from grace is that it takes a lot of space for a worth-while crop. Since sugar peas are eaten immature, when the pods just begin to form seed, it takes a big batch to make an adequate amount for dinner, and there's your crop eaten up almost as soon as it starts. Furthermore, people have been disappointed in sugar peas that have not been picked at the judicious state of seed formation—if picked too late, the pods get stringy, and one wonders, "Why was this considered such a delicacy?" If you miss the proper day for picking, best let the peas develop and eat them as regular garden peas.

Sugar peas must be stemmed and strung like string beans before they are cooked. Cook them barely tender—I should think they'd be wonderful done by "waterless" cooking—and serve them swooning in melted butter.

BE FAIR TO CARROTS Most people find it easy to drool over peas, even just reading about them. But not carrots! We had them in winter, we have them in summer. Even the sweet young ones, slim and pointed and needing only to be brushed clean before cooking, rate at best a "Well, they aren't bad when they're fresh from the garden." Some people try to take the curse off carrots by mixing them with peas, a preparation that does disservice to both vegetables. All this is grossly unfair to carrots, as I found out originally in a distinguished restaurant in Brussels. That was over twenty years ago; Flemish Carrots have by now been time-tested by family and friends, and I offer them in the serene conviction that, if given a fair trial both in the cooking and the eating, they will make carrots a gustatory treat.

June is the ideal month for Flemish Carrots, when the roots are young and delicately sweet, but they are good even in December, though winter carrots from the storage cellar profit from standing in cold water for ½ hour after slicing.

FLEMISH CARROTS

> 12 young carrots
> ½ teaspoon sugar
> ½ teaspoon salt
> 1 tablespoon minced parsley
> 3 tablespoons butter
> 1 teaspoon flour (optional)
> ½ cup cream (optional)

Scrape the carrots (in June they will likely need only scrubbing) and slice them lengthwise in long thin strips like matches. (They really do cook better cut this way than in even the thinnest slices, which are certain to stick together.) Put them in a saucepan with the sugar, salt, parsley, butter, and 2 tablespoons of water. Cover the pan and let them cook briskly until tender—7 minutes. Drain off (and of course save for the soup pot or other purposes) any butter unabsorbed by the carrots. At this point they approach perfection, but you may wish to add cream blended with flour, stirring well as the cream thickens slightly.

> *Time required: 25 minutes*
> *Quantity produced: 4 servings*

Even Flemish Carrots require some thought in menu planning. The Flemings serve them in the European manner, as a separate course, with French bread and a crisp bunch of watercress for each plate. Or you may wish to try them with Swiss steak, with pot roast, with broiled or baked liver.

Later on, when the carrot crop is at peak yield, you may find yourself put to it to make use of all the carrots that are just right for pulling. Chapter II may help, and the answer for next year, of course, is shorter rows and succession planting. But that's a year away. Most people don't cram their freezers with carrots—though I hope that Flemish Carrots may tempt you to try freezing a few cartons. With the carrots cut julienne, they need only 2 minutes' blanching before packaging to be ready for a wintertime reminiscence of the pleasures of June. You may be able to give away bunches to apartment-dwelling or non-gardening friends—though you may find that some other gardening cook has got there first.

Undoubtedly the time will come when you'll look for summer-time tricks to vary the family menu. Riced carrots, for instance—cook them soft in very little water with a dab of butter added. Rice them, then sprinkle with chopped parsley and onion butter made by sautéing 1 tablespoon of grated onion in 2 tablespoons of butter. This adds richness to the clean carrot taste.

If you really feel apathetic toward carrots even when they're fresh from the garden, use them for a spot of color. In creamed celery, for one. For another, shave them into coleslaw, potato salad, chicken salad. Three or four carrots grated into a rice ring (with of course lots of chopped parsley too) dress up that familiar favorite, and the result is particularly good with baked tongue.

We've been mentioning rice ring on and off for quite a while now, and June, when parsley thinnings, scallions, and carrots are handy, is a good time to bring it down to specifics. The best rice rings are built on the pilaf principle, in which the rice starts out sautéed in butter and is then simmered in stock, with the addition of judicious seasonings. The final effect may be approximated by using 3 cups of boiled rice moistened with ½ cup of chicken stock —canned or a bouillon cube will do. Savory Rice Ring is the making of a main dish of ham, chicken, or lamb, as well as tongue. It is also excellent with shrimp creole, but water should replace the chicken stock.

SAVORY RICE RING

> 1 cup raw rice
> 3 tablespoons butter
> 1½ cups chicken stock
> ½ teaspoon salt
> 2 carrots
> ½ clove garlic
> 4 scallions, tops and all
> 3 stalks celery with leaves
> ½ cup chopped parsley

Sauté the rice in 1 tablespoon of the butter for 5 minutes in a heavy saucepan, stirring constantly, then add the stock and salt, and simmer, uncovered, until the rice is just tender and most of the stock absorbed (about ½ hour). Meanwhile grate the carrots, sliver the garlic, scallions, and celery, and chop the parsley. Sauté these in the remaining butter for 5 minutes. Turn the rice into the skillet of seasonings and stir to absorb all the buttery sauce. Pack in a buttered ring mold and bake for 30 minutes in a 350° oven.

Time required: 1½ hours over all

Quantity produced: 6 servings

The rice need not be baked in a ring, so long as rice and vegetables are thoroughly tender. Savory Rice can be piled in the center of a platter and surrounded by slices of meat.

If a spot of Savory Rice is left over, stir it into a can of consommé or chicken broth for tomorrow's lunch. Or you can make double quantity to begin with, with an eye to using leftover meat. Cubed lamb, chicken, or beef, browned in fat, may be mixed with Savory Rice for a tasteworthy supper dish. Add curry powder and serve it with chutney, and you can almost believe you have an authentic oriental dish.

Come autumn and the hunting season, you can adapt Savory Rice to accompany duck by using wild rice and replacing the carrot with ½ cup of sliced mushrooms.

But it's June, and carrot time. Perhaps best of all for the season of peak yield, when the heat of summer sets in and even appetites droop, are Dill-Spiced Carrots. This dish is made to order for the gardening cook, who likely is drooping herself and longing for something out of the usual to tempt the palate, something crisp and cool and refreshing. Something, too, that's easy to make ahead of time and that doesn't require her to stand over a hot stove. Dill-Spiced Carrots are a surprisingly tangy concoction that can serve as salad or relish or vegetable, or as all three, depending upon how the meal shapes up. It can be relish for a hot dinner, it can double as salad and garnish for a platter of cold meats, or it can be vegetable with cold chicken and tossed salad. The preparation of Dill-

Spiced Carrots is simplicity itself, so long as you allow 24 hours for chilling.

DILL-SPICED CARROTS

> 8 young carrots
> 1 cup dill-pickle juice
> 2 tablespoons fresh-cut dill
> 1 tablespoon minced chives
> 1 cup sour cream

Trim and scrape the carrots and cut them in quarters lengthwise. Put them in a saucepan, cover with dill-pickle juice, and let them simmer until they can be easily pierced with a fork. This will take from 20 to 25 minutes, depending upon the age of the carrots. They never cook really soft, but retain a pleasant crunchiness. Let them cool, and then chill in the pickle juice overnight.

When ready to serve, drain off the juice and sprinkle the carrots with fresh-chopped dill and chives. Give them a generous topping of sour cream, or pass the sour cream separately in a bowl.

> Time required: 25 minutes, exclusive of overnight chilling
> Quantity produced: 4 servings

AND BE FAIR TO SPINACH   Spinach is another underrated vegetable that deserves friendly imagination in the cooking and a fair trial in the eating. The worst sins commonly committed against spinach are overcooking and underdraining. Crisp young spinach, fresh from the back garden, needs only 4 to 5 minutes' rapid boiling, and no water beyond what clings to the leaves after washing (a good trick is to dribble salt among the spinach leaves as you pack the pot).

Cooked like this, spinach retains its cheerful green, and the only problem remaining is the excess juice. Drain it through a strainer rather than a colander, press the greens with the back of a spoon to squeeze out all the water pockets, and of course save the juice. The spinach may now be comfortably chopped and sauced and reheated for table.

The sauce is where the friendly imagination comes in. Spinach is fun to experiment with. Butter, with a trickle of lemon juice and a few drops of onion juice? By all means, but let's occasionally vary the garnish of hard-boiled egg: slivered toasted almonds or sliced mushrooms sautéed with lemon and parsley make a welcome change—the latter especially delicious with creamed chicken and sweetbreads.

Vinegar? Not for me, I prefer the French version: a sauce made of bacon fat, flour, and the spinach juice, flavored with onion and lemon juice, seasoned with salt and paprika. Or the German variant, in which the juice is thickened with a roux of browned flour and butter, seasoned with onion juice, and spiced with nutmeg. In preparing spinach for French or German seasoning, I've found I can do the whole thing in one operation right in the original saucepan. A small tin can trimmed at the open end so that the edge is sharp, with a hole nicked in the closed end to let air out, makes an excellent spinach chopper. I chop the spinach right in its own juice, then sift a little flour on top, stir it in quickly, and beat hard to keep it from lumping; the seasonings are then added, and there's the spinach, with only one saucepan to wash.

For a rich and handsome dish—this too is French—put seasoned chopped spinach hot in a casserole, spread it with whipped heavy cream, sprinkle it with chopped toasted almonds, and brown it quickly under the broiler.

The Italians make a fine egg-and-cheese dish that offers a good way to ease the family into eating their spinach. The Italians call it Frittata di Spinacio; it's really more like a pancake than an omelet, because Italian cooks let it fill the skillet, don't let it rise too much, and finish it by browning under the broiler. Then they serve it cut like pie, well sprinkled with more Parmesan.

ITALIAN FRITTATA

> 1 clove garlic
> 1 small onion, minced
> 4 tablespoons olive oil
> 6 eggs
> 1 cup toasted coarse bread crumbs
> 1 cup cooked spinach, very coarsely chopped

¼ cup minced parsley
¼ teaspoon thyme or marjoram
⅛ teaspoon nutmeg
½ cup grated Parmesan or Romano cheese
Salt and pepper

Split the clove of garlic and spear it with toothpicks for easy re-
moval. Then brown it in a big skillet with the onion in 2 tablespoons of the oil. Cook slowly until the onion is yellow, then remove and discard the garlic. Beat the eggs lightly in a bowl; add
the remaining ingredients and the rest of the olive oil. Spoon the
onions into the mixture. Stir it all lightly with a fork, then pour it
into the skillet, cover, and cook over low heat until the sides shrink
away from the pan. If the Frittata puffs up in the middle prick it
with a fork. Brown under the broiler to finish cooking. Serve at
once, with additional Parmesan for a garnish.

Time required: 30 minutes
Quantity produced: 6 servings

STRETCHING THE HARVEST OF GREENS Spinach in
the garden delights the eye with its bright dark leaves and pretty
open heart. If you live in the northern states and if you don't need
to eat it up fast to make room for the late sowing of corn, make
a practice of cutting the head at the root line instead of uprooting
it: you may be able to induce a few new leaves from the crown—
useful for the salad bowl if not enough for a serving as vegetable.

It's too bad, in a way, that so many greens reach their crest in so
short a span of time. Hardly have we said adieu to dandelion greens
when along comes spinach, and with the spinach there are the beet
thinnings and turnip—even kale thinnings. I'm no fanatic on turnip
tops even when they're mixed in with beet tops and kale, though
this combination is palatable enough with spicy or salty entrées
like ham or corned beef. Be sure, in adding turnip or radish tops
to other greens, to cut off all roots; they're not like the beetlets
that add so much, both in flavor and color, to a fine mess of beet
greens. I like best the quick-cooked beet greens, done like spinach
with no additional water and seasoned with onion, lemon juice,
and chopped bacon.

You'll break your heart when the dish comes to table, by the way, if in washing greens of any kind you try to pour the water off the greens instead of lifting them out of the water bath. Pouring off the water merely washes the sand back into the leaves. The trick is to do the same as for dandelion greens: fill a big dishpan with water, lift the greens up and down in it, then leave it all for 5 or 10 minutes so the sand can sink to the bottom. Then lift out the greens, empty and rinse out the pan, and start over. Three good sloshings like this should make your greens immaculate.

If you're a lover of greens, you're probably already soaking more seeds of New Zealand spinach, ready to plant between the disappearing spinach rows, over which it can sprawl when the early spinach has gone the way of all greens.

You are probably also harvesting your Swiss chard properly: cutting for cooking the leaves that are young and tender, under 12 inches long, and pulling off and discarding the large old leaves that have lost their succulence. By not pulling the whole plant for a meal, or cropping the top so the plant stops growing, you thriftily assure your supply of chard until the first hard freeze.

I'm doing neither of these things; for me it's a happier thought to turn to the strawberries we've been enjoying all this month.

STRAWBERRY FESTIVAL Strawberries and cream run third on my list of favorite ways to feast on strawberries. When the berries come plump and sweet from the garden patch, there is, to my mind, nothing to surpass washing them gently, leaving the hulls on, and serving them chilled in a wide circle surrounding a little heap of powdered sugar. They are a beautiful sight; each berry, frosted white as you lift it mouthward, becomes an adventure in taste, whereby the quality of each individual berry is savored to the full. With a demitasse of strong black coffee and a liqueur of, say, Cointreau (no cake or cookies, please), such a dessert, by its very simplicity, attains gastronomical distinction.

My second preference happens to be strawberries with sour cream (sprinkled with lots of granulated sugar), but you may not be a sour-cream addict and may consider this a waste of good berries. The combination of sweet and sour for strawberries is worth exploring, however. The contrast in flavors can enhance the sturdy sweetness of the berries. A good example of this is Honey-Cream Strawberries, a delicate dessert in which honey offsets the cool ferment of sour cream and the combined flavors enrich the sharp sweetness of the berries. This concoction, American in origin, is French in effect, reminiscent of *crème d'Isigny*. The main preparation is done the day before, and a few minutes' attention shortly before serving completes the dessert.

HONEY-CREAM STRAWBERRIES

> 2 3-ounce packages cream cheese
> 1 cup sour cream
> 4 tablespoons strained honey
> 1 quart dead-ripe strawberries
> ¼ cup granulated sugar

Mash the cream cheese with the sour cream and honey into a smooth blend. Pack it in a bowl or, preferably, in individual custard cups and set to chill for 24 hours in the refrigerator. If you make the honey cream by the hand method as described, it will have solidified nicely; done in a blender, it stays soft and creamy. Shortly before serving, crush the berries lightly with the sugar; you may like to add a little brandy. Spoon the berries on the honey cream, whether brought on in individual custard cups or ladled from a bowl into sherbet glasses.

> *Time required: about 20 minutes in all*
> *Quantity produced: 6 servings*

If you want your strawberry tarts to have a French touch, make a strawberry-orange glaze to pour over the berries laid out on the custard in the tart shells. Simmer ¾ cup of very ripe berries with an equal amount of water, the shaved-off rind of an orange, and 2 tablespoons of lemon juice. Crush the berries and press the rind as they cook. When all the juice is extracted, strain it out; there should be about ¾ cup. Add an equal quantity of sugar, and cook to the jelly stage. Cool it before pouring it over the berry tarts.

When the berry season is at its height, strawberry jam is in order in nearly every gardener's kitchen. It's impossible to improve upon good homemade strawberry jam, but spiced jam makes a pleasant change: ¼ teaspoon each of powdered allspice, cinnamon, and cloves, plus 2 tablespoons of vinegar added to your own preferred recipe for 2 quarts of berries, will yield a fine strawberry relish, one you may like to jot down as a possible Christmas remembrance for discriminating friends.

WOULD YOU HAVE TUTTI-FRUTTI IN DECEMBER? Also with an eye to December, there's the old-fashioned delight, tutti-frutti, which starts with a stone crock, a cool dark spot, and a quart of strawberries in June. Scald the crock, wipe it dry, and pour in a bottle of cognac. Add also a tablespoon of finely grated orange peel and a tablespoon of whole spices, such as allspice, cloves, cinnamon stick, and thyme. Now goes in a quart of strawberries, sound and ripe, washed and hulled, plus an equal amount of sugar. Fit a tight cover to the crock—heavy aluminum foil tied down around the sides is practical—and store the crock for a week in a cool, dark place. From now on you add to it, as the season ripens, a quart of fruit, an equal amount of sugar, and more brandy as needed to keep the fruit covered. Stir the crockful every time you add fruit and between times as you think of it (Grandmother used to do it daily). Stemmed and pitted cherries, raspberries, blackberries, peaches, gooseberries, currants, plums, apricots, grapes halved and seeded: there goes the summer's bounty for winter's dearth. Even pineapple can go in. As the crock fills, more spices may be added, and you can give it a flavor of almonds by adding a few blanched peach kernels. Be sure the brandy keeps abreast of the fruit, and when the crock is well filled, set a china plate on top to keep the fruit below the brandy level. Cover the crock tightly and let it stand for 2 or 3 months, the longer the richer, before packing the tutti-frutti in sterilized jars. Our family used to make a celebration of Thanksgiving Day by opening the crock for tasting; one had to be twelve years old before being allowed to take part in this rite, and then only one sip.

THE ENERGETIC STRAWBERRY As June and the early crop of berries draw to a close, perhaps you're lucky, perhaps you have some ever-bearing strawberries coming along for fall feasting. If so, you're also energetic, for it takes twice-a-week attention in June, when you're busy enough anyhow, to keep the blossoms picked off and the runners cut back. Strawberries are so delectable, however, that few of us would grudge the effort for a double crop.

I have one friend whose passion for strawberries has inspired artistry in their culture. She grows an extra round of strawberries as a border to the rose bed, alternating June-bearing and ever-bearing plants. The June-bearing strawberries come from plants raised the previous year in the main berry patch: she sinks three-inch pots filled with rich soil beside the mother plants and roots the runners at their nodes in the pots. Then in early spring these new plants are transplanted two feet apart along the borders of the rose bed. Between the June bearers she sets out ever-bearing Mastodon. Of course neither is allowed to set runners, and all she has to do is to keep straight in her mind which plants are to be de-blossomed for the fall crop. If you're short of space for strawberries, this might be an idea to try; neatly mulched with buckwheat hulls or saw-dust, the plants make an attractive border, and while reveling in the scent and beauty of the roses, one can stoop to sample a few berries.

There are the strawberry barrels—these often grow unevenly un-less so placed that all the plants can sun evenly (they really ought to swivel)—and the novelty aluminum terrace beds, a bit tricky but, if the strawberries do well, handsome as the focus of a formal flower garden. The only thing I don't like about these is the blatant shine of the aluminum—couldn't they be painted either dark green or earth brown?

Any way you look at it, raising home-grown strawberries takes time, trouble, and space. One has to let the mind linger on the delight of the eating to offset the work required. . . . Perhaps a few quarts of strawberry juice to bottle up and blend with orange or grapefruit juice for a cool August drink? Perhaps fresh berries mashed with sugar, rolled up in sour-cream pancakes (French pancake-wise) for supper tonight? Surely some red beauties frozen to prolong the delights of June.

CHAPTER VI

July

START PICKING

Hardly have we bade au revoir to the strawberries when the sour cherries are red on the tree and the raspberries give promise of ripening. In the offing are the big oxheart cherries, the blueberries, blackberries, currants, and gooseberries, the peaches, pears, apricots, and nectarines. Then a reprise on strawberries, and at last the lush season of melons and grapes. What wealth, the fruits of summer! How lucky the house that has an orchard!

Maybe you can't crowd a sample orchard into the back yard, but you can grow at least some of the small fruits in even a small garden. Raspberries and blueberries, for example. High-bush blueberries, once established in suitably acid soil, produce their bounty year after year even with scant attention. They can be grown along a fence as a hedge or, as a neighbor of mine does, as a rim for the turn-around of the driveway. Raspberries, if you don't let them deteriorate into brambles, are sightly, and their load of berries gives an air of opulence to the garden border.

Then there's the fruit we sometimes forget: elderberries. Time was when no New England homestead was safe from witches without an elder bush in a corner by the garden patch: now elderberries are a beloved rarity. Gardeners who know cherish the elderberry shrub for its showy clusters of white flowers which bloom with the viburnums in June and, later, the heavy-hanging purplish-black berries. Even if you don't crave elderberry pie, an elder bush is an ornament to the garden that has room for it. If you respect witches and have a moist corner, Sambucus is the genus and canadensis the sweet elder you want.

Elderberries can be forgotten, so far as I'm concerned, in pie, unless you cut in a tart apple and a few green grapes and spice them with cinnamon. Elderberry jelly is better—when made two to one with crab apples. Elderberries at best are on the insipid side flavor-wise. But elder-blossom fritters are worth while, not only for their fragrant delicacy of taste, but for the ease with which the chief ingredient is attained. Elderberries for pie or jelly require that the berries be painstakingly stripped from the stems, a nuisance even when one reserves a coarse comb for that purpose. But elder blossoms for fritters: look for a wild bush if you haven't one of your own. Clip the heads with a bit of stem to use for a handle; wash them, shake them dry, dip them in fritter batter, and crisp them in deep fat. They come out like lace doilies, each blossom cased in a tiny fritter. Dust them with powdered sugar, nibble them from the stem: a dainty conceit for dessert or tea.

RASPBERRIES—NOT FOR THE BIRDS Raspberries are
my choice for back-yard fruit. They're the most perishable of the
summer fruits, and it's difficult to find them just right in market.
If underripe, they are temptingly handsome but dry and tasteless
on the tongue; if even slightly overripe, they slump soddenly. If
they are perfect, rush them home and eat them right up, for they're
not good keepers. Yet they freeze well, either dry, with sugar, or in
syrup. For "dry" freezing, wash the berries the day before right on
the bush with a fine spray, then gather them next morning
after the sun has dried the dew. If they must be washed in the
house, do only a few at a time, dipping them in and out of iced
water and draining them thoroughly. The simplest way to freeze
them is to lay them out on a tray, not touching each other; slip the
tray into the deep freeze, and next day they'll be frozen hard as
marbles, easy to package in bags or cartons. Next winter, when
you bring them out from the freezer, try mixing ¼ cup of sugar
and 2 jiggers of rum to a package of frozen raspberries to make
sauce for a pistachio ice cream sundae.

No one can resist a raspberry, and since mine run along a
section of low fence, it's a race between the birds and the boys
for the first and most berries, unless I put the old Scottie on guard,
who thinks it's all play. Boys respond to reason, but birds don't.
Even with a birdbath at hand, they prefer the water in the fruit
and peck for it voraciously from berry to berry. If extreme measures
are needed to protect the precious bramble patch, tobacco cloth is
the best bet. This needn't be too unsightly if you are one who re-
strains the canes between wires attached to crossbars nailed to
stakes. The cloth can be stretched like a tent from stake to stake
and tied to the crossbars.

No book for gardening cooks should ever give recipes for raspberries. Doctoring them up is heresy. There comes a time, however,
when we find on the bushes berries which are just past that luscious
state when it would be sacrilege to eat them any other way than
perfectly plain or heaped in a bowl with sugar and cream. Then is
the time for Norwegian Rôdgrôt, which demands berries that are
almost overripe, almost oozing their ruddy nectar.

I have never been in Norway, but my imagination has it a cool, even chilly, land. It must, however, have summer days of still, hot sunshine, for how else should one of the best hot-weather desserts hail from that northern country? Never try to tell a Norwegian there's Rôdgrôt for dessert: just bring on the bowl, and the proper pronunciation will be supplied: "Ah, the good Rôdgrôt!"

Take thought for the bowl in which you serve Rôdgrôt, for it deserves a proper setting. Silver, yes, but one gets hot in July thinking of the polishing. Perhaps a blue-lined bowl to accent the ruby red of the Rôdgrôt, or the dead-white milk glass of our grandmothers. And with it, crisp cookies or, best of all, macaroons.

NORWEGIAN RÔDGRÔT

> 1 quart ripe red raspberries
> 1 cup currant jelly
> 1½ tablespoons cornstarch
> ½ cup cream, whipped
> ½ cup almonds, blanched and slivered

Wash the berries carefully, then crush them through a fine strainer, extracting every possible drop of juice. (With my particular strainer there is usually still some pulp left on the seeds, which I boil up with a spoonful or two of water, then re-strain.) Now simmer the raspberry juice with the currant jelly until the jelly is completely dissolved. A short piece of stick cinnamon may be simmered with it, but I prefer the fruit flavor undisguised. Stir in the cornstarch rubbed to a smooth cream with 3 tablespoons of cold water; let the Rôdgrôt thicken to the consistency of thin boiled custard. Pour it into a shallow bowl and let it cool, then chill it thoroughly in the refrigerator. At serving time pile it high with whipped cream and sprinkle slivered almonds on top. You will need sherbet cups or little bowls for individual servings, as the Rôdgrôt should never be thick enough to hold its shape on a plate.

Time required: 20 minutes, plus chilling
Quantity produced: 4 small servings

There is another good hot-weather combination of raspberries and currants. Fresh-extracted currant juice, sweetened, poured over perfect ripe raspberries, chilled and frosted with powdered sugar, makes a colorful and piquant fruit cocktail. If you wish it a fruit cup for dessert, give each portion a spoonful of kirsch. And have you tried crushing a few raspberries in lemonade to make it pink and pretty?

Once more I commend to you sour cream. Jo, in *Little Women*, need not have wept because the cream for the berries at her famous dinner had turned sour. All she had to do was bring out the sugar shaker with a flourish, and lo, a distinctive dessert. The secret is to be profligate with sugar—preferably superfine or granulated rather than powdered—on the cream, not the berries. With raspberries, with blueberries, with peaches, as with strawberries, sour cream is delectable.

And a hint for home canners: raspberry juice and apple juice, half and half, make a fine, firm jelly.

SIN OF OMISSION It's odd that so few cookbooks count blueberries in on the jam-making. Strawberry, raspberry, blackberry, cherry jam, yes. But blueberry jam, a blank. Perhaps it's too easy. Perhaps we're so busy eating blueberries and cream that the idea of jam doesn't occur.

BLUEBERRY JAM

> 2 cups blueberries
> 1 tart apple (1 cup, chopped)
> 3 cups sugar
> 1 teaspoon lemon juice
> 1-inch stick cinnamon if desired (I like it without)

Wash and drain the blueberries; quarter, core, pare, and chop the apple. Cook them together with ¼ cup of water, the sugar, and lemon juice (lacking a lemon, 6 green grapes, seeded, will give the tart touch). Add the cinnamon if desired. Stir frequently, crushing the berries as you do so. Bring the jam to a boil and cook until thick and syrupy—about 20 minutes. Jar and seal.

> *Time required: ½ hour exclusive of sealing*
> *Quantity produced: about 1 pint*

Some July Sunday when the gardening cook has time to loll in the hammock, get the man of the house to make blueberry pancakes for breakfast. Don't let him get away with using even the best pancake mix; give him this recipe:

SEWARD'S BLUEBERRY PANCAKES

> 2 cups flour
> 3 teaspoons baking powder
> 3 teaspoons sugar
> ⅓ cup butter, melted
> 3 big eggs
> 1 scant teaspoon salt
> 1½ cups milk
> ½ cup or more of blueberries

Seward does sift the flour, baking powder, and sugar, but for the rest he just throws it all together (except the blueberries) and beats it up with a few swift strokes. If the consistency doesn't suit him—he likes it about like thin custard, to make thin pancakes— he adds a little water. Then he pours three cakes on the griddle and on these sprinkles some blueberries. These burst when the pancakes are turned, so the griddle often needs extra greasing. Seward works two griddles at once, so we each get two pancakes at a time. These pancakes you don't serve with syrup or honey; brown sugar's the trick. They really don't need any extra butter, but you may have some if you wish.

> Time required: 15 minutes
> Quantity produced: enough for 3

Our native American blueberry dishes—our juicy pies, our feathery muffins, our bursting roly-polies—they are all so good, why look further? But you'll sometimes want a change. Or perhaps on occasion you may have more than enough berries for muffins, not quite enough for a really bursting pie, and surely not enough to feed the whole family on blueberries and cream. The answer will be a pudding which is native to another country of blueberry lovers: Iceland.

In Iceland blueberries are so common that one has only to climb the hill behind the house to gather enough for any purpose. Everybody eats them, everybody preserves them. In winter, blueberry jam is the stuffing for pancakes folded into triangles. In summer, the fresh berries are combined with what are in Iceland much rarer, apples, to make the Icelandic version of our brown betty. The combination of blueberries with apples is a happy one, and zwieback crumbs give the dish a subtly distinctive flavor.

Icelanders, who are lavish with butter and cream, use twice as much butter and cream—and sugar—as the directions here given, but doubling these ingredients makes the dish overrich for my taste.

BLUEBERRY PUDDING

> 2 cups diced tart apples
> 1 cup sugar
> ¾ cup butter
> 1 cup coarse zwieback crumbs
> 2 cups blueberries
> ½ teaspoon cinnamon
> ¼ teaspoon salt
> 1 cup cream, whipped

Cook the apples with the sugar and 2 tablespoons of water until soft and transparent. Melt the butter and use a little to coat a baking dish. Fill the dish with thin layers: first crumbs, then melted butter, apples with a little juice, uncooked blueberries, a dusting of cinnamon, and a dash of salt. Repeat until the dish is full. Pour over the top any remaining butter and syrup from the apples. Bake the pudding for thirty minutes in a moderate oven (375°), then let it cool and chill. Serve it cold, smothered in whipped cream.

> Total time required: 1 hour
> Quantity produced: ample for 4

If in blueberry season you ever make a cheesecake—that luscious, cool, summertime dessert—you might like to copy the hausfrau's trick of folding a handful of floured berries into the cheese filling.

Going back for a moment to blueberry pie, don't forget the dash of cinnamon and the spoonful of lemon juice to give it zest. And if you have enough crust left over from your pie making, try a few open blueberry tarts, with a tablespoon of cherry or peach brandy in the syrup in which you soften the berries.

HOW MUCH FOR HOW MANY? If you're considering putting in some of the small fruits, you'll want to figure how many and which varieties. You'd better select the varieties according to what does well in your climate, remembering that the berry season can be stretched by planting some early and some late varieties. If you're too far south of Mason-Dixon to risk raspberries, there are the dewberries, young-, boysen-, and nectar-; for California, the loganberries. As for yield, when full-bearing under favorable conditions, you can expect about a quart and a half of raspberries from each cluster of fruiting canes; twenty-five roots should supply a family of four, unless the whole family goes in for canning, preserving, and freezing. From strawberries, expect up to a quart per plant; thus for four, fifty plants (twenty of the ever-bearing should do). Four blueberry bushes, they say, take care of four people, with an average four quarts from each bush (it wouldn't do for our household). Currants and gooseberries yield a little less—around three quarts—but before you start growing them, make sure yours isn't one of the areas susceptible to the danger of white pine blister rust. Blackberries can yield up to ten quarts—a third of a bush would be enough for me.

. . . An old English cookbook recommends brandy in the blackberry jam in the last 10 minutes of boiling down: quart for quart, fruit and sugar, with a wineglassful of brandy.

REALLY FRENCH, AND A MOUSSE Gooseberries, if you can and do have them, should go first into Gooseberry Fool, which raises fond memories of old England, is really French and a mousse. It is a delicious dessert, and the kitchen diplomat is wise to promise it for dinner as a spur to the family harvesters who in the hot July sunshine must strip the bushes for the year's supply of gooseberry jam, conserve, and pie. When the first quart of gooseberries is brought in, you can start your Fool, for you'll need about 4 hours' freezing time.

If you have time to chill but not to freeze, you can serve Gooseberry Fool as a pudding, piled high in a bowl or in individual sherbet cups, decorated with sprigs of mint.

GOOSEBERRY FOOL

> 1 quart gooseberries
> 1 cup sugar
> 1 tablespoon brandy
> 2 drops green coloring (more, if you like)
> 2 cups whipping cream

"Head and tail" the berries, which means remove the stem and blossom ends, and wash them well. Put them in a pot with the sugar and 1 cup of water (less if your variety of gooseberry is very juicy) and cook them slowly until tender—perhaps 30 minutes. Rub the fruit through a fine sieve, then add the brandy and a few drops of green coloring. Stir this mixture well and let it cool thoroughly. Now whip the cream stiff, fold in the gooseberry sauce, and turn it into the freezing tray to solidify. Freezing will require from 2 to 4 hours, depending upon your refrigerator.

> Time required: 1 hour of intermittent attention
> Quantity produced: 6 servings

Many home gardeners don't fully realize how versatile gooseberries are. Pie, of course (don't forget the cinnamon), and equally of course, jam and conserve. Seeded raisins, by the way, make a good addition to gooseberry conserve, in the proportion of 1½ pounds of raisins to 4 quarts of gooseberries.

Too few of us nowadays make that prime old-fashioned favorite, four-fruit jam. A quart each of gooseberries, red raspberries, sour cherries, and currants, plus 5 pounds of sugar: these are your ingredients. Once the fruits are prepared, the rest is easy, as jams go. The trick is to mash the fruit slightly to start the juices running, stir in the sugar, and let the mixture stand for 1 hour before cooking. Twenty minutes' rapid boiling produces your jam, a rich ruby red in color, ready to pour into sterilized jars.

Gooseberries combine well with blackberries, too, in jelly. Try it with 2 quarts of gooseberries to 4 of blackberries, and cut in a green apple to assist the jellying. The gooseberries and blackberries should be cooked separately with a little water, then combined. You then proceed as usual, using a cup of sugar to each cup of fruit juice.

When you harvest your gooseberries, give a thought to next winter and make a batch of Spiced Gooseberries to serve with roasts and stews and steaks. Spiced Gooseberries are delicious with almost all meats and, if next fall you haven't time to make chutney, you'll find them a welcome substitute adornment to meat curries.

SPICED GOOSEBERRIES

> 2 quarts gooseberries
> 4½ cups brown sugar
> 1 cup cider vinegar
> 2-inch stick cinnamon
> 8 cloves
> ¼ teaspoon ground nutmeg
> 2 whole allspice

Wash the gooseberries; head and tail them. Put the sugar, vinegar, and spices together in a large enameled pot with ½ cup of water and boil for 5 minutes. Now add the gooseberries and simmer them about 30 to 40 minutes. When they are tender and the syrup thick, turn them into hot sterile jars and seal.

> Time required: 1 hour
> Quantity produced: about 3 pints

GOOSEBERRY CHUTNEY

> 2 quarts gooseberries
> 1½ cups seedless raisins
> 4 good-sized onions, chopped
> 3½ cups brown sugar
> 1 heaping teaspoon mustard seed
> ½ teaspoon cayenne pepper
> ¼ teaspoon turmeric
> 2 tablespoons salt
> 3½ cups vinegar

The gooseberries of course must be headed and tailed, then all ingredients can be tossed into an enameled kettle, stirred round, and brought slowly to a boil. Two hours' simmering completes the chutney, ready for hot sterile jars and sealing.

Time required: 3 hours over all
Quantity produced: about 4 pints

CHERRIES WITH A BOUNCE It was in France that I learned the trick of putting a little bag of crushed cherry pits in the syrup for Brandied Cherries to strengthen and intensify the flavor. Here's the superlative recipe to serve with vanilla ice cream.

BRANDIED CHERRIES

> 2 pounds bing cherries
> 2 cloves
> 2 cups dry red wine
> 1 cup sugar
> 4 tablespoons cherry brandy

Pit the cherries—it comes easily with a new hairpin to loop around the pit. Crack a couple of dozen pits and tie them in a muslin bag with the cloves. Then combine the red wine, sugar, cloves, and pits; bring to a boil and cook for 5 minutes. Add the cherries and simmer, covered, for 10 minutes. Lift the cherries with a perforated spoon and dispose them in a serving dish to cool. Discard the bag of cherry pits and boil the syrup briskly until it reduces to 1½ cups, then strain and cool it. Just before serving, stir the brandy into the sauce and pour it over the cherries.

Time required: 30 minutes
Quantity produced: about 2 pints

I was a gullible child. Once a year I was permitted—nay, urged— to climb the wild-cherry tree that grew by the roadside. It was the annual family project, Cherry Bounce. Of course I was thrilled to be allowed to participate in such an enchanting-sounding mystery and picked the cherries I could reach and shook the tree with vigor. It was always smilingly implied that I would share in the end result of the Bounce, which was represented as a nice cool drink. My enthusiasm dampened when I was told that it would have to ripen, untouched, for two months. I suppose my parents thought I'd forget all about it in two months, and mostly I did. In the one or two years when I remembered to inquire about the state of the Cherry Bounce, it was as much a mystery as ever, for the invariable answers were either that it wasn't ready yet or that it had all been used up. So I never did get to taste Cherry Bounce as a child. But here's the family recipe.

CHERRY BOUNCE

> 2 quarts black cherries
> 1 pound loaf sugar
> 1 tablespoon whole allspice
> 2-inch stick cinnamon
> 1 tablespoon whole cloves
> 1 quart whiskey (it doesn't say which, but I'd guess bourbon)

"The cherries must be washed and stemmed and put in a wide-mouthed 2-quart jar in alternate layers with pieces of loaf sugar and the spices. When the jar is nearly full, pour the whiskey in. Screw on the cap and hide the jar on a cool back shelf for at least two months. Leave it longer, if you can, it improves as it ripens."

> *Time required: 10 minutes, exclusive of tree climbing*
> *Quantity produced: about 2 quarts*

I'm not one for gelatin salads as a rule—always excepting a fine tomato aspic—but a black-cherry gelatin made from the juice of canned black oxhearts boiled up with sugar and spice (cinnamon, cloves, allspice, and nutmeg) is delicious. Serve it as a ring center-filled with chicken salad, with popovers, and you've a company lunch for July.

A LITTLE OF THIS AND A LITTLE OF THAT One of the beauties of cooking by the garden calendar is that, as the season moves along, our cooking style imperceptibly changes, keeping step with the fortunes of the garden, the orchard, the herb corner. Non-gardeners, too, follow the crops, of course, and take advantage of home-grown asparagus, the new peas, the raspberry festival, the first-picked Golden Bantam, the short spell of the Concord grapes.

But they follow at a distance and, thanks to our market luxuries of greenhouse and import, are able to rove backward and forward, so that for them the trail is less distinct. And they miss the minor delights of the shifting season—the chance to explore the delicacy of eggplant the size of a small pear, or plum-sized acorn squash split, sautéed in butter, sprinkled with salt and parsley, and eaten skin, seeds, and all.

They miss the happy season of "a little of this and a little of that," which is upon us now in July. A handful of new beans in the lamb stew, an unaccountably early cucumber for the salad, the first heads of dill to sprinkle on buttered new potatoes. We find ourselves using oddments from the garden on the spur of the minute to enhance the good eating of other foods. Chicken broth, for instance, surpasses itself as a summer soup if in the last 3 or 4 minutes of boiling chopped parsley, watercress, spinach leaves, and lettuce, plus paper-thin slices of scallions and celery, are added. Well-seasoned tomato juice makes a fine cold soup for a hot day if you grate into it carrot, celery, green pepper, and onion. Chives, chervil, fresh leaves of tarragon and basil go into the mayonnaise for chicken or crabmeat salad; a scallion, some celery leaves, and a few cooked peas add color as well as flavor to sweetbread salad.

Later on the problem will be one of abundance; now is the season to revel in the newness of the staple vegetables. It isn't often we find in market baby beets the size of cherries, but there they are in the garden, and it's a virtue to enjoy them, because the ones we pull now make room for the rest to grow plump in. There are the cocky heads of broccoli, and from our own garden we can make sure of cropping them in tight bud.

THE TIGHTER THE BUD, THE BETTER THE BROCCOLI
We've been misled about broccoli. Even the handsome seed catalogue pictures of it show the heads too far developed in bud for best eating. Broccoli by rights should be cut when the head is as tight as cauliflower and cooked just to the bare edge of tenderness: 10 to 15 minutes is plenty. Haven't you noticed the buttery tenderness of the underdeveloped axillary heads when you've cut some to eke out enough broccoli for dinner? Perhaps not, for likely

they've cooked to nothing by the time the main bunch is done. Another time in this dilemma, try adding them to the pot at least 5 minutes after you've started the bigger heads. In any case, split the lower ends of broccoli stalks four ways, so that they will cook tender as fast as the tops. Broccoli, of course, can be cooked like asparagus—wearing a collar of foil and steamed upright in boiling water—but the variation in size of stalks and heads of home-grown broccoli leads me to prefer letting it lie in the pan, with precautions taken so that all parts will cook at the same rate. You can, for example, lay the split-stemmed broccoli flat in a skillet with half a cup of water, cover the skillet tightly, and cook it over high heat. In 7 or 8 minutes—by the time the water has boiled away— the broccoli will have steamed tender, and you can serve it with melted butter and a drizzle of lemon juice.

There are two excellent easy sauces for broccoli which can also be used as dressing for almost any vegetables: cabbage, summer squash, cauliflower, string beans, asparagus. One is sour cream with caraway. Sour a cup of whipping cream with the juice of half a lemon: warm the cream, stir in the lemon juice, and let it thicken. Meanwhile mash 1 teaspoon of caraway seeds in a mortar, add them to the soured cream, and let it all heat but not boil.

The other sauce is brown butter with pecans. This calls for ¼ pound of butter put to brown in a saucepan while you chop fine ¼ cup of pecan meats. At the last minute add these to the butter with 1 teaspoon of tarragon vinegar. Stir it quickly as it steams up, turn off the heat, and there's your sauce.

Ever tried broccoli soup? It's even good in winter, made with frozen broccoli; it's wonderful in July, when you can cut heads and side florets and a crisp leaf or two from your own garden. You can serve it hot or cold: for summer let's have it chilled, with salmon loaf or cold cuts and potato salad to follow.

ICED BROCCOLI SOUP

> 1 pound broccoli
> 1 quart chicken stock
> ¼ cup chopped onion
> ½ cup chopped celery and tops

¼ cup diced carrots
¼ cup chopped parsley
1 teaspoon salt
¼ teaspoon cayenne pepper
2 tablespoons cornstarch
1 cup light cream
1 tablespoon chopped chives
1 teaspoon minced fresh rosemary

Cut off the bud heads of the broccoli and dice the stalks coarsely. Put the stalks (not the heads yet) into the stock with the onion, celery, carrots, parsley, salt, and pepper. Simmer for 15 minutes, then add the broccoli heads and simmer for another 5 minutes. Lift out the heads and save them to chill for a garnish for the soup bowl. Now add the cornstarch rubbed smooth with a little water, and bring the soup to a boil, stirring constantly as it thickens. It should then be pressed through a food mill—or blended in a blender—and set to chill thoroughly. When ready to serve, stir in the cream, drop in the broccoli heads, and sprinkle the chives and rosemary on top.

Time required: 35 minutes
Quantity produced: about 3 pints

DOWN WITH BEAN SLICERS We'll be eating snap beans now for several weeks, so it's well to plan on succession cooking to match our succession planting. The very first of the round, tender-podded green beans should never be Frenched or cross-cut; they're delectable cooked whole, with only the ends snapped off.

Again I sing my song of undercooking; where standard cookbooks recommend "15 to 25 minutes," they're not thinking of the younglings fresh from the garden, which deserve 15 minutes at most. When the super-long flat beans (bush or pole) are young, the same applies; and they can be served like asparagus, with melted butter and a squeeze of lemon juice, with hollandaise, or sprinkled with grated mild cheese *all' Italiano.*

Think, too, what whole green beans contribute aesthetically to a platter of garden vegetables. Not the drab vegetable plate of dieting dowagers, but the picture-book array of the garden's pride:

the centerpiece of cauliflower, triumph of the home gardener when he succeeds with it, surrounded by slender whole carrots, little white onions, baby beets, and the slim green beans. French-fried eggplant sticks or corn fritters provide contrast; the whole is garnished with sprigs of fragrant herbs. No sauce, no juice should blur this beauty; after the guests help themselves to samples of this and that, pass them a bowl of melted butter spiked with lemon juice. It is only perfection in garden produce that merits such lavish attention. Only a six-burner range makes it possible, unless you've kept the triple saucepots from the old steam cooker. Too, the gardening cook must forgo her apéritif in order to see to it that each separate vegetable is cooked to the nice point of crisp tenderness.

The cutting of beans has a definite effect on their flavor and texture and certainly affects cooking time. When I can take the time, I like to cut snap beans the true French way, which is to slice them diagonally in thin strips. They cook in 12 to 15 minutes and retain their bright color and wonderful freshness of taste. Slit lengthwise or split with a bean cutter, they seem to me to dissipate their flavor even with very short cooking and inevitably mat down flabbily when served. Cross-cut beans keep the beaniest taste and do well sprinkled with chopped chives and crumbled bacon; wax beans I ignore as a pale understudy of the real thing.

Lest we move from joy to pleasure to resignation with respect to beans, let's consider summertime ways in which this unhappy progression may be reversed. After the first flush of delight in the new beans in their own buttery juice, what next? Perhaps beans in cream sauce, onion-flavored, blanketed with Parmesan cheese, and well browned under the broiler; possibly that German favorite, Bohnengemüss, which is simply diagonally cut green beans mixed with diced potatoes, well seasoned with salt and pepper, and dashed with vinegar and caraway seeds.

If the time comes when beans are frequent leftovers, there's string bean salad, which is delicious when the beans are first marinated in French dressing, then smothered in a thin mayonnaise. But when this time comes, it's high time to give the family a respite and to get on with canning and freezing instead so that

you'll be ready for Chapter II again next March. If the bean surplus gets ahead of you, it's well to remember that beans past their prime needn't be eaten up or frozen but may be left on the vines to mature fully and be harvested as shell beans for next winter's baking.

But let's put a comma to the good young beans with two French recipes, Green Beans à la Niçoise, and Green Beans Poulette.

GREEN BEANS À LA NIÇOISE

> ¼ cup olive oil
> 1 onion or 6 scallions, sliced thin
> 2 juicy tomatoes, peeled and quartered
> ½ green pepper, cut small
> 1 stalk celery with the tops, chopped
> 1 teaspoon salt
> ¼ teaspoon pepper
> 2 cloves
> 1 bay leaf
> 6 sprigs parsley
> ½ teaspoon chervil
> 1 pound green beans, diagonally sliced

Heat the olive oil in a skillet and simmer in it the onion, tomatoes, green pepper, and celery with ¼ cup of water and the salt and pepper. Add to this brew the bouquet garni of cloves, bay, parsley, and chervil tied in muslin. Meanwhile cook the beans separately, drain them, and keep them hot. When the vegetables are tender and the sauce cooked down—about 15 minutes—remove the bouquet, stir in the beans, heat thoroughly, and serve.

Time required: 40 minutes
Quantity produced: 6 servings

GREEN BEANS POULETTE

> 1 pound green beans
> ¼ cup sliced onion
> 1 sliver of garlic
> ¼ cup chopped celery
> 1 teaspoon salt
> ½ teaspoon sugar
> 2 egg yolks
> ½ cup heavy cream
> 2 teaspoons lemon juice
> Dash of pepper and paprika

Use young beans, ends clipped, and cut in half. Cook them in ½ cup of water in a heavy saucepan with the onion, garlic, celery, salt, and sugar. When they are cooked tender—15 minutes or so— let them cool slightly while you make a sauce by beating the egg yolks and adding the cream and lemon juice. Heat this over boiling water until it thickens, then add the warm beans. Reheat, but don't let it get too hot lest it curdle.

Time required: 35 minutes
Quantity produced: 4 servings

CHAPTER VII

August

THE PROBLEM OF PLENTY

It sounds wickedly ungrateful to Nature and I hate to confess it, but bountiful August is far from my favorite month in the garden. The kitchen I don't mind so much; it's airy and the house is cool. But the garden! Relentless sun, whirring, biting insects, back and disposition strained from endless stooping and squatting for interminable picking! I keep wishing so many things wouldn't reach fruition at the same time. April, May, June, July, they're hard work too, but there's always the rich promise of harvest to egg us on.

And here it is, the harvest, its thrill beclouded by the urgency of what to do with it all.

With that off my chest, I can cheerfully hunt out a couple of cucumbers cool under their leaves and retire to the kitchen to retrieve my disposition. One thing about August, plenty's a pleasant problem, and simple meals are justified to enable us to keep abreast of canning, preserving, and freezing the surplus.

This is the month it's especially in order to do a little quiet planning to spare the energy of the gardening cook. Simplicity's the August keynote, and informality. Not so many tossed salads, for one thing, and more relish bowls of fresh young raw vegetables instead. Cauliflowerets, strips of sweet pepper, sticks of cucumber can now be added to the scallions, carrots, and radishes, and this sampling bowl saves the extra plates and the steps involved in assembling the salad array of seasonings, oil, and lemon juice. Fewer table dinners and more picnic suppers with paper cups and plates; fewer roasts and more ham slices or shish kebabs broiled on the outdoor grill to save messing up the oven. More casserole dishes prepared while the morning is still cool; more basic soups which can be varied from day to day. Fruit for dessert instead of pie and pudding. And vegetables and more vegetables, garden-fresh, imaginatively prepared, to crown the summer menu.

TAKE A COUPLE OF CUCUMBERS Those two cucumbers, for instance, go into sour cream, one of my favorite cook-savers. When cucumbers come gloriously thick and fast—and even when they don't—our household likes to keep Sour-Cream Cucumbers on hand, ready to serve instead of, or even in addition to, salad.

Sour cream is the cucumber's friend. It enhances the flavor and smooths over the sharp edge of indigestibility for which this innocent vegetable is often held accountable. Even people with settled convictions that they "cannot touch cucumbers" have been lured into eating them with impunity when they are smothered in sour-cream dressing. Sour-Cream Cucumbers go with practically everything: cold meats, hamburgers, hot dogs, baked ham, chicken, tongue, steak, stew, cutlets, omelet, or scrambled eggs. With fish they are superlative. Take this for an August supper party: iced broccoli soup, boiled salmon with hollandaise, Sour-Cream Cucumbers, corn on the cob served as a separate course—you can even send the guests out to pick and husk the corn while you put the kettle on to boil—and for dessert, blueberries. The colors in this supper are in themselves enough to cool you off on a hot night. This particular recipe comes from Hungary, that country whose ingenuity with sour cream amounts to genius.

SOUR-CREAM CUCUMBERS

> ½ teaspoon salt
> 1 scant tablespoon sugar
> 2 tablespoons cider vinegar
> 1 cup sour cream
> 2 tablespoons chopped chives or a grating of onion
> 2 tablespoons chopped fresh dill, head and leaves
> 1 teaspoon celery seed
> 2 firm fresh cucumbers

Start with the dressing: stir in a bowl the salt, sugar, and vinegar. Then add sour cream and stir it smooth. (These measurements are accurate for our taste; you may like more—or less—vinegar, salt, or sugar, but don't let it get too sweet.) Now throw in the chives, dill, and celery seed, and finally the cucumbers, which need only to be scrubbed and sliced paper-thin, rind and all. Paring and soaking cucumbers is outmoded, especially when they are fresh from the home vine. The creamy bowlful should now be chilled, and the dish is ready. You'll find it tastes better with keeping, for the flavor of the cucumbers soaks into the dressing.

> Time required: 10 minutes
> Quantity produced: enough for 4, if not gluttons

Cucumber lovers hardly need to be reminded what a fillip cucumber gives to salad—not only sliced in tossed salad, but also cubed in chicken or potato salad or coleslaw. And do you like, as I do, a diced cucumber (well drained) in mayonnaise for boiled fish? It makes a piquant sauce, especially if a few tarragon leaves are cut into it to fleck it with green.

But it's a shame to waste cucumbers on anything but themselves.

If sour cream doesn't fit your taste, pare the cucumbers, slice them, and marinate them in French dressing. Then drain the slices and press them back into the shape of the whole cucumber to serve as an accompaniment for meat or fish. A gardening friend of mine has worked out a formula for French dressing which is excellent for this and many another purpose. Two teaspoons of salt, 1 each of dry mustard and garlic salt, 6 peppercorns, 5 cloves, ¼ cup of red wine vinegar, and 1 cup of olive oil are put in a bottle, shaken vigorously, and allowed to "ripen" before using. This recipe makes an especially fine marinade not only for cucumbers but for any vegetable salad—try it next time you make potato salad, and be sure to marinate the potatoes while they are still warm.

Those who can't eat cucumbers raw may slice and boil them tender—10 to 15 minutes—in salted water. This is well worth a try for a change, especially if the cucumbers are dressed with a sauce made by melting 3 tablespoons of butter with 2 of lemon juice and adding 1 tablespoon each of capers and minced parsley. Worth trying, too, are Sautéed Cucumbers and, for a novelty, cold Cucumber Soup.

SAUTÉED CUCUMBERS

> 1 teaspoon chopped onion
> 2 or more tablespoons butter
> 2 medium-sized cucumbers
> ¼ cup flour
> ½ teaspoon salt
> 2 tablespoons chopped parsley

Mince fine a slice of onion and fry it yellow in the butter. Meanwhile wash and peel the cucumbers and slice them ½ inch thick. Dry the slices on a clean cloth; shake them in a paper bag containing the flour and salt. Then sauté them briskly in the onion butter. Five minutes on a side should give a crisp golden coating. Don't overcook them. Drain on brown paper; serve at once sprinkled with parsley.

> Time required: 15 minutes
> Quantity produced: 4 servings

ICED CREAM OF CUCUMBER SOUP

> 3 large cucumbers
> 3 tablespoons butter
> 3 tablespoons flour
> Salt and pepper
> 4 cups chicken broth
> ½ teaspoon onion juice
> ½ cup heavy cream
> 1 tablespoon chopped chives
> 1 teaspoon dill

Pare the cucumbers and slice them into the butter to sauté gently for 10 minutes. Sift the flour, salt, and pepper over the cucumbers, stir it in smoothly, and gradually add the broth and onion juice. Let the soup simmer and thicken for 15 minutes, then put it through a food mill or blender and set it in the refrigerator to chill. Before serving, stir in the cream and strew the chives and dill on top.

> *Time required: 40 minutes*
> *Quantity produced: about 2 pints*

NO BLIGHT, NO PESTS, NO DYING VINES   I had beginner's luck growing my first cucumbers. I read in a garden book about cucumber "hills" and built up two little mounds of a fine mixture that was almost all dried manure and peat moss. Four seeds went to each hill as directed, and I watered my hills and waited for the cucumbers to come up. Which they did, in profusion, climbing all over the privet hedge and bearing a mammoth crop. No blight, no pests, no dying vines. The next summer I had my comeuppance. "Hills," I discovered during a drought, should be wells to catch rain, and there's a cucumber beetle. So I learned painfully what any good gardener knows. Now I make my "hills" of flowerpots sunk in the soil, with the seeds planted in a ring around. I'm still lavish with peat moss and dried manure, which I pack into the pots so that fertilizing and watering are all one easy operation. As for the beetles, that's easy too: a screened top for an old box to cover the seedlings until they start to vine.

BUTTERED AND BAKED Mention eggplant, and many people automatically think: "French-fried." That's not the only way to enjoy this delicately flavored vegetable, and it's a way better suited to March than to August. Sautéed eggplant slices (dip first in milk, then flour before frying) are a proper August delicacy—and that smooth golden crust is achieved with olive oil, not butter. Best of all and one of the easiest and most delectable ways of preparing eggplant is to bake it in slices. Those who relish eggplant for itself unadorned should try this if it isn't already a specialty of the house.

Pare the eggplant and cut it into slices about ½ inch thick (draining them under a weight—a flatiron in the old days—is now considered an old wives' superstition). Spread the slices with soft butter generously on both sides, dust with salt and paprika, and range them on a cooky sheet for a 15 to 20 minutes' baking in a 400° oven. They need to be turned once and whisked immediately to table before they have a chance to grow limp. Sprinkled with chopped parsley and chives, garnished with a slice of lemon, they grace any meal.

And I, for one, in the heat of summer prefer having the oven on for a few minutes to standing over a deep-fat fryer!

Eggplant is such a beautiful fruit that stuffed eggplant has rich appeal to the eye of the imagination: purple splendor adorning the supper table. Actually, of course, stuffed eggplant is a visual disappointment, since the skin becomes drab and wrinkled as it cooks. My advice to eggplant admirers, therefore, is to put your favorite stuffed-eggplant recipe into a casserole and capitalize on the glorious color of the vegetable by using little eggplants from the garden as a centerpiece with lemons and green and red peppers on a bed of grape leaves.

Choices among casserole concoctions of eggplant depend upon whether one prefers to feature the eggplant flavor, as in Julia's Stuffed Eggplant, or to use it as a base for the blending of many ingredients. One example of the latter is a "one-dish-meal" variant of the way in which the Greeks prepare this, to them, favorite among vegetables. With garlic bread, sliced tomatoes and cucumbers, and cheese, fruit and coffee to follow, Eggplant Casserole makes an excellent summer supper.

EGGPLANT CASSEROLE

> 1 small onion, minced
> 1 clove garlic, minced
> 2 tablespoons olive oil
> ½ pound ground raw lamb (or 2 cups cooked and diced)
> 1 medium-sized eggplant
> 2 tablespoons chopped parsley
> 2 tablespoons soft bread crumbs
> 2 tablespoons Parmesan cheese
> 4 ripe olives
> 1 teaspoon salt
> ½ teaspoon each of fresh marjoram, thyme
> ¼ teaspoon ground pepper
> 1 egg

Sauté the onion and garlic in the oil for 5 minutes, then add the lamb and sauté for another 5 minutes, breaking the meat into small chunks as it browns. Meanwhile pare the eggplant and dice it into ½-inch cubes. Add these to the meat sauce and sauté for 5 minutes more.

The dish is now ready to be assembled. Scrape the contents of the skillet into a buttered casserole; put 2 tablespoons of water in the pan to loosen any fragrant brown bits and pour this on the eggplant and meat. Add the parsley, crumbs, cheese and seasonings, slivering the olives into the mixture. Beat the egg lightly with 1 tablespoon of water and mix all together. If it seems a little dry, another tablespoon of water may be added. Bake for 30 minutes in a 400° oven.

> Time required: 1 hour total
> Quantity produced: 4 servings

JULIA'S STUFFED EGGPLANT

> 1 large eggplant
> 3 tablespoons chopped onion
> 2 tablespoons butter, melted
> 1½ cups coarse bread crumbs
> 1 tablespoon minced parsley
> 1 teaspoon salt
> ½ teaspoon pepper
> 2 eggs
> 3 tablespoons grated mild cheese (optional)

Parboil the whole eggplant in salted boiling water for 15 minutes. Split it lengthwise, and carefully, without breaking the skin, scoop out the pulp and chop it coarsely. Fry the onion lightly in the butter for 3 minutes, then add the eggplant pulp, stir it round, and let it cook for 2 minutes more. Remove from the stove, add 1 cup of the bread crumbs, the parsley, salt, and pepper. Beat the eggs and add them too. If the resulting mixture is too stiff, add a little milk to give a soft but not runny consistency. Fill the eggplant shells with the mixture, top with the remaining crumbs and the cheese, dot with butter, and bake ½ hour in a 350° oven.

> Time required: 1 hour
> Quantity produced: 6 servings

Eggplant combines well with several other vegetables, notably tomatoes. A quickie for the gardening cook is to lay alternate layers of thickly sliced eggplant and tomatoes in a buttered casserole; each layer should be sprinkled with salt and pepper and a few dabs of butter. When the dish is full, chop a slice or two of bacon on top and bake in a moderate oven until tender—about 40 minutes. A sprinkling of fresh dill, if you like, as it goes to table, and there you are.

In experimenting with eggplant combinations, it's hard to go wrong if you start in the traditional European manner by frying onion, garlic, and parsley in oil, browning the eggplant in this sauce, and proceeding from there as taste and the contents of the refrigerator dictate. Okra might be added and a few peas or green beans; with mushrooms and chopped ham or chicken, you create a luncheon ragout.

An eggplant that feels light for its size is what you want to pick. When it's heavy with seed it's past its prime; better cut eggplants at the peak and store them in a cool corner until wanted in the kitchen. You can freeze them, of course. Marie Essipoff, in *Making the Most of Your Food Freezer*, advises not to blanch them; just peel them, slice them ½ inch thick, slip wax paper between the slices, reshape the eggplant, wrap, and freeze. In freezing eggplant, one has to work quickly to prevent discoloration (or drop the slices in water and lemon juice).

THE SNOWY HEART OF CAULIFLOWER If your household complains of the odor of cooking cauliflower or cabbage, watch that you aren't committing that sin of overcooking. There's not too much odor in the first few minutes, it's the extras that offend. Cooked cauliflower is at its best slightly undercooked: it stays snowy and firm and retains the essential delicacy of its flavor.

Try steaming a compact whole head with some of the tender green leaf shoots left on. Barely cover the bottom of a heavy saucepan with salted water, put in the cauliflower, clap on a tight cover, and let it steam for about 15 minutes, and on no account more than 20. Cauliflower broken into flowerets needs only 8 to 10 minutes.

This method, to my mind, is the making of that simple and delicious dish, cauliflower with buttered bread crumbs. Crumbs for cauliflower are best rubbed coarsely from the center of stale bread, sautéed in melted butter to which salt and possibly a touch of nutmeg or ¼ teaspoon of curry has been added. You may pat the crumbs into the head of the cauliflower and brown it under the broiler. Or you may just spread the crumbs on top and add a sprinkling of grated sharp cheese.

Cauliflowerets parboiled for 5 to 8 minutes give the start of Cauliflower Casserole.

CAULIFLOWER CASSEROLE

> 1 cup chopped mushrooms
> ½ teaspoon minced onion or 1 teaspoon chopped chives
> 4 tablespoons butter
> 2 tablespoons flour
> 1 cup milk
> ½ teaspoon salt
> ¼ teaspoon fresh-ground pepper
> ¼ cup chopped parsley
> 1 large cauliflower, parboiled in flowerets
> 1 cup cooked peas
> ½ cup grated Parmesan cheese

Sauté mushrooms and onion in the butter for 5 minutes, then lift out with a perforated spoon. Stir flour into the butter remaining in the pan, and when it bubbles, add gradually a cup of milk to make a white sauce. Season with ½ teaspoon salt and ¼ teaspoon of fresh-ground pepper, and add the parsley.

Now dispose the parboiled cauliflowerets in a casserole. Sprinkle them with the mushrooms and the cooked peas; pour over all the white sauce. Give the casserole a topping of grated Parmesan cheese. Bake in a hot oven (450°) for 30 minutes.

> Time required: 45 minutes
> Quantity produced: 6 servings

Italian tricks with cooked cauliflower include a sauté in which a minced clove of garlic is cooked slowly for 5 minutes in 3 table-spoons of olive oil. Salt and pepper are added, and in this mixture undercooked cauliflowerets are cooked gently for another 5 minutes, with 1 tablespoon of chopped parsley stirred in just before serving. . . . Flowerets of cauliflower and broccoli nestling together in the same dish (separately cooked, of course) make a stylish combination, and a natural for flavor.

Raw cauliflowerets, crisped in iced salted water and well drained, are a distinguished addition to the apéritif hour. A few spikes of fresh green pepper give color to the bowl, and the sauce dip may be mayonnaise flavored with curry powder or a combination of chili sauce and horseradish.

You're an aristocrat among gardening cooks if you succeed in growing market-grade cauliflower and celery, which need special conditions of climate and soil; there's no shame in sticking to broccoli and celery cabbage instead. But what about a corner of the garden to try celeriac, which does well in cool, moist soil and can be stored for winter use? Too few cooks appreciate celeriac.

CINDERELLA OF THE CELERY FAMILY Mostly this gnarly root gets relegated to the soup pot, where, to be sure, it plays a worthy role, imparting a delicate background flavor of celery to the whole brew.

But that is only one of its virtues. Celery root makes an excellent salad, and knowing gourmets look for this among the hors d'oeuvre at French restaurants. Home gardeners need not go so far afield; they may pull a few young roots and do as the French do: scrub and pare them and slit them into long thin strips—the kind the French call julienne. Then all that is needed is to marinate them overnight in a French dressing to which a dash of onion juice has been added.

For a special salad to go with cold meat or fowl, celery remoulade is your dish. For this, the celeriac is first cooked, then chilled in a mayonnaise sauce spiced highly with capers and herbs. Start with a cup of mayonnaise, add a scant teaspoon of mild prepared mustard plus ½ teaspoon of anchovy paste; then season with 2 teaspoons of capers chopped fine, 1 teaspoon each of chopped chervil and celery, and a couple of tarragon leaves, minced. This remoulade sauce is good, too, on parboiled cauliflowerets.

Or for a hot meal, again something French, a simple stew with an aristocratic name: Ragoût aux Céleris. This concoction might well be called meat balls in masquerade. If you relish the flavor of celery, you will find it a far from commonplace variant of an old favorite.

It is a bit difficult to give an accurate timing for the cooking of celeriac; so much depends upon the age and condition of the root. Young ones, cubed or sliced, will be tender in 15 to 20 minutes (2 to 3 minutes in a pressure cooker). Large-girthed, venerable roots may take up to 2 hours. This recipe, calling as it does for cooking the celery root ahead, allows you to size up your own roots and time the cooking accordingly.

RAGOÛT AUX CÉLERIS

> 1 pound celery root
> 1 pound chopped beef
> ¼ cup oatmeal
> ¼ cup milk
> 1 teaspoon minced onion
> ½ teaspoon fresh marjoram
> 2 tablespoons butter or drippings
> 2 tablespoons flour
> Salt and pepper

Pare the celeriac, carve it into half-inch cubes, and boil it in 2½ cups of water with ½ teaspoon of salt. When tender (see above), lift it from the liquid and keep the liquid at hand. Meanwhile prepare meat balls by combining the beef, oatmeal, milk, minced onion, and marjoram with ½ teaspoon of salt and ¼ teaspoon of pepper. Form this mixture into 1-inch balls. Brown these in butter or drippings, then boil up the celery liquor and pour it on the meat balls. Let them simmer for about 15 minutes—they are ready when they rise to the surface. Thicken the sauce with the flour smoothed to a thin paste with water; add the celery cubes, heat well, and serve.

> Time required: ½ hour, exclusive of cooking celeriac
> Quantity produced: 4 servings

Mashed potatoes sprinkled with chives, or rice with a generous grating of Swiss cheese, go well with this ragout.

When the season for game and fowl approaches, keep celeriac in mind as an addition to wild rice or for a soufflé or timbale. A cupful of puréed cooked celery root is about right for the standard recipe. With duck or pheasant, a celeriac timbale baked in a ring and center-filled with peas makes connoisseur fare.

THE BRIGHT GREEN PODS Green peppers have never come into their own as a cooked vegetable. We tend mostly to use them in a green salad or a lamb stew, or we stuff them to dress up left-over oddments of meat and vegetable. Yet this vegetable has a pleasing distinction of taste which deserves more recognition. As a change from the summer parade of greens, how about a mess of sweet peppers stewed in the Italian manner with tomato, olive oil, and an herb or two?

It makes an admirable accompaniment for ham slices, Swiss steak, or omelet, is easy to prepare, and gives the gardening cook an opportunity to boast that every ingredient—except the olive oil—has come from the vegetable patch.

SWEET PEPPER SAUTÉ

> 1 clove garlic
> 1 onion
> 4 tablespoons olive oil
> 4 large green peppers
> ½ teaspoon salt
> Pepper
> 3 large tomatoes
> 4 to 6 leaves sweet basil (or ½ teaspoon dried)
> 1 teaspoon marjoram leaves (or ½ teaspoon dried)

Start by slivering the garlic and onion and setting them to sauté gently in the oil for 5 minutes while you prepare the peppers. Remove seeds and stem ends and cut them into large squares. Add them to the onion with ½ teaspoon of salt and a grating of fresh pepper and continue sautéing for 10 minutes.

Peel the tomatoes; cut them and the herb leaves into the pot. Chili enthusiasts may want to add a piece of hot green chili pepper. Clap on a tight cover and let all simmer over a very low flame until the peppers are tender—about 15 minutes. When done, the oil and most of the juice will have been absorbed.

> Time required: 35 minutes
> Quantity produced: 4 servings

In this dish the skins of the peppers give a slightly sharp taste, to my mind not unpleasant. This can be obviated if you have the

patience and skill—which I have never had—to parboil the peppers
and skin them before adding the onion.

Another quick and easy serving is green peppers browned in
butter with onions, allowing 1 onion to 2 peppers. Excellent with
broiled steak, as are also French-fried peppers. A distinguished
garniture for steak, by the way, is to combine green pepper rings,
onion rings, and bushy sprigs of parsley, all French-fried in the
same deep fat.

Try mixing green peppers with other vegetables, to be served
with a cream sauce generously flavored with cheese, plus a dash of
Worcestershire. Celery, okra, even cucumbers, half and half with
green pepper, do well combined in this manner: just pop the prepared vegetables into a heavy saucepan, add a minimum of water
and a tablespoon of butter for each cup of vegetables, season with
salt and pepper, and cover them with lettuce leaves. Now, with
a tight cover, they may be left to their own devices over a very
low flame until just tender. Then cream-sauce them.

Given one large fine green pepper, our household is likely to
find itself enjoying an old family favorite which bears no name
but "Green Pepper, Cheese, and Eggs." The title tells the story:
it is a version of the rarebit, in which the flecks of green pepper
contribute more than color. We make it at table in a chafing dish,
and, summer or winter, a fine hearty supper it is. Don't, I beg you,
use the rubberoid cheese that comes in a package: get a cut off
the drum of a ripe, semi-sharp Cheddar.

GREEN PEPPER, CHEESE, AND EGGS

> 1 tablespoon butter
> 1 large green pepper, chopped fine
> 1 pound American Cheddar cheese, broken in pieces
> 1 cup rich milk
> 6 eggs
> ½ teaspoon salt
> 6 slices toast

Put the butter and green pepper in the top part of a double boiler
and sauté for 5 minutes over direct heat. Then set it over boiling

water; add the cheese and stir until it melts, then add the milk beaten with the eggs and salt. Stir all constantly until the mixture is about the consistency of a rarebit and just beginning to show signs of lumping. Remove it from the fire when this consistency is reached, as it will thicken up quickly. Serve on toast.

Time required: 30 minutes (longer in a chafing dish)
Quantity produced: 6 servings

SCALLOP, CYMLING, OR PATTYPAN Squashes are called by lovely names: Cocozelle, Cymling, Pattypan, Scallop, Butternut, Crookneck, Straightneck, Zucchini. Vegetable marrow I wouldn't touch, but cocozelle, on the reverse principle of "a rose by any other name," I like. All these summer squashes can fit into an average home garden if one gets the bush variety, and all should, if for no other reason than that they're easy on the cook. They make simplicity pay off. Pick those you can puncture with your thumbnail, snip off the stem end, cut them into as little boiling salted water as will keep them from burning, cook them rapidly 12 to 15 minutes, by which time all the water should be absorbed. Now a quick mashing with a wire masher, a lot of butter and fresh-ground pepper. For my taste, there's no more delicious summer dish. No frills, no doctoring. You may stuff your cocozelles, put orégano in your crooknecks, and pan-fry your zucchini or cook it with tomato and green onions; for my point of personal privilege, plain buttered and peppered summer squash.

It's worth freezing this way, too, which is again easy on the cook. All she has to do is cook a double batch at one time, cool and package half of it, and there increases the winter stock as the summer crop dwindles.

Lima beans are another vegetable I prefer as they are in summer, though of course I never turn down succotash. Frozen limas in winter I pep up with some chives or green onion and a little cream. They can be baked too. Defrost the package, mix in some chives or green onion, add a couple of tablespoons of sour cream, and salt and pepper to taste. Bake the beans in a covered casserole in a 300° oven until tender, which should be in 35 minutes. But in August let's keep the keynote simplicity.

DON'T SHELL THE LIMAS Save your shelling energy for the lima beans you're going to can or freeze; the ones you're going to eat can be cooked before you depod them. They take a little longer in the cooking—say, 25 minutes at a brisk boil; a rinse with cold water will let you handle them to slip off the pods, and they're ready to heat up with salt and pepper and butter. Limas cooked before shelling seem sometimes a trifle dry, but a little cream offsets this nicely.

Do you know your succotash? New Englanders in the know say there's nothing to compare with cranberry beans in a succotash. These are the French or dwarf horticulturals whose pods under favorable growing conditions are streaked and speckled with carmine. For a dish of plain cranberry beans buttered with cream or for succotash the beans are right for picking when they begin to swell out the pods, but don't use them all up that way. Let some stay on the bush until full maturity and treat them as shell beans for baking.

Not many gardening cooks grow shell beans, but these are worth having a go at if there's extra space in the garden. They mature in 60 days to the green-shell stage, so time the planting for them to ripen with the corn. Another 30 days sees them to the ripe-shell stage. They should be harvested before the pods crack open, and spread to dry in a warm, airy spot—a dry attic for choice—until thoroughly dried out. They can then be shelled and packed in tins or jars.

A LAVISH HAND WITH VEGETABLES Some Sunday morning raid the garden for Poulet aux Lauriers. This is a superbly simple chicken casserole which you can assemble before ten, pop in the oven as you leave for church, and forget about for two hours. Poulet aux Lauriers is a real potpourri; anything goes—except beets. You'll definitely need potatoes, onions, carrots, tomatoes. From there on, let the garden be your guide. A small turnip or two, a green pepper, a handful of beans, peas, spinach, brussels sprouts; some flowerets of cauliflower or broccoli—what have you? One thing: admire the casserole with all the dress-parade vegetables before you stow it in the oven.

POULET AUX LAURIERS

> *4 small potatoes*
> *4 small onions*
> *4 carrots*
> *3 tomatoes*
> *12 mushroom caps*
> *Assorted vegetables, such as small turnips, a few cauliflowerets, celery stalks, green pepper, a handful of green or lima beans, peas, spinach leaves (anything but beets)*
> *1 strip bacon or salt pork*
> *1 roasting chicken, cut in joints*
> *2 bay leaves*
> *1 sprig rosemary*
> *Salt and pepper*

Prepare the vegetables as necessary; cut to size for easy serving. The potatoes and unpeeled tomatoes should be halved. Lay the bacon strip in the bottom of a high-sided casserole and on it dispose the chicken. Sprinkle with salt and pepper. Then arrange the vegetables on the chicken, salting and peppering as you go along: the potatoes and lumpy vegetables on the lower layer, greens and mushroom caps above, with the tomatoes topping it off, cut sides up. Tuck the bay leaves and rosemary among the upper vegetables and pour in ½ cup of water. Cover the casserole tightly, slip it into a moderate oven (375°), and leave it to its own devices for at least 1½ hours; at most, 2 hours. If too much liquid accumulates, uncover the casserole for the last ½ hour of baking.

> *Time required: 2¼ hours over all*
> *Quantity produced: 4 servings*

Two or three days in a row cook a little extra of all your vegetables, save out some oddments of meat, and on the fourth day there'll be meat salad for supper. Leftovers can be used if they've not been buttered, but it's fun to see the salad grow from day to day: a couple of potatoes, half a cup of limas hoarded from Monday's dinner, Tuesday some cauliflowerets and a couple of carrots,

Wednesday green beans and beets. All these, neatly diced and marinated in French dressing made with lemon juice (better do the beets separately and add them at the last minute), are mixed with diced meat, ham, beef, lamb, veal—any or all of these are excellent. The giblets and liver from Sunday's Poulet aux Lauriers can go in too, and cubes of cheese and slivers of salami make an excellent addition. Some shreds of garlic, a little chopped onion and green pepper, and maybe some capers are needed for zest, and the dressing should be mayonnaise made bland with sour cream. Ring the platter round with sliced tomatoes and halves of hard-boiled eggs, and you have a pretty dish for a terrace supper. All you need besides are corn muffins keeping hot in the bun warmer and beakers of iced tea.

Any cook who enjoys eating has a spirit of quest, and her ally is the adventuring gardener. I felt mildly favorable to brussels sprouts with butter and lemon juice, but it wasn't until I stayed with friends who specialized in raising them that I was inspired to do elsewise with them. I had never really wanted to hunt down recipes for brussels sprouts until I saw their strange and comical habit of growth, with the plume of top leaves tossing a challenge. It didn't take long to discover the charm of combining brussels sprouts with chestnuts in a cream sauce blended of milk and chicken stock. Thus is one's repertory enlarged.

SIX MINUTES A-BOIL And so to corn. As with peas, my early memories of corn go back to childhood summers in Connecticut. Mother would put on a huge pot of water, and I'd be sent up the hill to the farmer's. He would lead me to the corn patch and let me help select the perfect ears, creamy and solid, with little pearl kernels at the tips. When the basket was full, I'd tear downhill, careless of dust and pebbles, and the whole family would gather to help strip off the husks and rush the corn into the kettle. Six minutes a-boil, and there on the supper table was the high-heaped platter, with a mound of butter and the big salt shaker nearby.

No gardening cook needs to be told how quickly that platterful would disappear. The rites of corn are enacted daily in homes all across the corn belt in this rich season. For those of us who can eat our corn on the cob within 20 minutes of the picking, there is no other way to enjoy this queen of the crops.

I favor serving corn on the cob as a separate course, not only for full relish of the corn, but also in the interest of having it good and hot. Keeping corn hot for seconds and thirds is a problem. Once is enough for anyone to discover that it must never, never be allowed to stand in the kettle of water after it is cooked; or that it can't be kept hot over steam without deteriorating into flavorless sogginess. The best way is to rush it to table well wrapped in napkins in a hot serving dish and abandon conversation until everyone has had his fill. If it is impossible to serve corn when the perfection of 6-minute boiling is reached, a salvaging operation is required: run cold water on it at once to curtail its cooking; then you can wrap the ears in a napkin and heat them quickly in the oven.

And let's not forget the delight of "roasting ears," whether on a picnic or the back-yard grill. To prepare corn for roasting, tear off the biggest outer husks and fold back the inner ones so that the silk may be rubbed off. Refold the husks and line the ears on the grill over hot coals. They'll need to be turned several times; when the husks are dry and brown—15 to 20 minutes—they're done to a sweet and nutty turn.

If your garden is too small for raising corn, take heart. Corn on the cob may not be perfection if it is a few hours old, but it still is good, especially if kept chilled until time to cook it. It may even be parboiled for 2 minutes in the morning and then cooked for 4 minutes at suppertime. Be sure to cool it quickly in cold water after the parboiling. If you have more corn than you can eat at one sitting, cook it all; it will retain its flavor better cooked than raw, and there are so many ways to enjoy cooked corn.

It seems presumptuous to discourse upon corn off the cob, for every corn lover has his stubborn favorites. Fritters hot off the griddle (have you tried adding ⅛ teaspoon of nutmeg to the batter?); corn chowder or Corn-Curry Soup; scalloped corn; succotash (remember the cranberry beans)—the list is long and enticing. One of our favorites is fried corn, made by frying diced bacon, then adding minced onion and green pepper to sauté dry and crisp, and finally the corn itself. When the corn has absorbed all the liquid in the pan and begins to brown, the dish is ready.

Another family favorite is my mother's Corn-Tomato Casserole. I am surprised to find this concoction not listed in my standard reference cookbooks; perhaps it is too homely, too easy. But it is a fine hearty dish, and its four major ingredients are to be had for the picking in any self-respecting home garden. This casserole is an ideal summertime one-dish supper, especially when served with a bowl of crisp greens and fresh, homemade bread. It is good with Canadian bacon or with sausage. Or let it be the hot dish in a meal of cold cuts and cheese and rye bread, with peach pie to follow.

CORN-TOMATO CASSEROLE

> *3 cups corn cut from cob, preferably raw*
> *6 tomatoes, sliced thick*
> *½ onion, chopped fine*
> *1 green pepper, chopped fine*
> *2 tablespoons butter*
> *Salt and pepper*
> *1 cup coarse bread crumbs*
> *3 slices bacon, diced*

Spread half the corn in a casserole, cover it with slices of tomato packed closely, sprinkle with half the onion and green pepper, and dot with half the butter. Give this layer a good dusting of salt and pepper. Add another layer in the same order. Top the casserole with bread crumbs and diced bacon. If raw corn is used, the casserole will need about ¾ hour baking in a moderate oven (375°); with cooked corn, ½ hour is ample, and even less if you sauté onion and green pepper for 5 minutes in butter before assembling the casserole.

> *Time required: 1 hour*
> *Quantity produced: 4 good servings*

Corn and tomatoes are a jolly combination which Nature obviously endorses since she brings them forth on the same time-table. It is traditional good eating to have sliced tomatoes instead of salad when corn on the cob is on the menu; baked tomatoes stuffed with succotash, a chowder of corn, tomatoes, and okra are familiar friends. Then there's Indian Corn Stew, another of those one-dish, top-of-the-range dinners that is the delight of the gardening cook in August. There's also that rich and delicate combination of Corn Custard with Fried Tomatoes. Corn custards can be cooked on top of the range; they take a little longer this way, and the molds should be battened down with wax paper held in place with rubber bands.

CORN CUSTARDS WITH FRIED TOMATOES

> 1 cup raw scraped corn
> 4 eggs
> 1 teaspoon finely minced onion
> Salt and cayenne pepper
> 1½ cups milk
> 6 small tomatoes
> ¼ cup flour
> 3 tablespoons butter
> 1 cup cream

Scrape the corn by ripping down the rows with the tines of a sharp fork and then pressing out the milky pulp with the side of the fork. Combine the corn with eggs, onion, ½ teaspoon of salt, and a good dash of cayenne pepper. Scald the milk and add it gradually to this mixture. Pour into buttered custard cups or a ring mold and place on several thicknesses of paper in a pan of hot water. Bake in a 325° oven for 30 to 40 minutes, or until the custard is set. Then unmold onto a serving platter to be assembled with the fried tomatoes.

Meanwhile slice the peeled tomatoes; sprinkle them with flour and salt and fry them quickly in the hot butter over a high flame. Two or 3 minutes a side should be enough to sear them well and cook them through. Surround the custards with the fried tomatoes, and let it all stay hot in the oven while you sprinkle a little more flour in the skillet, blending it into the butter. Add the cream, let it thicken, and pour it as a sauce upon the tomatoes.

> Time required: 50 minutes over all
> Quantity produced: 6 servings

INDIAN CORN STEW

> 1 pound ground beef
> 2 tablespoons butter
> 1 onion, chopped fine
> 1 clove garlic, shredded
> ½ cup chopped green pepper
> 3 cups raw corn cut off the cob (or 1 package frozen)
> 1 can tomato soup
> 1 tablespoon Worcestershire sauce
> 2 teaspoons sugar
> 1½ teaspoons salt

Brown the meat in the butter, stirring frequently; then add the chopped onion, garlic, and green pepper, continuing the frying for 5 more minutes. Toss in the remaining ingredients and stir well; cover and let simmer for ½ hour.

> Time required: 1 hour
> Quantity produced: 4 generous servings

A word about scraped corn. Next to corn on the cob, for pure enjoyment of corn, comes corn scraped from the cob as described in the Corn Custard recipe. Cooked for not longer than 10 minutes in butter and cream, it is a rare and delicate delight upon the tongue. Poached in cream in the oven, it is equally good but takes longer, about 1 hour at 225°. The proportion of corn to cream is two to one, with 1 teaspoon of salt. Some like to add 1 teaspoon of sugar. Scraped corn, too, is the basis for corn soufflé—and the making of a good corn soufflé is to cook the corn pulp with 1 tablespoon of butter until most of the moisture has been absorbed before adding it to the cream sauce.

QUEEN OF THE CROP Tomatoes have been in and out of the pages of this book right along. Back in Chapter IV I yielded up my favorite way of serving raw tomatoes, and I hope you've been enjoying them all summer long. Now the time has arrived when we can indulge that other delight of the gardening cook: fresh, home-made tomato juice. Don't, I beg you, can it all.

There is no time like August, when the crimson flood begins to run high, to fill a gallon jug and stow it on ice, ready to be used in half a dozen ways. What more cooling, these hot days, than a tall thin glass of chilled tomato juice, either seasoned only with salt or with a slice of lemon afloat in it and a spray of basil tucked in like the mint in a julep?

If the day turns chilly, heat the juice with a little lemon juice and a dash of Worcestershire and serve it as soup, with a blob of whipped cream for a garnish. Or cream it and give it a sprinkling of chopped chives and dill or basil and serve it with garlic bread. You can mix tomato juice with clam juice or with chicken or beef stock and serve it hot or cold. You can use tomato juice instead of milk in a cream sauce, add grated cheese, and have a quick tomato rarebit.

Or—and this I recommend especially—spice the juice as you make it. Again, a gallon jugful is not too much for even a very small family. The juice, chilled, makes a spicy herb-tomato cocktail, ready for any emergency. You can have it different every day by crushing a different herb sprig in it. It forms the basis of a superb aspic to go with meat or fish or to serve as salad. Tomato aspic ring, for example, filled with shrimp and flanked with cucum-

ber slices, makes a perfect supper for a hot August night. Spiced tomato juice makes a fine garden soup to be served cold and colorful as the prelude to lunch or dinner. This recipe for Garden Soup lists my own personal preferences for the basic seasoning of tomato juice; it's an all-purpose seasoning that can be varied later by adding one or another of the fresh summer herbs.

GARDEN SOUP

Group I   2 quarts (about 10) well-ripened tomatoes
           2 stalks celery with leaves
           6 or 7 sprigs parsley
           1 small onion
           1 bay leaf
           1 teaspoon whole peppercorns
           4 cloves
           4 allspice (or ¼ teaspoon ground)
           ½ teaspoon Worcestershire sauce
           2 slices lemon
           2 teaspoons salt

Group II   ½ cup grated carrot
           ½ cup grated green pepper
           ½ cup grated celery
           Sour cream

Wash and quarter the tomatoes (no need to peel, but remove the stem end). Put them in an enameled kettle with all the other ingredients of Group I. Crush the tomatoes a little so they won't stick to the pot, and stir them from time to time, letting them cook gently until soft—15 minutes or so should accomplish this. Let them cool, and then press all juice and pulp through a fine strainer or whirl it in the blender. To this purée add the grated vegetables. (If time is short, you can use a food grinder, but the crisp grainy quality of the vegetables is lost.) Chill and serve cold, with 1 tablespoon of sour cream atop each bowlful.

                Time required: 1 hour or less
                Quantity produced: about 3 pints

Quick freezing is a godsend to the gardening cook in coping with August's problem of plenty. By no other means can we so preserve the summer sweetness of what we grow; even canning doesn't admit of the flexibility of freezing. Tomato juice, for instance, can be frozen into ice cubes and packed in bags. No problem of opening a can and using only part of it. As many cubes as you want, there they are, handy. The same trick can be applied to raspberry juice: crack up a few cubes to make a pink lemonade on some hot October afternoon, or melt down enough to make Rôdgrôt. By gauging the family appetite for this or that vegetable, one can package the fresh vegetables in bags or containers of a size for just-right portions. I like to stock-pile mixed ingredients for some of my favorite recipes. The onions, leeks, and butter, for instance, for Vichyssoise, stewed together and frozen in recipe-sized cartons. Garlic, onion, celery, parsley, cooked in butter, ready for soups, ragouts, and sauces. Stems of asparagus, of broccoli, for the soup pot; boiled baby beets, celeriac, for the hors d'oeuvre tray.

And quantities of Minestra, in pints and quarts, against the lean months of winter.

CHAPTER VIII

September

REVELING IN FRUIT

Nature did well to give us peaches for the still hot days of August and September. Merely to think of biting into a peach is to feel the refreshment of cool juiciness on the tongue. To pause and straighten up from picking limas, saunter over and pluck a peach in the orchard is celestial thirst quenching.

Such luxury is not for many of us small-time gardeners, though why not? Perhaps we haven't sufficiently explored the possibilities. Espaliered peach trees, for instance, against a sunny wall, or on trellises to define the garden, the service yard, or the driveway. Even a small back yard can usually sustain one or two espaliered fruit trees: with twenty feet of sunny wall or high fence, one could have a peach, a pear, and an apple. Espaliered fruit trees can be purchased already trained and on their way to maturity, but the real amateur will want the triumph of training his own.

With a little more space—even as little as a patch twenty-five by fifty feet—a miniature orchard of dwarf trees, peaches, pears, apples, could be managed, reserving the trellis and the sunny wall for grape-vines and raspberries. There's a classic book of information about fruit trees for the small garden that would inspire even the laziest connoisseur who takes his fruit seriously. It is *Fruits for the Home Garden*, by U. P. Hedrick, listed in the Bibliography.

Don't think, however, that growing one's own fruit is the Utopia of setting out a little tree and a few months later picking a perfect peach without even climbing a ladder. There's the slow reach toward maturity. There are frost dangers to contend with; one is at the beck of Nature in matters of spraying, pruning, drought, and flood. There's the art of auspicious fertilizing. But the satisfaction of achievement! The pride of success! Perhaps that's what spurs the hobbyist on through the years of nursing and nurturing: to be able at last to bring in his own bowl of peaches which, fresh-cut and with the pot of thick cream beside it, seem to promise an evening breeze.

It's no accident that peaches are second only to apples in popularity; peaches are indeed a boon to the home gardener's table and the gardening cook's repertory. Unblemished peaches picked with a sprig of leaf or nesting in grape leaves in a chilled bowl bespeak the perfect hot-weather dessert. Peaches and cream, peach short-cake, of course. But next to eating a whole ripe perfect peach, let's have them peeled and halved and chilled in honey and brandy, and I'll take sour cream for a garnish.

I can't say too much for the distinction that liqueur and honey give almost any fruit, fresh in summer, canned or frozen in winter. Peaches, for instance. For 2 cups of sliced peaches, ¼ cup each of strained honey and brandy is about right. Rolled round in this mixture and set aside to chill for an hour or two, the fruit doesn't darken. One hardly tastes the brandy, but it brings out the ambrosial quality of the peach flavor, a subtle sweetness and coolness of taste. Mix, if you like, pitted black cherries or seedless white grapes with the peaches, and use kirsch instead of brandy. These liqueurs, with their edge of sharpness, go better with peaches than do the more commonly used sherry or madeira, which for my taste are too cloying.

Other variations on the versatile peach:

. . . Peaches and cream, pure and simple, may still be the favorite with most of us. But it is possible to vary the flavor delicately by sweetening sliced peaches with brown sugar, maple syrup, or honey, by adding a whiff of cloves, cinnamon, or almond essence. . . . By the way, peaches can be kept from discoloring by slipping them as you peel them into water and lemon juice, or pineapple juice.

. . . Dab a spoonful of currant or mint jelly in the center of a halved peeled peach, add a topping of whipped sweet cream, and you have a quick, dressy dessert.

. . . Combine well-ripened, quartered peaches with figs cooked in syrup; again a spoonful of brandy or kirsch adds distinction.

. . . It's really gilding the lily, but crushed macaroons or ground almonds, toasted to a light brown, may be spread on an open peach pie before serving, to simulate a top crust.

. . . Have you ever tried broiling peaches? Peel and halve them and lay them cut side up in a shallow pan. Dot with butter, sprinkle with brown sugar, then broil them slowly until the sugar melts and crusts. You can bring them to table flaming by pouring on warmed kirsch when you take the pan from the oven, touching a match to it at once. Brandywine Baked Peaches are the winter version of broiled peaches. . . . A slight difference produces Peach Crumble: water and lemon juice—say 1 teaspoon of juice to ¼ cup of water for 8 peaches—are poured over sliced peaches in a buttered shallow casserole; 1 cup of light brown sugar sifted with ¾ cup of flour and blended with a couple of tablespoons of butter is crumbled on the peaches, and they are baked to a soft and golden brown in a moderate oven (375°).

Peach Fritters are gourmet fare when done with a French twist. It is well to plan a meal which will build up to the climax of the dessert: a cup of Vichyssoise, say, to begin with, and broiled chicken, cucumber salad and bread sticks to follow. Then the fritters, crisp and cinnamon-sugared.

PEACH FRITTERS

	6 dead-ripe peaches
	1 teaspoon grated lemon peel
	3 tablespoons honey
	½ cup madeira wine
	2 cloves
Batter:	2 eggs
	2 tablespoons brandy
	1 tablespoon olive oil
	1 cup flour
	⅛ teaspoon salt
	2 cups fat for frying
Garnish:	½ cup powdered sugar
	1 tablespoon cinnamon

Plunge the peaches in boiling water for 1 minute and slip off the skins. Halve them, remove the pits, sprinkle with the lemon peel, add the honey, wine, and cloves, and roll them around until they are thoroughly coated. Let them stand thus for 2 hours.

Mix sugar and cinnamon for the garnish.

Now mix the batter. Separate the eggs and whip the yolks until thick with the brandy, olive oil, and ½ cup of water. Stir in the flour and salt. Beat the egg whites frothy and fold them in. The batter should be not too thick, should pour easily from the tip of a spoon.

Heat frying fat in a deep fryer to 370°. Drain the peaches from their winy bath with a perforated spoon, immerse them one at a time in batter, and fry in deep fat until golden brown—probably 3 to 4 minutes. When each fritter is done, lift it to brown paper spread in a hot oven with the door left open, and when all are ready, sprinkle with the sugared cinnamon and serve promptly.

Time required: advance preparation, 20 minutes
batter and frying, 30 minutes
Quantity produced: 6 servings

The winy mixture in which the peaches were soaked may be saved and used next day as dressing for peaches with cream. Any batter left over can go into pancakes for breakfast!

That smooth-skinned peach, the nectarine, though less robust in body and flavor than its bloomy sister, responds to whatever culinary treatment the peach will. However, it is my own conviction that nectarines, like apricots, red plums, pears, and ripe figs with their dusky flush of rose, are best in the plain state of natural goodness, to be eaten as "munching fruits." Put a bowl of these assorted beauties on the porch table for casual sampling, with a peach or two and some black cherries thrown in, and it's hard to decide where to start and when to stop.

FOUR POUNDS OF BLUE PLUMS Is there some coffee-cake dough in the house? If so, it's a day for *Zwetschenkuchen*, that monstrous tart bulging with sugar-crusted blue plums and trickling red juice. Line a 7-x-11 pan with a ¾-inch layer of risen coffee-cake dough, and an hour will make and bake you the *Zwetschenkuchen*. You'll need about 4 pounds of freestone blue plums and a good cup of sugar, with some butter. Split and stone the plums and pack them into the pan of dough. Let each half stand on its edge, leaning backward a trifle to expose its juicy interior. Have them crushed so close together that there is no room for more. Sprinkle with the sugar and fleck the top with butter; ½ hour's baking in a moderate oven completes the operation.

Next to peaches, my summer favorites are melons. From the Netted Gems and the Honey Rocks to the honeydews, casabas, crenshaws, and Persians—I wish sometimes that my climate combined North and South so that I could vine-pick them all. There's no surer way to tell when a melon is sweet for eating than to press a finger against the stem and see if it snaps lightly off the vine. The next best way to ensure perfect melon eating is to get established in the good graces of a knowledgeable vendor. This is done not by open flattery but by communicating a keen sense of appreciative appetite and a serene confidence in his judgment. It isn't enough, either, to accept what he chooses and find it good. Reporting back on the merits of the specific melon is what puts him on his mettle. It's worth many a special phone call or visit to market, for once your vendor is your partner in good eating, your melon future is assured. Add salt, and for the green-fleshed melons a crescent of lemon, and feast.

When using honeydew melon as a first course, don't forget the fine Italian hand which puts a wedge of lime on the melon, and beside it shavings of the ham called prosciutto. Smithfield or Virginia ham will do if you can't get to an Italian market, but the ham must be literally shaved from the shank.

A sprinkling of powdered sugar and kirsch, cognac, rum, or sauterne lends piquancy to almost any kind of melon. You might even like to try spiking a watermelon with champagne! To do this, cut a plug 3 or 4 inches deep from a ripe watermelon and gradually pour in a quart of champagne. Replace the plug and chill for several hours. The melon can be served either in wedges or scooped out in balls.

Why does anyone trick out the luscious fruits of summer in a fruit salad slathered with mayonnaise or even French dressing? It's anathema when the pure delectability of the fruits themselves is considered. The fruit's the thing, and each should be arranged to show to best advantage and to set the others off by contrast in shape, in texture, in color, in taste. Laid forth on grape leaves impeccably prepared, peach halves center-filled with the last of the raspberries, melon balls of honeydew, cantaloupe, watermelon, crescents of pears with the rosy skin left on, neat rounds of pineapple, bananas split and quartered; these stand on their own merits, need no furbishing. A twist of lemon or lime for the bananas, at most. One of the most inviting first courses ever offered me at a Sunday brunch was a tray of peeled melon crescents, honeydew on one side, cantaloupe on the other, fanning out from clusters of red Malaga, blue Concord, and white seedless grapes. The arts of hostess and connoisseur combine in the creation of such taste-provocative arrangements.

The judicious combining of fruits is indeed an art. If your refrigerator is big enough to chill it, one of the prettiest and most delicious buffet-party desserts is a watermelon "boat" piled high with the colorful fruits of late summer. The trick of advance preparation is to slice off the top third—lengthwise—of a ripe watermelon and save it to cover the boat during the chilling. The watermelon is scooped out (let the children have some for lunch, since you'll want only about a third of the pulp) and the shell filled with balls of watermelon, honeydew, cantaloupe, plus seedless grapes, blackberries, blueberries, and chunks of fresh or frozen pineapple, a few late strawberries—and whatever else your fancy suggests. The packed watermelon can then be covered with its top shell and chilled until suppertime, when you whisk off the cover, decorate the fruit with lemon mint, and serve the "boat" in a bed of ice.

Melon and fruit served like this are, to my mind, best eaten plain or with a sprinkling of lime or lemon juice, but some like powdered sugar and a bowl of grated coconut on hand.

For a small party, Honeydew Surprise, a French version of the fruit-filled melon, is a happy inspiration. This recipe is given in detail as a basic pattern which the imaginative hostess can vary to suit her own taste in fruit. Seeded grape halves, raspberries, pineapple chunks, whole strawberries, even banana slices, are among the seasonal variations that can be used in Honeydew Surprise.

HONEYDEW SURPRISE

> 1 large honeydew melon
> Confectioner's sugar
> 1 cup watermelon balls
> 1 cup cantaloupe balls
> ¼ cup blueberries
> ¼ cup blackberries
> A few Bing cherries
> ½ cup each peach and apricot cubes
> 1 package frozen raspberries
> ¼ cup granulated sugar
> ½ cup kirsch

Cut a 3-inch circular plug from the top of a ripe honeydew melon; scrape out the seeds and remove the pulp with a ball scoop. Then dust the inner shell with confectioner's sugar. Prepare the rest of the fruit except the raspberries: cherries should be pitted, the apricots and peaches cubed and dipped in water and lemon juice to prevent darkening. Mix these fruits and fill the melon shell. Then make a strained purée of the raspberries, flavoring it with the sugar and kirsch (brandy may be substituted). Pour this over the fruit, replace the plug, and wrap the whole airtight in aluminum foil. Chill for at least 2 hours. Serve the melon upright on grape leaves in a deep bowl of cracked ice.

Time required: ½ hour exclusive of chilling
Quantity produced: 4 servings

DON'T BE AFRAID TO BE SIMPLE Have you ever, on a hot September evening, tried the rustic menu which dates back to classical days of Greek myths? It's so easy—bread and cheese and milk, with grapes and honey—but it can satisfy the hungriest stomach and the most discriminating palate.

No "store-bought" bread, please. Fresh-baked homemade bread is my choice, with Vienna or French bread cut in chunks a close second; either of these supplemented by thin slices of dark sour pumpernickel. Sweet butter, of course, and comb honey, and plenty of milk in a tall stone pitcher. The cheeses can be any kind you choose, but a good sharp Cheddar should be among them, a cream cheese, and a goat's-milk cheese like the Italian Bel Paese. The chilled grapes, misty clusters of Concords, Malagas, white seedless, spread on grape leaves in a flat basket, form the center of attraction.

Simple, too, but more sophisticated, is White Grape Dessert in crystal cups, served with macaroons or the French pastry called "elephant ears."

WHITE GRAPE DESSERT

> 2½ cups white seedless grapes
> ¼ cup strained honey
> 1 teaspoon lemon juice
> ½ cup brandy
> 1 cup sour cream

Remove all stems but leave the grapes whole. Mix them in a bowl with the honey, lemon juice, and brandy, and chill overnight. Just before serving, stir in the sour cream. Serve decorated with sprigs of lemon mint.

Time required: 10 minutes
Quantity produced: 4 servings

Since we're concentrating on simplicity, do you know the quick and easy method of making uncooked grape juice from the Concords on your garden trellis? All you need is a quart jar, sterilized and hot, 2 cups of washed and stemmed Concord grapes, 1 cup of sugar, and boiling water. Put the grapes and sugar in the hot jar and fill to overflowing with boiling water. Seal the jar at once and set it aside to stand for three or four weeks. By this time you'll have a pale, clear infusion with delicate grapy flavor which needs only to be strained as you pour it from the jar.

MIX YOUR OWN DRINKS This grape juice is really too delicate to waste in a mixture of fruit juices, but there are fine quick combinations to make with commercial grape juice for a cooling draught. Grape juice with lemonade is well known; it's also excellent blended two to one with grapefruit, orange, pineapple, or apple juice. You can even mix a fine mélange of all the flavors.

If you've been freezing fruit-juice cubes or canning juices as the season rolls around, you're well fixed for exploring hot-weather drinks, and how welcome they are in the inevitable September hot spell. Grind up a few assorted cubes in the ice crusher, pack a glass full, pour on sparkling water, and there you are. Try a cup each of currant juice, orange juice, raspberry juice, and a dash of lemon sweetened with honey.

Until I discovered the virtues of honey as a sweetener for fruits, I laboriously bottled up simple syrup, and we always ran out of it in hot weather. Now the bottle of strained honey is always within arm's reach. If the fruit juices are ice-cold, dissolve the honey in a little warm water so it will blend easily. Raspberry juice half and half with pineapple juice, adding one eighth part of lime juice— and again, the honey—is a notable combination. Peach juice, pineapple and lemon juice; apricot juice in lemonade; pineapple and papaya juice; orange and cranberry juice—they're all worth trying.

Any of these fruit punchettes needs some dilution with sparkling water or ginger ale—I like neither, so I take my concoction in a glass packed with cracked ice. If the wind turns chill, a spike of rum or brandy circumvents goose-pimples.

If the home freezer is first aid for the gardening cook, the electric blender is her prime kitchen gadget. No particle of the good of our garden produce is lost in blending, as it must be when sieve, strainer, or food mill are depended upon. For soups, vegetable bisques, purées, a blender is unsurpassed in preserving the rich flavor of the nutrients; in exploring fruit drinks it invites adventure. Fruit still good but past table freshness can be popped into the blender for a quick cooler. A velvety peachade, for one: ½ cup of sliced peaches, ½ cup of cold milk, ½ cup of vanilla ice cream, with a pinch of salt and 2 or 3 drops of almond essence.

You can play your own variations. With chipped ice you can make an instantaneous punch; say a handful of seedless white grapes (no need to peel them) in a cupful of pineapple juice with a touch of lemon juice. A whole mélange of fruits can go in with orange juice as a base—a principle of fruit-drink mixing is to keep one main flavor predominant, and the best are orange, lemon, pineapple, or grape—only don't use blueberries: they come out an unappetizing, gloomy gray. A mint syrup for iced tea or lemonade is quick as a flash: just cut a handful of spearmint into a cup of simple syrup and give it a whirl; pretty, too.

For the freshest of apple flavor now that the early transparents are ripe, save a couple out from the applesauce, core and cut them, skin and all, into a blender with 1 tablespoon each of lemon juice and honey, ¼ cup of water, and ½ cup of cracked ice.

Or, with a little more preparation, an Eau de Melon.

EAU DE MELON

> 1 small honeydew melon
> ½ cup sugar
> 2 tablespoons kirsch
> Soda water

Scoop the pulp from a smallish honeydew—to make about 2 cups in all—and add it to the sugar which you've brought to a boil with a cup of water. Let the mixture cook gently for 5 minutes, then set it aside to steep for 2 or 3 hours before chilling it. At serving time run it through the blender with the kirsch and ½ cup of cracked ice, and serve it in tall glasses, decorated with lemon mint, with a splash of sparkling water.

Time required: 15 minutes

Quantity produced: 4 servings

. . . How is your tutti-frutti coming along? By this time it should be bursting with the fruits of summer. Better check to see if it needs more brandy at this point; its time for ripening is at hand. . . .

FINE KETTLE OF FRUIT And put on the apron; it's time, too, for jelly, jam, conserve, marmalade, fruit butters, chutneys. The books are full of them. But the books aren't full of some of the choicest concoctions: Plum Chutney, Grape Butter, Beach Plum Jelly.

PLUM CHUTNEY

1½ pounds blue plums
1½ pounds red plums
1 pound greening apples
½ pound onions
4 cups vinegar
2 cups sugar
2 tablespoons salt
1 teaspoon ground cinnamon
1 teaspoon allspice
1 teaspoon ground cloves
1 teaspoon ground ginger
1 pound seedless raisins

Stone the plums and quarter the fruit. Core the apples and chop them fine; peel and chop the onion. Meanwhile bring the vinegar to a boil with the sugar, salt, and spices. Add the onion and fruit, including the raisins, and simmer until the mixture thickens—

about ½ hour. It can then be poured into hot sterilized jars and sealed.

Time required: 1½ hours
Quantity produced: 3 to 4 pints

SPICED GRAPE BUTTER

> 6 cups Concord grapes
> 3 cups sugar
> 2-inch stick cinnamon
> 1 teaspoon whole cloves
> ½ orange
> ½ lemon

Wash the grapes; squeeze off the skins, which are to be put through the coarsest cut of the food grinder. Heat the pulp for about 10 minutes, or until the seeds come out easily; then press the pulp through a sieve to remove the seeds. Combine the pulp with the ground grape skins and measure: there should be about 4 cups. To this add the sugar, the spices in a bag, and the orange and lemon in thin crescents.

Boil rapidly until the butter thickens—it will take 20 minutes to ½ hour to reach the sheeting stage. Remove the spice bag and seal the grape butter in sterilized jars. Spiced grape butter makes a fine accompaniment for venison.

Time required: 1¼ hours
Quantity produced: about 3 pints

THE TANG OF BITTERSWEET There are those, I'm told, who do not relish the bittersweet tang of Beach Plum Jelly, but there are many more who consider this seaside specialty the quintessence of jellied delight. Thus those who are lucky enough to live along the shore lines of New England and other coasts where the handsome, purple-fruited beach plum flourishes have an opportunity, indeed almost an obligation, to do up Beach Plum Jelly in vast quantities for the benefit of inland friends. It's a good idea to store your Beach Plum Jelly in screw-top jars, which will travel well, come Christmas, to the far-off fellow addicts.

September is the very last call for Beach Plum Jelly; actually the little maritime plums, no bigger than cherries, ripen during the latter part of August, and you don't want them all fully ripened when you make the jelly.

BEACH PLUM JELLY

8 to 10 quarts beach plums
10 to 12 cups sugar

Most of the beach plums should be fully ripe, but some should still have the reddish flush of underripeness. Pick them over and wash them, then stew them in a kettle with just enough water so that you can see it among the plums. Boil until the plums are very soft (about 30 minutes), then mash them thoroughly with a potato masher. They now go into a jelly bag for overnight extraction of juice. Measure juice and sugar cup for cup and boil until the jelly stage is reached—220°—which should take no longer than 20 minutes. Seal in sterilized jars.

Time required: about 1½ hours of cook's attention
Quantity produced: 12 to 14 glasses

EDIBLE MUSHROOMS ONLY Mushrooms may not be strictly a product of the home garden, but they have certainly come into their own in the gardener's kitchen.

Time was when these delectable, tender fungi were considered foreign and exotic, even suspect when gathered in the fields by enthusiasts. Now cultivated meadow mushrooms are in everyday supply in the markets and are more and more often being grown in prepared flats in home cellars, as will be advertised in garden magazines come fall. Properly moistened and covered, these produce successive flushes of opulent, fleshy mushrooms; you can keep a constant supply on hand by succession starting of flats. And what a rich dividend to offset the cost of the flats: the fine manury spore bedding, when the mushrooms are spent, makes a lush top dressing for the asparagus bed or the strawberry row.

But that's for the future. If you know your mushrooms—and be certain you know them—September's the month to gather them wild. Meadow mushrooms (the pink gills), and puffballs are the only two I'm dead sure of, and I double check even them. But there's many a fine mess of mushrooms I've gathered in the past. In my golfing days—which ceased when I discovered the equally expensive and time-consuming but far more soul-soothing pastime of back-yard gardening—we used to carry a brown paper bag on the links and between shots collected enough mushrooms to feed the whole family, with enough left over for preserving.

Mushrooms sautéed in butter with a generous sprinkling of chives and parsley, for instance, are not only superb in themselves but will stretch and make memorable that last sparse picking of peas or the late crop of snap beans or limas. They are good in stewed tomatoes or a casserole of eggplant. If you wish to try them in a manner typically Italian, sauté them as suggested above, but add a sliver of garlic and a pinch of marjoram.

A spinach ring filled with creamed mushrooms makes a perfect accompaniment for baked tongue or ham; a combination of chestnuts, celery, and mushrooms, cooked separately but creamed together, is excellent with roast chicken. In our household mushrooms are a must in stuffing for turkey or chicken or braised flank steak. They give distinction to baked fish fillets: haddock, for example, may be dressed up for company by slicing mushrooms and onions on top of the fillets in a baking pan, dotting with butter, moistening with white wine, then baking as usual.

One of my most cherished recipes is Rumanian Stuffed Mushrooms. This dish is essentially simple and perhaps for that reason gives us mushrooms at their best. Stuffed mushrooms are delicious served as a hot canapé at the cocktail hour—Rumanians often serve them as an appetizer before dinner with a liqueur or fruit brandy. They are passed with small squares of dark pumpernickel rye bread, and one spears first mushroom, then bread with a toothpick, making one bite of both.

For canapés, small mushrooms should be used, but you may also use big ones and serve them on toast as the *pièce de résistance* for supper. With sliced ham or chicken, salad and cheese and coffee, what better on a warm September evening?

RUMANIAN STUFFED MUSHROOMS

> 1 pint mushrooms
> 1 tablespoon lemon juice
> ½ cup chopped parsley
> 1 teaspoon chopped chives
> ½ teaspoon salt
> 3 tablespoons butter
> 1 tablespoon olive oil

Wash the mushrooms, then remove the stems and peel the caps; drop the caps into a bowl containing the lemon juice mixed with 3 tablespoons of water. Make a fine mince of stems and skins; add the parsley, chives, and salt and sauté in the butter for 5 minutes. Meanwhile oil a flat ovenproof dish, letting the oil run all over the bottom and up the sides. Lay the mushroom caps in this pan, hollow side up. Pour the remaining lemon water into the stewing stems and stir well. Now put a spoonful of the mince in each mushroom cap, using it all up, including the buttery juice.

The mushrooms are now ready to cook, and at this point may be set in the refrigerator for as much as half a day. Final step is to broil them for 10 minutes or bake them in a 400° oven for 20 minutes.

> Time required: 20 to 30 minutes
> Quantity produced: 4 servings

If you're a reliable mushroom identifier, gather your supply. If you're in any doubt, lay in a stock of cultivated mushrooms when the market price is low. But in any case, preserve them. Mushrooms are something you want when you want them. Might as well have them in instantly usable form. Mushrooms may be canned, of course, but an old French cookbook gives directions for preparing the caps for main dishes, the stems for sauces or soup in such a way that they may be kept for weeks in the refrigerator. Sort your mushrooms according to size and work with a pint at a time.

PRESERVED MUSHROOMS

> 2 pints fresh plump mushrooms
> 4 tablespoons lemon juice
> 6 tablespoons butter
> 1 teaspoon salt
> 3 tablespoons minced onion or shallot
> ½ cup parsley, minced fine

Select fresh white mushrooms so that no washing is needed; a damp cloth may be used to brush off any flecks. Button mushrooms should have their stems cut off level with the caps and then be sliced; larger mushrooms should be peeled, stemmed, and sliced. Discard a thin slice from the base of the stems and reserve stems and peelings for later. As you prepare the caps, roll them in the lemon juice mixed with 4 tablespoons of water.

First, the caps: 2 pints of mushrooms will produce about 2½ cups of sliced caps, which when cooked will shrink to about 1 cup. Melt 3 tablespoons of the butter in a skillet. Lift the sliced caps from the lemon; cover and simmer them gently in the butter with ½ teaspoon of salt for 8 minutes. Cool the pan in iced water; spoon the mushrooms, butter and all, into a small jar and stow it in the refrigerator, ready for instant use in creamed dishes, casseroles, sauces. The butter will rise to the top and form a seal.

Now the stems and peelings: I chop these fine with my spinach cutter (Chapter V) and find that the stems and peelings from 2 pints of mushrooms yield about 2¼ cups chopped and shrink to 1½ cups in the cooking. Melt the 3 remaining tablespoons of butter in the same skillet the caps were cooked in; add the onion and ½ teaspoon of salt and simmer 3 minutes. Toss in the mushrooms and parsley and any remaining lemon water (the caps will have absorbed most of it) and continue simmering, covered, for 5 minutes. This mixture may be bottled in the same way, ready for gravies, soups, sauces.

Time required: 45 minutes
Quantity produced: 1 cup caps; 1½ cups stems

Mushrooms preserved in this manner freeze well: package them in recipe-sized packets.

Stuffed raw mushroom caps, mouthful size, impeccably white and crisp, are an exotic addition to the canapé tray. The filling can be prepared ahead of time, but stemming and peeling the mushrooms is a last-minute job; they must not stand, or their pristine whiteness will vanish. The filling is up to your imagination: try combining cream cheese with chives and a drop of Worcestershire, or cream cheese with a little anchovy paste. And a rare bite they make, the clean, woodland taste of the mushroom contrasting with the piquant cream cheese.

PUFFBALL SURPRISE Puffballs are surprising. Our common puffballs of the Lycoperdon genus are a fairly safe find in the woods, but even so the uninitiate had better check with an expert to be sure of what he has. Break off the outer casing, and there's the clean white meat. When sliced, it looks and almost feels like angel cake—and its flavor borders on the angelic, delicately reminiscent of eggplant. My happiest memory of puffballs is of a giant one found by my friend. Big as a football, it supplied two families for Sunday-morning breakfast. Sliced, dipped in beaten egg, fried golden in butter, then sprinkled with salt—that was all there was to it—except the exquisite pleasure of savoring it.

CHAPTER IX

October

THEY NEEDN'T BE DULL

They needn't be dull, those "winter vegetables" our forefathers manfully choked down day after long winter day. Why do we scorn them so? We don't have to let them grow big and tough and stringy as our forebears did in order to be sure the family's provender would last out the frozen months. We don't have to live on a solid diet of cabbage and turnips and parsnips and onions; we can intersperse them with peas and asparagus and snap beans all year round. What has prejudiced us? Is it the heritage of unpopularity that has dogged them from pioneer days? Does their stronger flavor give them less taste appeal?

How many of us, for example, approach turnips with an open mind and an unprejudiced palate, ready to give this homely vegetable a chance to show its merits? Far too few, would be my guess. Turnips have never been a popular vegetable, to begin with, and turned-up noses at table end by infecting the cook with a defeatist attitude that does nothing to create enthusiasm for the cause of the turnip. Yet turnips, given a fair try, may surprise us. Shavings of raw white turnips—or kohlrabi—crisped in iced water and sprinkled with ground salt crystals, are as good as radishes on the appetizer tray—and there they are in the garden, which the radishes now are not. And no housewife need be apologetic about serving plain boiled turnips if she applies a bit of imagination to her cooking.

Young white turnips diced raw into ¼-inch cubes will cook tender and delicious in 10 to 15 minutes. The trick is to cook them in butter and water—2 tablespoons of butter and 4 of water to 2 cups of diced turnips—in a heavy saucepan that has a tight-fitting cover. Salt, of course, and, if you like, a few grains of sugar to smooth down the bitter taste. By the time the turnips are tender, all the liquid, except for a buttery trickle, is usually absorbed. The best of the true turnip flavor is brought out in this simplest of methods.

Creamed turnips need just the further step of adding cream blended with a little flour, and a good sprinkling of chopped chives and parsley.

That more solid-fleshed turnip, the rutabaga, can be baked whole —scrub them but don't peel them, and bake them at 375° for about 1¼ hours. Then cut them in two and send them to table decked out with minced parsley, sweet butter, and a dash of lemon juice.

Gardening cooks whose families are skeptical about rutabagas and turnips may find sour cream helpful. Half a cup of sour cream stirred into either when cooked as described completely disguises both the turnips and the sour cream: the combination tastes of neither but has an elusive sour-sweetness of its own. A leaf of basil cut into the dish may find favor with the still reluctant.

Turnips are, after all, one of the strong-flavored vegetables, and one needs to take care in fitting them into the menu. Creamed or sour-creamed turnips are good with chopped beef, with steak, with baked ham or roast turkey (Thanksgiving is not far off!). They don't belong, to my mind, with lamb, veal, or pork, although mashed rutabagas are excellent with pork if mixed in two-to-one proportion with mashed apples. With pot roast or Swiss steak I've found it good to serve a green vegetable and, instead of potatoes, a turnip purée. Better let the family know the purée is of turnips; there's nothing more disconcerting to the palate than to be prepared for one taste and find it something else.

TURNIP PURÉE

> 8 medium-sized white turnips
> ⅛ teaspoon ground caraway
> 3 medium-sized onions
> 3 tablespoons chopped parsley
> 1 teaspoon lemon juice
> 3 tablespoons salt butter
> Salt
> 2 tablespoons sweet butter

Pare and slice the turnips and boil in salted water with the caraway until tender and soft—about 20 to 25 minutes. Meanwhile peel the onions and shred them into a skillet. Add the parsley, lemon juice, salt butter, and ½ teaspoon of salt. Let all sauté gently over a low fire until the onions are transparent but not brown.

When the turnips are cooked, drain off the water and mash them with the sweet butter. Pile them in a hot serving bowl, make a depression in the center, and fill this with the sautéed onion.

> Time required: 40 minutes
> Quantity produced: 4 servings

I don't know what my family did to kohlrabi and parsnips, but once I left the parental roof I never touched them for twenty years, until a gardening friend badgered me into having a try at them. She showed me how to select the pale little knobs of kohlrabi not two inches in diameter, had me cut a slice from the root end and peel them like a tangerine. Then I was told to slice them very thin, cook them barely covered with salted boiling water for 10 minutes.

Drained, dressed with pepper and lemon juice and melted butter, they astonished me by being highly palatable. I was next instructed to try them cooked and cubed, baked in a casserole with chopped hard-boiled eggs, covered with cream sauce, and blanketed with grated cheese. This was good too, so I approached the parsnips with more confidence.

They gave me the surprise of my gastronomical life. They were sugar-sweet and melting on the tongue. My mentor had dug her parsnips in the fall and wintered them in a heap alongside the garage, covered with earth. One February day we went out together, brushed off six inches of snow, and dug out half a dozen icy roots. These she scrubbed and scraped and quartered lengthwise (sometimes there's a woody core that has to be removed) and cooked tender in salted water—about 20 minutes. The final touch was to brown them in butter in a skillet and shake on salt and pepper.

After that I explored parsnips. Baked in cream, they are a delicious addition to an oven dinner: simmer them tender, whole, then slip off the skins and lay them lengthwise in halves in a buttered baking dish. Sprinkle them with ½ teaspoon each of salt and paprika and spread on 1 tablespoon of brown sugar mixed with ¼ teaspoon of dry mustard. Dot them with butter and pour over them a cup of cream. A half hour baking in a 400° oven should see them golden brown.

Parsnips are good in croquettes, but if I'm to go to all that trouble I'll sieve a cupful of parsnip pulp and make a parsnip soufflé. This is superb with fricasseed chicken: pour some of the gravy on the soufflé and see if your tongue can analyze the rare charm of the combination.

QUEEN OF THE CABBAGES I find it difficult not to grow lyrical about red cabbage. What lovelier sight is there than red cabbage ripening in the garden with misty red-veined leaves and crisp-curled heart? What more striking in the kitchen when, stripped to its red heart, it discloses whorls of crimson and white as you slice it? What more mouth-watering than red cabbage, cooked to perfection, in a heaping bowl on the dinner table?

Yet I find cooks who have not discovered the real worth of red cabbage. They cook it as they cook green cabbage, and it tastes much the same. But what a horrid-looking mess! Red cabbage, cooked plain like green cabbage, quickly turns a repulsive purplish-gray as it cools. This proud beauty of the garden row, this queen of the cabbages, deserves better than to be robbed of all charm in the cooking.

Perhaps that's what spurred cooks on to experiment with ways of dressing up red cabbage. Most good recipes call for bacon drippings, vinegar, and brown sugar, and this vegetable does require something fat, something sour, and something sweet to bring out its best qualities of taste and color. Our recipe follows this principle, but with ingredients that lift red cabbage to a new distinction. Red cabbage becomes Cinderella at the ball when the fat is butter; the sour, red wine; and the sweet, grape jelly. The taste is superb, the color a rich ruby red.

This particular recipe, one of my proud possessions, comes from the Black Forest of Germany. It calls to mind nostalgic memories of roast duck, potatoes with caraway seeds, *Apfelkuchen*, and the rest of the bottle of good red wine.

RED CABBAGE DE LUXE

> 1 small red cabbage
> ½ onion
> 1 big apple
> Salt and pepper
> 1 tablespoon butter
> ½ cup red wine
> ¼ cup grape jelly

Chop or shred the cabbage and onion; pare, quarter, and core the apple. Set all these to cook in 1 cup of boiling water. Add 1 teaspoon of salt, a light sprinkling of pepper, the butter and red wine, which should be of the burgundy type. Cover the pot and let the cabbage cook briskly for ½ hour. Then add the grape jelly. Ten minutes' further boiling completes the cooking, and the dish is ready for table.

Note that with fairly brisk boiling the cabbage will usually absorb most of the sauce. If it is too runny, 1 teaspoon of flour sifted over the cabbage and stirred well will thicken it. Or you may pour off the liquid and cook it down, reheating the cabbage in it before sending it to table.

Time required: 45 minutes
Quantity produced: plenty for 4

Gourmet fare, indeed, worthy of company dining. A favorite menu for friends in our household centers in an enormous pot roast, Red Cabbage de Luxe, and homemade noodles with fried bread crumbs. Pot roast is something special when you get several pounds of the tip of the rump, brown it dark on all sides, add salt and ½ cup of water, then cover it and let it simmer long and slow until it melts with tenderness. No onion, no vegetables mar the rich flavor of the beef itself; the gravy alone—and this roast produces an abundant gravy—is allowed a dash of onion juice. Red Cabbage de Luxe can also enhance roast turkey or pork or, if you are so lucky, a partridge.

Here are some tricks to try: a spoonful of caraway seeds in red cabbage cooked with drippings, vinegar, and brown sugar; slivers of raw red cabbage for color contrast in a tossed green salad; red cabbage slaw side by side on a platter with green cabbage slaw— the former with some grated apple, the latter with green pepper, both with boiled dressing.

Perhaps you may want to try cooking red cabbage with chestnuts, raisins, and apple. The principle of fat, sweet, and sour remains, but the method differs. Chestnuts, raisins, and apple are first made into a sauce with butter and white wine, and in this the cabbage is simmered.

RED CABBAGE WITH CHESTNUTS

> *3 cups red cabbage, shredded*
> *¼ cup vinegar*
> *½ cup chestnuts, peeled and blanched*
> *½ cup white wine*
> *1 tablespoon sugar*
> *¼ cup seedless raisins*

½ cup tart apple, *sliced*
2 tablespoons butter
½ teaspoon salt
1 tablespoon flour

Put the shredded cabbage in a bowl with the vinegar; cover it with boiling water and let it stand for 10 minutes. Meanwhile prepare the chestnuts and set them to simmer until tender with the white wine, sugar, seedless raisins, and ½ cup of water. After 20 minutes add the apple and continue cooking for 10 minutes. While the chestnuts are simmering, melt the butter in a skillet; add the cabbage and salt. Let the cabbage cook 10 minutes, browning slightly, then stir the flour in and turn it all into the chestnut mixture. When all is well blended, the dish is ready to serve.

Time required: 40 minutes, exclusive of
peeling chestnuts
Quantity produced: 4 servings

Don't treat green cabbage as you would red. You'd overcook it. Fresh from the garden, cabbage tastes best when it retains its light green tinge and has a slightly crunchy feel in the mouth; 4 minutes' brisk boiling at the most. In winter it's another matter. Cabbages that have long been whitening in the storage pit will profit by a somewhat different treatment. If you want winter cabbage plain, try chopping it loosely and letting it soak up cold water for an hour before you cook it. Pour off this water and set the cabbage to cook in an inch of salted water that is thoroughly a-boil. Let it bubble for 8 minutes, drain it dry, give it a prodigal spoonful of butter, stir it over a hot flame until the butter is melted and the cabbage smoking hot, then rush it to table.

Sour cream makes a good change from the melted butter, or you may make a mustard butter sauce: melt ¼ cup of butter in a saucepan; blend into it ½ teaspoon each of dry mustard, sugar, and salt; give it 1 teaspoon of lemon juice before pouring it on the cooked cabbage.

If you have no time for shredding cabbage, cook it in wedges. Cut the wedges 1½ inches thick and spread them—don't pile them up—in a broad skillet. Sprinkle the cabbage with caraway seeds—

or grate nutmeg on it—give it some fresh-ground pepper, a few grains of sugar, and ½ cup of water. Cover the pan and let it come to a quick boil. Then lower heat and let simmer for 15 minutes. Serve it with chopped parsley and melted butter.

And a trick for coleslaw: shred the cabbage into a colander, set the colander in a bowl, pour boiling water over it, and let it stand for 60 seconds. This quick parboiling refreshes old cabbage, reducing its chewiness without destroying its crispness. And don't forget that sour cream dressing for cucumbers (Chapter VII) tastes just as good on coleslaw.

If you cook cabbage with meat, that's something else again. The role of the cabbage becomes supporting, not stellar, and its virtue must be subservient to the main ingredient. But even with corned beef and cabbage, that notable New England staple, I prefer to use the core and outer leaves for flavoring the beef, cooking separately that which is to be eaten as vegetable.

However you like your winter cabbage, save enough whole outer leaves to make a Sarma, which is the stuffed cabbage of the Yugoslavs and a meal in itself. This dish is doubly cabbagy, since it combines fresh cabbage with sauerkraut. You will probably want mashed potatoes and applesauce with the Sarma, as do the Yugoslavs. Connoisseurs of this dish tell me that it gains flavor by being cooked the day before, needing only thorough warming before serving.

SARMA

12 large cabbage leaves
1 tablespoon chopped celery
1 teaspoon chopped onion
2 tablespoons chopped green pepper
2 tablespoons olive oil
1 clove garlic
1 pound veal and pork ground together
¼ cup rice, parboiled for 10 minutes
1 teaspoon salt
½ teaspoon pepper
3 cups sauerkraut, fresh or canned

> 2 cups tomato juice
> 3 tablespoons fat (butter or drippings)
> 2 tablespoons flour

Pour boiling water on the cabbage leaves and let them stand for 10 minutes while you sauté the celery, onion, and pepper in olive oil for 5 minutes. While these are frying, rub a big bowl with garlic and mix in it the ground meat, rice, salt, and pepper. Add the sautéed vegetables when ready. This is the stuffing for the Sarma. Divide it into 12 portions, and roll each in a leaf of cabbage, lapping over the corners to make compact rolls.

Spread a layer of sauerkraut on the bottom of a heavy kettle, pack in the cabbage rolls, then cover them with another layer of sauerkraut. Pour the tomato juice over all, adding a little water if necessary to just cover the top layer of sauerkraut. Sprinkle on salt and pepper generously, cover the pot, and let the Sarma cook gently, either on top of the stove for 1½ hours or in a slow oven for 2 hours. Shortly before serving, brown the flour in the fat and stir it in to thicken the sauce.

> Time required: 2 hours
> Quantity produced: 6 servings

A BETTER FATE THAN BOILED TO DEATH   Most cookbooks—and most cooks—give kale and its southern sister, collards, scant attention, lumping them with other pungent greens such as turnip, dandelion, and mustard greens. And indeed, if kale is to be treated in the time-honored manner, boiled to death with pork hocks or salt pork and served smothered in vinegar, they're right.

Kale doesn't deserve this unconsidered brush-off. The garden-minded like to grow kale, a dependable green which improves in flavor with the frost that puts a finish to the chard crop. One ardent gardener grew such a fine stand of kale that his wife was literally forced into inventing a kale dish the family would eat repeatedly so the crop wouldn't be wasted. Her ingenuity turned up a potpourri of kale, late vegetables, and sausages, and the recipe became a standard fall favorite.

This concoction has the connoisseur's touch of imagination and is an ideal dish for the end-of-the-garden season. It belongs in the repertory of every gardening cook. Potpourri of Kale makes a fine, hearty, one-dish dinner. Try it with popovers or hot cheese biscuits or with French, Vienna, or pumpernickel bread. Apple dumplings or fruit and cheese round out a worthy meal to usher in October.

POTPOURRI OF KALE

4 large link sausages
4 to 6 large onions
1½ pounds kale
4 large tomatoes
4 to 6 okra pods
1 teaspoon salt
Fresh-ground pepper

Simmer the sausages in water for 5 minutes while you peel the onions and wash and dry the kale. Cut off the stems and any tough midriffs. Now prick the sausages and set them to brown in a large deep skillet. As the fat accumulates, slice the onions into it and fry until sausages begin to brown and onions are transparent. Cut in the tomatoes and okra (first remove stem ends) in chunks. Then add the kale, as much as the skillet will hold. Cook briskly, stirring frequently so that the liquid will be absorbed, until the kale is just tender but not limp—say 15 minutes. The curly leaves should stand up in the pot. Just before serving, give the Potpourri a teaspoon of salt and grind fresh pepper generously on top.

Time required: 45 minutes
Quantity produced: 4 good servings

When the stalks of kale are young and tender, they may be boiled like asparagus and served with hollandaise. And don't forget that a handful of young kale leaves lends zest to a green salad!

Traditional methods of treating kale as boiled greens should be considered outmoded in this day of quick cooking of vegetables. Fifteen minutes' brisk boiling in a small amount of water gives kale a fresh, crunchy texture; the seasoning may be crisp-fried salt pork with a little of the drippings, plus grated onion, with perhaps a dash of lemon juice or, for variation, a tablespoon of chopped green pepper with some chili sauce for seasoning.

MINCED KALE WITH GARLIC DRESSING

> 1 pound kale
> 4 slices bacon
> 6 tablespoons bacon fat
> 1 large onion
> 1 clove garlic
> 1 teaspoon salt
> ½ teaspoon fresh-ground pepper

Wash the kale well, then boil it in a small amount of water for 15 to 20 minutes. Drain it and keep it hot. Meanwhile fry the bacon crisp; lift it from the pan and mince it for a garnish. In 6 table-spoons of the bacon fat fry the onion, sliced thin, and the garlic in slivers. Add the hot kale, salt, and fresh-ground pepper and heat for 5 minutes. Before serving, garnish the dish with the minced bacon.

> Time required: 30 minutes
> Quantity produced: 4 servings

THE BREAD-AND-BUTTER VEGETABLES—POTATOES AND ONIONS Those winter-keepers, beets and carrots, have been discoursed upon elsewhere; salsify we'll ignore. One can't ignore potatoes and onions, which are such staple items of good eating year round and which go so well together in so many combinations.

I particularly don't want to ignore them right now because I've just checked six standard reference cookbooks and have made an amazing discovery: only one of them mentions the one thing that makes scalloped potatoes really good—onion. Some cookbooks even recommend making scalloped potatoes with cream sauce, which I consider not only a lot of extra work but out of character with the dish. It's such a homely, easy way of preparing potatoes, just to build up the casserole with layers of thin-sliced potatoes, each layer dusted generously with flour, salt, and pepper, dotted with butter and chopped onion. I use the whole of a small onion, chopping a good slice onto each layer of potato. Then milk just to the topmost layer, and the casserole can be forgotten in a 350°

oven for 1½ hours. It's a delicious dish for a chilly October day and can be made into a whole good homespun meal by laying pork chops atop the potatoes. These bake and brown with the milk lapping at their undersides, and fat from the baking chops seeps into the potatoes, enriching their flavor.

One beauty of baked potatoes is that they'll cook through at any temperature from moderate to very hot, which makes them a cook-saver de luxe. All you have to do is adjust the length of time: about 40 minutes at 450°, almost double that at 350°. Baked potatoes invite herbs and spices. Have you tried the sprinkling of dill and spoonful of sour cream mentioned back in May? Have you tried a grating of fresh nutmeg? Have you tried Stuffed Baked Potatoes with Herbs?

STUFFED BAKED POTATOES WITH HERBS

> 4 large potatoes
> 4 tablespoons butter
> ⅓ cup rich milk or cream
> 1 teaspoon fresh chives
> 1 teaspoon fresh chervil
> 1 teaspoon fresh thyme or marjoram
> 1 teaspoon salt

Bake the potatoes until soft when pinched, then make boats out of them by slicing them lengthwise. Scoop out the potato and mash it to a fluff with the butter and milk (it may need more milk), adding also the herbs and salt. Pack this mixture lightly into the boat shells, letting it stand up in peaks at the top. Reheat them in a moderate oven and slip them under the broiler at the last to brown the peaks.

> *Time required: 25 minutes after baking*
> *Quantity produced: 4 servings*

The Dutch have a family supper dish that is equally appropriate to the kitchens of American home gardeners, and seasonable now that the time is here for harvesting the ingredients. This Dutch treat, affectionately called Hemel en Aarde (which, translated, means "heaven and earth"), is simply a mixture of mashed potatoes and applesauce, but the combination produces taste and texture unlike either. Hollanders would serve it for supper with broiled bacon, sliced cucumbers, coffee cake, and cocoa. Simplicity itself, and a menu I commend to you for some mellow October evening. As a welcome change from the conventional, try it also as a companion piece for roast pork, roast duck, or broiled Canadian bacon. Hemel en Aarde may be prepared ahead of time and browned just in time to be eaten; if you chill it, however, you'll need to increase the baking time.

HEMEL EN AARDE

> 2 cups potatoes mashed while hot
> 4 tablespoons butter
> 2 cups unsweetened applesauce
> 2 tablespoons sugar
> ½ teaspoon nutmeg
> ½ teaspoon salt

Whip the butter into the hot mashed potatoes and then add the remaining ingredients. Taste it; you may find you want a little more sugar, but don't get it too sweet: its charm is the tart surprise of apple blended with the bland potato. Let it cool. Turn the mixture into a casserole, lifting rough peaks with the back of a spoon. Bake in a 400° oven for ½ hour. If by this time the surface hasn't gilded nicely, slip it under the broiler to brown.

> Time required: 1 hour
> Quantity produced: 6 servings

Once as an experiment because it sounded good I tried making Hemel en Aarde with sweet potatoes instead of white. The result was entirely different. The sweet-potato flavor predominated, the applesauce disappeared into a slight tang as of vinegar. Substituting a little more of brown sugar for the granulated and adding a few chopped black walnuts turned it into a good sweet-potato pudding —but what a squandering of good applesauce!

Yet of course apples do combine well with sweet potatoes. We are all familiar with the sweet-potato "pie" consisting of layers of cooked sweet potatoes alternating with layers of sliced raw apples, each layer sprinkled with brown sugar and dotted with butter. A fluffier version is a real pie made with a base of mashed sweet potatoes and sliced apples—it is more soufflé than pie and gives a fitting climax to an autumn dinner.

SWEET POTATO AND APPLE PIE

> ¾ cup granulated sugar
> ½ teaspoon nutmeg
> 1 teaspoon cinnamon
> 2 tablespoons rum
> 2 cups hot mashed sweet potato
> 3 tablespoons butter
> 1 cup milk
> ½ cup cream
> 2 eggs
> Baked pie shell
> 1½ cups thick-sliced apples
> ½ cup brown sugar
> Juice of 1 lemon (optional)
> Grated rind of 1 lemon (optional)
> ½ cup chopped walnuts (optional)

Add the white sugar, spices, and rum to the hot mashed potatoes, then whip in 1 tablespoon of the butter, melted, the milk, cream, and beaten egg yolks. If you choose to use them, the lemon and nuts go in too. Whip the egg whites stiff, fold them into the filling, and turn the mixture into a baked pie shell. Spread the apples on top, sprinkle them with the brown sugar, dot them with the remainder of the butter, and give a final dusting of cinnamon. Bake the pie ½ hour at 375°.

> Time required: 1 hour
> Quantity produced: 6 servings

To accompany pork roast or ham, you can make nut-rolled sweet-potato balls on somewhat the same principle as the sweet-potato pie. Use about 3 cups of hot mashed sweet potatoes; spice them with ¼ cup of brown sugar, ½ teaspoon of salt, and ¼ teaspoon each of cinnamon and nutmeg. Moisten the mixture with

⅓ cup of orange juice and grate in a teaspoon or two of the rind. Shape into 8 balls, roll each in chopped walnuts or pecans, and bake them on a cooky sheet along with the roast for 30 minutes.

Many are the fillings for acorn squash, whether baked, boiled, or steamed. By and large, they fail to catch more than my passing interest; I so much prefer the flavor of the squash unalloyed except for butter, pepper, and maybe a sprinkling of brown sugar or sherry. By far the sweetest, moistest, nuttiest-tasting acorn squash is achieved by baking it whole. It takes nearly 1½ hours in a moderate oven, but the aroma is heavenly when the squash is split in two. And incidentally it's much easier to cut and remove the seeds and fibers. A good blob of butter, a generous shaking of salt and fresh-ground pepper—what better with a slice of ham, which you can spread with mustard, sliced apples, and brown sugar and bake at the same time?

And those squash and pumpkin seeds. Of course you save them for the birds, but do you ever toast them for yourself? You don't wash them, but you do pull off the fibers. Then you stir them with enough melted butter to moisten them—about a tablespoon to a cup of seed—give them a good salting, and toast them, with an occasional stir, in a slow oven until they brown and crisp.

What are you going to do with the pumpkin pulp when you scoop out a jack-o'-lantern for Halloween? Make pumpkin pie, to be sure. Since there will be the makings of several pies, here are a few reminders of what can be added to your favorite recipe for adventuring in flavor. Two tablespoons of brandy in the filling goes almost without saying, but have you tried giving the pie a thin film of kirsch just before serving it? Pour a spoonful or so on the pie and tilt it to let the liqueur run all over the surface; then pile whipped cream lightly on top.

Instead of brandy in the filling, lemon—grated rind and juice— gives an elusive, unusual savor. Or chopped black walnuts or pecans may go in the filling or be spread on top of the pie and sprinkled with caramel syrup.

If you have filling for more than one pie but not enough for two, make some pumpkin tarts: put a teaspoon of orange marmalade in each tart shell before filling with the pumpkin mixture. Serve these with a topping of whipped cream or, if you are one of those who like it, marshmallow.

You may even bake your pie as a pudding instead of a pie. Use your favorite recipe (with brandy), replacing the milk with cream; pour the pumpkin mixture into a deep casserole which has been buttered and then spread generously with brown sugar. In the baking, set the casserole in a pan of water and bake at 350° until the pudding is set—about 1 hour. Chill it well before serving and garnish it with whipped cream.

But let's not turn all our pumpkin into sweets. A well-flavored pumpkin purée makes excellent company for roast pork, roast lamb, or mutton or duck. You may even want to try it instead of sweet potatoes or squash, come Thanksgiving, with the turkey.

PUMPKIN PURÉE

> 2 cups mashed cooked pumpkin
> 2 tablespoons butter
> ⅛ teaspoon ground clove
> ¼ teaspoon ground cinnamon
> ½ teaspoon grated nutmeg
> ½ teaspoon salt
> 1 tablespoon brown sugar
> ½ cup brandy

Mix all these ingredients in a heavy saucepan and set over low heat. Stir constantly until the butter melts and blends, then occasionally (to prevent burning) until the purée has dried out enough to keep shape when piled up.

> Time required: 20 minutes
> Quantity produced: 4 servings

Everyone has his own ideas about onions, but here are a few reminders of ways in which this sturdy vegetable may contribute to good eating: baked, with a glaze of butter and sugar (have you tried a dusting of curry powder on them?); stuffed, with peas and mushrooms, with sauerkraut, with mashed potatoes and crumbled bacon, with cheese, with their own hearts mixed with seasoned crumbs; scalloped, with cracker crumbs and milk; sautéed, with green pepper.

A crusty onion soufflé is a fine accompaniment for cold sliced turkey or for that roast beef dinner you've been saving up for. An onion soufflé (use 1 cup of puréed onion for the standard soufflé recipe) can bake right along with the roasting meat at 325°, though it takes both arithmetic and experience to figure the timing so both will be at the peak of perfection at the same moment. Thirty-five minutes before you expect the beef to be ready should be about right for popping the soufflé in the oven.

TIME-SAVER FOR COOKS Have you ever tried baking onions whole and unpeeled, like potatoes? All they need is a good washing and about 1½ hours in a 375° oven. When they are baked tender, slice off the root end and squeeze out the centers, discarding the outer shells. Dress them with melted butter seasoned with salt and paprika, and garnish them with grated cheese or minced parsley.

Our household likes sliced Bermuda onions baked in cream. Two big ones will serve four; they should be sliced very thin, spread in a flat baking dish, salted, covered with thin cream, and baked in a slow oven until soft.

Best of all, as a specialty of the house with steak, French-fried onions. These, like onion soup, are easier to prepare than is usually thought. To be truly "French" fried, they are never dipped in batter or in eggs: dip them in milk, then in flour, and fry a few at a time in deep fat. They may even be made a little ahead of time and kept crisp on brown paper in the oven.

TAKE YOUR TIP FROM THE SQUIRREL Before we eat
up the whole surplus crop, what are you doing about winter storage? Frosty days are coming and you need to have your weather ear
to the radio to get in the tomatoes and peppers at the very last
possible minute before the first frost. Better dig the sweet potatoes
right away and start curing them; perhaps you've already piled up
the squashes and pumpkins for their two weeks' sunning. No need
to worry about the cabbages and root crops until a hard freeze
threatens, but have you your plans made for wintering them over?
It would be a gastronomical horror to be caught short and faced
with eating them all up before they spoil. It would be garden
blasphemy to let them waste, the patient work of man and nature
put to naught.

If you're an old hand, with a vegetable storage room in the
cellar or an outdoor storage pit, you're sitting pretty. But what if
you live in an apartment or a "ranch-style" house where every inch
is dedicated to living space and the "cellar" is a cubicle for the
furnace next to the kitchen? You'll be able to ripen the tomatoes
and peppers—they wouldn't keep long anyhow—decoratively dis-
played on window ledges. Squashes, pumpkins, onions will do all
right for several weeks at least in a cool corner on the floor, if you
can tuck them where they won't be tripped over.

But what about beets and carrots and turnips? Will you have to
take to canning? You won't be able to keep them in the house,
they'd shrivel and rot. Perhaps you can store a few, packed in
cartons within cartons, in a cold corner of the garage. Have the
inner carton enough smaller than the outer one so that it can be
insulated on all four sides with torn paper, shavings, or sawdust.
You could bury a barrel on an angle in the garden or sink a metal
garbage pail up to its neck handy to the back door. With a tight
cover mounded over with straw and piled with soil if the weather
gets bitterly freezing, your hoard will be safe for several months.

If you're really cramped for space, you've probably already de-
cided to stick to canning and freezing the staples. But don't give
up all hope of wintering over some of the garden crop. Plant kinds
that can stay right in the ground where they grow: parsnips, salsify,

horseradish, leeks, even carrots, if the ground doesn't freeze too hard, can be covered with leaves or straw, battened down with boards, or mounded with soil. There'll come a thaw in January or February when you can chop a supply out of the frozen earth. Celery and Chinese cabbage can be packed in trenches in the garden row and covered the same as the parsnips. Kale is extremely hardy and will last well into December with a little protection with leaves and newspapers on very cold nights.

If your house is standard from attic to cellar, you'll be able to store everything from garlic braids and dried beans to cabbages, celery, and sweet potatoes. The attic, if it is frost-free, will do for the onions as well as the beans and garlic. The pumpkins, squashes, and sweet potatoes can lie on the cellar floor if you have a temperature not much above 55°.

But if you go in for supplying the family with home-grown produce on any scale at all, it will pay you in comfort, if not in money, to wall off a six-by-eight-foot corner of the cellar for a storage room. Bins for the apples and potatoes; sandboxes for the beets and carrots, turnips and rutabagas; slatted shelves for the squashes and sweet potatoes, lying so as not to touch each other. Put nails in the rafters for hanging the upside-down garden of pepper plants, tomato vines, and Chinese celery, narrow shelves for the canned goods, moist sand on the floor, and you're set. Except for one thing: there are three principles of vegetable storing— temperature, humidity, and circulation—and you must know how these apply to your various crops. The Cornell Extension Bulletin 846, *Home Storage of Vegetables and Fruits*, gives general directions to keep you straight, and your state service can fill in for local conditions. The storing of winter vegetables is an art not to be taken lightly; it's only too true that one improperly stored cabbage can fill the whole house with a miasma of foul odor.

There are tricks, too, not always mentioned in the general articles. Cabbages, for instance, if pulled up one week and allowed to dry out upside down on the shed floor, can the next week be wrapped in newspaper to survive even city living until April. The secret seems to be the drying out for a week; you then cut off the stems, tear off the loose outer leaves, and wrap each cabbage tightly in several layers of newspaper. By winter's end the outside leaves may have dried to paper, but the heart, if the cabbage was unblemished to begin with, is white and succulent.

The root trio of carrots, beets, and turnips have been known to do very well packed in crocks, kettles, and wash boilers, loosely covered. Their shapes assure circulation; moisture is provided by a jelly glass half full of water. Set it high enough in the container so it can easily be checked: if it gets cloudy, change it for fresh; if moisture condenses on the sides of the glass, reduce the amount of water in it. The vegetables store well this way even in a preserve closet or unheated sun porch, and you can pull out a crisp, sweet carrot as late as March.

TAIL END OF THE GARDEN The tail end of the garden has its own high moments. Fried green tomatoes should be one of the rituals of the first frost. The big shapely ones, showing the light green of impending ripening, you'd best wrap in paper, separately, and keep. But the knobby, small, blatantly underripe ones conceal unsuspected goodness in their hard green hearts. Slice them, dip them in salted flour, and fry them crisp and brown—almost charred—in butter; they're a feast dish. They're worth a Sunday breakfast party with baked corned beef hash.

Baked hash, by the way, is a gardening cook's easy trick: use 2 cans of corned beef hash with 1 can of pressed corned beef chopped into it. Add chopped green pepper and onion and a good measure of chopped parsley—I usually first sauté these in drippings. Spread mixture in a casserole, pop it in the oven, and it can bake for ½ hour while you fry the green tomatoes.

About this time of year cherry tomatoes become a problem. The novelty of decorating a salad plate with them wears thin, and munching them with salt at cocktail hour, so pleasant back in September, begins to pall. After all, these midgets can't compete in flavor or versatility with their big sisters. Yet here they are, a prolific crop that mustn't go to waste.

The answer is simple. Cherry tomatoes make superb pickles, crisp, translucent globules, good to look at, juicy to bite into, subtly pungent with dill and garlic. This particular recipe is apparently little known, except as it is passed from friend to friend. I have never found it in a cookbook, and I suspect that this may be a first public appearance. I commend it as a notable addition to the repertory of those who relish pickles.

LILLIAN'S CHERRY TOMATO PICKLES

> 1 quart small green cherry tomatoes
> 2 heads dill
> 1 small clove garlic, peeled
> Grape-sized piece of horse radish (about ⅝-inch cube)
> 1 teaspoon mustard seed
> 1 teaspoon mixed pickling spices
> Raisin-sized piece of alum (about ⅜-inch cube)
> 1 small hot pepper, red or yellow
> 1 cup white cider vinegar
> 1 teaspoon salt

For best results the tomatoes should be hard and green, with no blush of color. Wash and dry them, removing the stems. Sterilize a quart jar. Put into the bottom the heads of dill, the garlic, horse-radish, mustard seed, spices, and alum (this is to be had at drug-stores; if lump alum is not available, powdered may be used—scant ½ teaspoon). Now pack the jar tightly with cherry tomatoes, poking the hot pepper among them.

Make a brine by combining the vinegar and salt with 2 cups of water. Bring this mixture to a good boil, then pour it over the tomatoes, filling the jar to overflowing. Be sure the jar is still hot from its sterile bath—it is a good idea to keep it in the hot water while you pack it—so that the boiling brine won't crack it. Seal at once.

> Time required: 30 minutes
> Quantity produced: 1 quart

Any of the pygmy-sized tomatoes may be pickled by this recipe, or undersized green tomatoes may be used, with cherry tomatoes to fill out the jar. Or, if you like the flavor combination, you may pickle gherkins or burr cucumbers in the same way.

Making mustard pickles on the grand scale is a good occupation for a couple of bright October days. It's a big job, but one that gives you the smug satisfaction of putting to thrifty use the last of the garden crops. And as the kitchen grows more and more crowded with pots and jars and bowls and spoons and strainers, it's good to remember that a jar of mustard pickle, homemade by a time-honored recipe, will make a prized Christmas gift.

The recipe below is time-honored: it comes from the ample kitchen of a Nebraska farm, where from year to year generations of mothers and daughters have made "Miz D's Special Mustard Mix."

It's a good idea to assemble the utensils ahead of time. This recipe yields 10 to 12 quarts, and I suggest that if you have Christmas in mind you include some pint jars in your supply. You'll need at least six bowls in a variety of sizes, including a big one for the cauliflower, and a similar array of kettles and pots. You'll need to arrange to sterilize the jars. And so to mustard pickles.

"MIZ D's" SPECIAL MUSTARD MIX

> 1 quart (3 large) cucumbers
> 1 quart small gherkins
> 1 quart green tomatoes
> 3 heads cauliflower
> 2 quarts button onions
> 3 red peppers
> 3 green peppers
> Salt
> Vinegar
> 1 ounce powdered turmeric
> 4 ounces ground mustard
> 2 cups flour
> 6¾ cups sugar
> 3 quarts cider vinegar (may use a little less and dilute with water)

Prepare the vegetables: the cucumbers, if tender, can be left unpeeled; they should be cut in chunks or diced. The tomatoes, if large, should be cut in eighths; if small, quartered. Break the cauliflower into flowerets; slice the peppers in strips; peel the little onions. The gherkins are left whole. When ready, put each vegetable in a separate bowl, cover with brine made of one part salt to nine parts water, and let stand overnight.

In the morning drain the vegetables and cook each separately in salted water and vinegar, using one part vinegar to two parts water. Let them boil briskly until nearly tender—5 to 10 minutes, depending on the vegetable. Then drain them well.

Meanwhile make a paste by blending the turmeric, mustard, flour, and sugar, and adding 3 quarts of vinegar gradually until the mixture is smooth. Then boil it up, stirring constantly until it thickens.

Combine all the vegetables in a big kettle; pour the pickling mixture, boiling hot, over them. Bring all to a boil and let bubble for 10 minutes. Then pour into hot sterilized jars and seal.

Time required: 2 days, on and off
Quantity produced: 10 to 12 quarts

Did you know that you can use the liquid from any kind of pickles—except mustard pickles—to make quick and easy pickled onions? Take the small dry onions, peel them neatly, cut them in half, and let them stand for a week in a jar of pickle juice. They are then ready for the table.

If you still have gusto for pickling, perhaps you'll want to stock the provision shelf with Pickled Cabbage, which comes out crunchy like a glorified coleslaw, to give relish to ham, tongue, sausage, or cold cuts.

MRS. ABRAMS' PICKLED CABBAGE

> 1 medium-sized cabbage
> 1 green pepper, cut fine
> 1 cup sugar
> 1 cup cider vinegar
> 1 bay leaf
> 2-inch stick cinnamon
> Salt

Shred the cabbage, wash and drain it, and let it stand overnight in brine made of one part salt to nine parts water. In the morning drain off the brine and squeeze out the cabbage. Add the green pepper. Mix sugar, vinegar, and 4 cups of water; add the spices and boil for 5 minutes. Pack the cabbage in hot sterilized jars; pour on the pickling mixture while boiling hot. Seal and let ripen a couple of weeks before using.

Time required: 1½ hours in all
Quantity produced: 4 pints

In an old cookbook I once discovered a pickle recipe that is an especially apt reminder that we approach the close of the garden season. It is called "Tail End of the Garden Pickles" and reads: "Use whatever you have: lima or string beans, celery, carrots, green peppers. Prepare and cut into desired size. Soak each kind separately overnight in brine. In morning, drain off brine, cook each kind separately in boiling salted water until just barely tender (peppers, bring just to boil). Drain and pack into sterilized jars and cover with pickling mixture: 1 quart vinegar, 1 cup sugar, 2 tablespoons whole black pepper, 1 teaspoon grated horseradish if liked, 1 piece stick cinnamon, ¾ teaspoon mustard seed, and ½ teaspoon whole cloves. Heat to boiling, boil 3 minutes, pour into jars, filling to overflowing, seal at once. Ripen for 6 weeks."

Pickle enthusiasts must beware, however, for, as in making mustard pickles, this kind of mixed pickling can quickly turn into a major project, with the kitchen crowded with little bowls of vegetables soaking in brine and many more jars needed than one originally bargained for.

WHY NOT A KITCHEN-WINDOW GREENHOUSE? I hate to see October depart. It's a season of good-bys; good-by to the mellow fruitfulness of the garden, and as one looks up bare rows to the horizon of trees, good-by to the colors of autumn. Good-by, too, to the gardening mistakes of the summer and the sins of culinary omission. Good-by to shorts. October's a time when we follow the sun instead of the shade and feel the anticipatory shiver of winter.

One always wants to do something to preserve the green garden growth into the brown months of winter; October's the last call for potting up a few hardy herbs for the kitchen window. Actually it should have been done long ago from seedlings or root cuttings started early enough to be ripe for transplanting before frost. October's the time when the pots come indoors for good, having been nicely hardened up with sunny days spent outside and cold nights safe in the house. Herbs won't do well in the kitchen, however well prepared for the adjustment, if proper arrangements for their care aren't made. A narrow tray for the window ledge, filled with pebbles kept wet with water, is the start, for the little plants will need plenty of light and air and moisture. Don't let the pots ever stand in water: give them a good soaking every couple of weeks, and water from the top in between times if they dry out. Parsley, chervil, chives, mint, basil, marjoram, rosemary—all these and many others can adorn the shelf, to the joy of the gardening cook.

I've always wondered why some ingenious soul hasn't invented a kitchen-window greenhouse that can be put on or off like a storm window. Something like a portable bay window, with glass shelves where plants could drink up the sun by day and be warmed from the kitchen by night, and where moisture and warmth could be controlled easily by lifting or lowering the kitchen-window sash. How wonderful for the gardening cook to be able to move the whole herb garden indoors and pick her *bouquets garnis* and *fines herbes* as palate moves her! She might even try dill, which they say dwarfs itself as a house plant, or do a little succession raising of radishes in flowerpots.

CHAPTER X

November

FRUITS THAT LIKE FROST

One autumn someone gave me a whole bushel of quinces and we went on a spree. We picked out the ripest and most perfect, the ones blushed by a touch of frost, baked them with a sliced orange, and had them for dessert. We made quince jelly plain, with apples, with honey (for the sweetening, strained honey and sugar, half and half). This last was the best of the jellies, for the honey gave the quince a distinctive flavor and texture. We made quince and sweet apple preserves. We made *cotognato*, the Italian quince paste. We made quince marmalade. We made quince honey. We still had quinces, so we extracted quince juice and bottled it and made it into jelly later on when we revived.

Quince addicts know the tricks of quinces: you don't eat them raw—they pucker your mouth. You don't use the cores, as sometimes recommended nowadays, for they are gummy and spoil taste and texture. You always use an enameled or earthenware pot in cooking quinces. You always boil up the skins and use the liquid (only addicts do this). The longer you cook quinces, the darker they get. Most important, you keep the fruit, once pared, in cold water so that it won't discolor.

You have to be a quince addict to work with this hard-fleshed fruit; it's hard on the hands. I have a little double-bladed scraper that fits in the palm of the hand: with quick, short pulling strokes one can pare potatoes, apples, carrots in a jiffy. With quinces it's not that easy, but it works. Furthermore, quince, like orange and lemon peel for marmalade, has to be cooked soft before the sugar is added, or it stays hard and tough. At breakfast, lunch, or dinner, however, when the end product appears at table sweet and fragrant, all the effort entailed is discovered to have become a labor of love.

And so to some recipes for quince. Quince recipes are hard to come by. Many cookbooks ignore this historic favorite entirely: some palm you off with quince jelly; a few carry a scattering of jellies, conserves, jams. One or two treat quince as a dessert. The most appreciative treatment of quinces I've run into recently is Flora Harris', in her volume, *Pickling and Preserving*. No desserts, of course. With this general dearth in the literature, I've found myself for years collecting quince recipes from friends and enemies. Here are some of the spoils I consider worthy the attention of gardening connoisseurs.

Quince Honey, oddly enough, is not made with honey. Its color and general consistency are that of thick marmalade; its taste the ineffable tang of quince.

QUINCE HONEY

> 6 large quinces
> 12 cups sugar, more or less

Quarter and pare the quinces, discarding the cores. Drop the fruit into a bowl of cold water, the skins into 3 cups of water boiling in an enameled pot. They should be just covered with water; use more or less, as necessary. Meanwhile put the quince meat through the food grinder. After 30 minutes' boiling, strain the skins out of the liquid, and into it put the pulp of the quinces. Measure the quince in its liquid, and measure 1½ cups of sugar for each cup of pulp plus juice. Boil the grated quince and juice for 20 minutes; then add the measured sugar and stir until it is well dissolved. Boil for 5 minutes.

During the boiling processes, sterilize 10 jelly glasses and keep them hot. When the Quince Honey is cooked, pour it in. They may now be sealed, labeled, and stored.

Time required: 2 hours, paring to sealing
Quantity produced: 8 to 10 glasses

Here is a roster of good things to spread your Quince Honey on: homemade bread; muffins or biscuits; corn bread; pancakes or waffles; fried mush; scrapple. If you are willing to be extravagant with your handiwork, use some in glazing a ham.

If you can lay hands on only 3 quinces, make half and half quince and apple honey by the same method. Apple cores and skins go right along with the quince skins. The apples of course don't need to be ground or grated: if sliced, they'll disintegrate while the quinces are cooking. A lemon, grated rind and juice, should cook with them.

Quince-jelly making saves two of the steps of Quince Honey: separate cooking of skins and grinding of pulp. The quinces are quartered and cored, covered with water, and boiled rapidly for 30 minutes—crush them to see when they're good and tender. After straining through a jelly bag, boil the juice for 20 minutes with ¾ cup of sugar, or honey and sugar half and half, to every cup of juice.

Tip to the thrifty: don't discard the pulp from the dripbag when you make quince jelly. Make it into quince jam. Press the pulp through a food mill to remove the skins; put 3 cups of sugar to 4 cups of quince pulp and add 1 cup of quince juice. Mash it all in an enameled pot and let it cook until thick—about 20 minutes. But be careful not to let it stick and burn.

WHAT'S IN A POUND? One of the exasperating things about cookbooks—including this one—is this vague business of pounds, cups, and numbers. It can come out different every time. I have had distinctly different flavor blends from a perfectly reputable recipe for Paradise Jelly, which calls for 4 pounds of tart apples, 10 quinces, and 2 quarts of cranberries. A quart isn't always a pound, although with cranberries it usually is, so I'm reasonably safe in my order of 2 pounds. But 10 quinces! Big, little, or medium? On the answer to that depends the final flavor. You can really be sure only by weighing. The advice in ancient cookbooks, "cook with an equal weight of . . ." was sound advice and probably accounts for the steady excellence of our great-grandmothers' jellies, jams, and marmalades.

Gardening cooks who go in for grand-scale jelly and jam making are wise if they follow great-grandmother in relying on kitchen scales and go her one better with a cooking thermometer. But how many scales are there in American kitchens today, I wonder? And how many discouraged cooks who can't quite make it jell?

Next best to weighing is measuring by cupfuls. But if I were to start a cookbook campaign to Put All Measurements in Cupfuls, PAMIC would get complaints. How many should I start with to get 4 cupfuls? Do I pack the cup down? How small must I chop? Why go to all that bother when I can just slice them into the preserving kettle?

There's no final answer to this dilemma, unless every alternative is dully spelled out to read: 4 pounds of apples which, if the size of tennis balls, will number approximately 15 and come to 2½ quarts; when pared and cored and chopped to ¼-inch dice, will yield 11 cups, packed down. For my own purposes, and I hope yours, it seems better to work in ratios based on measurement of juice or, for jams and marmalades, of fruit cooked and in its own juice. This sometimes puts on the experimeter the burden of figuring out how much to start with, but it allows of working flexibly as to quantity and gives some assurance that the result will be what the recipe intends.

Then there's this matter of "cook until tender"—but back to quinces.

Quince and apple jelly is made half and half quince juice and apple juice; Paradise Jelly adds cranberries, to make it all thirds. Sugar goes in ¾ of a cup for every cup of fruit juice.

Quince is a good combiner in jams; its sturdy flavor stands out even with other strong-flavored fruits. The general principle (which you may of course vary) is equal amounts of the various fruits: quince and apple; quince, apple, and pear; quince, pineapple, and orange. The sugar ratio is the same as for jelly: ¾ cup to 1 cup of fruit in juice. Always make the extract of skins of quinces (include apple and pear skins, if you're using these) by barely covering them with water and boiling 30 minutes. Use this juice to cook the quince in. Apples and pears don't need this pre-cooking; they can be measured and added with the sugar. Pineapple, chopped up, and orange and its peel, put through the food grinder, do need pre-cooking with the quince. Once the sugar is added, boil the concoction rapidly to the jellying stage—about 20 minutes.

QUINCE CONSERVE

> 2 cups ground quince
> 1½ cups ground orange
> ½ cup ground lemon
> 2 cups seedless raisins
> 2½ cups sugar
> 1 cup chopped walnuts

A couple of sizable quinces, 2 small oranges, and a biggish lemon will likely produce the amounts given above. All can go through the coarse blade of the food grinder. Pare and core the quinces; it's a good idea to squeeze out the lemon and orange juice first—or at least have a drip dish under the grinder handle. Combine fruit and raisins with 2 cups of water and boil rapidly for 10 minutes. Then add the sugar and simmer until the mixture clears and thickens. It will take about 30 to 40 minutes. Add the nuts just before removing from the fire, and pour the conserve into hot clean jelly glasses.

> Time required: 2 hours
> Quantity produced: 12 to 14 glasses

Quinces, cored and quartered and cooked to the edge of tenderness in the juice of their skins, make an excellent dessert compote. Sugar—about ½ cup to 2 quinces—and the juice and peel of a lemon are then added, and gentle simmering is continued for 15 minutes. The quince quarters should at this point be lifted out and the liquid boiled down to a rich syrup. A good ¼ cup of rum is the final touch; the quinces steep in this heady sauce as they cool, and are served chilled. Rum, too, is the making of Baked Quince.

BAKED QUINCE

> 4 ripe quinces, preferably
>   frost-nipped for flavor
> 1 orange
> ¼ cup sugar
> ¼ cup honey
> ¼ cup rum

Quarter, core, and pare the quinces; let the flesh stand in cold water, and do the usual with the parings and a cup of water. Slice the orange thin and spread it in a shallow baking dish. Pour the quince water over it and let it simmer for 10 minutes on top of the stove. Now slip the quince quarters under the orange slices, sprinkle with the sugar and honey, and set the dish to bake, covered, in a 300° oven until deep red and tender. This will take about 2 hours. Add the rum for the last 15 minutes of baking. Serve cold.

> *Time required: 1 hour, exclusive of baking*
> *Quantity produced: 4 servings*

I'm somewhat baffled about what to recommend about quinces garden-wise. If you live in quince country, that's one thing, of course; and your quince tree is an ornament to your place, lovely in flower, leaf, and fruit. If you don't, although the quince is relatively hardy, the experts seem to disagree. Hedrick, in his *Fruits for the Home Garden*, states roundly that every owner of a fruit garden should have two or three quinces. Leonard Wickenden, in *Gardening with Nature*, while he acknowledges the delights of quince eating, seems to think poorly of the rewards of quince raising and makes one dismal suggestion, "To prevent wormy fruit, cover with cheesecloth from July 1 to harvest."

AN APPLE A DAY KEEPS THE COOK BUSY With apples it's different. The apple, with its hum of bees, its gnarled and twisted trunk, its spreading crown and grateful, fragrant shade, is universally beloved of orchardists, whose only problem seems to be which varieties to settle on as most desirable. Leaving it to them, we'd all start spacious apple orchards of early, middle, and late ripeners, of table, pie, baking, and sauce apples. Lacking the space, the money, and perhaps the years of life to enjoy the fruits of the investment, the home gardener must bone up in order to get the most out of the few trees, or even one tree, he has room for. If he is clever, he can produce some early, some late, some sauce, and some eating apples all on one tree; even a dwarf apple can be grafted to produce more than one variety of apple. If he has a fellow enthusiast for a next-door neighbor, he may be able to work out a deal which will provide the two families multiple varieties of apples. Spraying and pruning can be jointly done too.

One good way to bone up for orcharding is to eat apples. That you can do now; you'll want a year to lay your tree plans. Start with baked apples, for instance, and enlist the interest of the gardening cook. Baked apples may seem like kid stuff to the kitchen mechanic, but the kitchen artist gives them no such brush-off. Connoisseurs of the baked apple consider the variety to begin with. Winesaps, greenings? For pie or applesauce, yes, but not for baking. Rome Beauty, Spy, Jonathan? By all means. It's fun to experiment with baking apples. By selecting several varieties and baking them all at the same time, the flavors can be compared and your own favorite specialty of the house settled upon. Keep an eye out for the good "bakers" among winter apples as they come along in market: besides the three mentioned above, there are Opalescent, Cortland, Guinea Golden, Spitzenburg, King.

Then there's the spicing. In the fall, when apples are at their best, you wouldn't dream of distorting their delectability with cinnamon or nutmeg; as the winter wears on, spice adds to the flavor, as does a sprinkling of lemon juice or rind. A stuffing of nuts and raisins mixed with brown sugar, cinnamon, and softened butter makes baked apples an enriched dessert.

Methods of baking can be varied too. You can pare the top third or leave the apples unpared. You can prick the skins so they won't split. You can bake them fast, medium, or slow. You can bake apple halves. Spoon out the cores after cutting the apples; fill the holes with sugared and floured raisins topped with a dab of butter. The apple halves should bake at 400° with a little water in the bottom of the pan for basting. You can bake apple slices sprinkled with lemon juice and sugar. If you put these in a 350° oven for 15 minutes, the apples will shrink and form juice. You then spread the slices with a meal made by kneading together 1 tablespoon of butter, ¼ cup of flour, and ½ cup of light brown sugar. Bake the slices uncovered until they start to brown, then cover and cook slowly, giving them a final browning, uncovered, at the last. These are delicious with vanilla ice cream.

You can steam-bake apples—try this with Rome Beauties—using the same stuffing as for oven-baked. You don't core the apples all the way through, else you lose the stuffing to the water in the bottom of the pan. Range the apples on a rack in a saucepan, with boiling water beneath the rack (keep it replenished as needed), cover tightly, and the apples should steam tender in 40 to 50 minutes. When they're done, sprinkle a little granulated sugar on top and give them a glazing under the broiler. Apples in Maple Caramel, too, are not oven-baked, but the effect is similar.

APPLES IN MAPLE CARAMEL

> 1 cup maple syrup
> 4 large, perfect apples
> 1 tablespoon butter
> 1 tablespoon cornstarch
> ½ cup cream
> 2 tablespoons brandy
> Salt

In a saucepan just big enough to hold the apples put the maple syrup with ½ cup of water and let it boil for 3 minutes. Meanwhile prepare the apples: core them first, then pare them. Put them into the boiling syrup and let them simmer until tender—20 to 30 minutes should do it—turning them occasionally to absorb the syrup. When tender, lift the apples to a serving bowl and keep them warm in the oven. Let the syrup boil down to ½ cup. Meanwhile in another pan melt the butter and add the cornstarch smoothed with the cream. Stir in the syrup slowly and let the sauce thicken. Add the brandy and a few grains of salt; pour the sauce over the apples and serve.

Time required: about 1 hour
Quantity produced: 4 servings

When the apples in the barrel begin to shrivel and wrinkle, they are full of concentrated sweetness, and that's the time to make Apple Crunch. Be sure your apples were tart to begin with: Baldwins, for choice, or McIntosh. The rest is easy.

APPLE CRUNCH

> *4 tablespoons butter*
> *1 cup brown sugar*
> *6 tart apples*
> *1 egg*
> *1 cup granulated sugar*
> *1 teaspoon vanilla*
> *1 cup flour*
> *½ teaspoon baking powder*
> *Pinch of salt*

Melt the butter in an ovenproof dish over a low flame, add the brown sugar, and let all melt and mingle. Meanwhile pare, quarter, and core the apples. Dump them into the butter-sugar mixture, stir them around until they are well coated, then prepare the following mixture: Beat the egg and sugar until light, add ¼ cup of boiling water and the vanilla, and then stir in the flour and baking powder sifted together. Pour this batter on the apples and put the Crunch into a moderate oven (375°) to bake until the top is crusty like a macaroon. This will take from ¾ hour to 1 hour. A tap of the fingernail will tell you when it is baked to a turn: there should be a sharp "ping."

Time required: 1¼ hours
Quantity produced: 4 servings

Apple Crunch is rich enough to need no sauce, but whipped cream flavored with vanilla and sprinkled with ground almonds dresses it up. Or serve it à la mode with vanilla ice cream.

There are tricks with winter apples. They are good extenders, for one thing. A sweet apple diced into chicken salad not only makes it go farther, if that is needed, but also adds to the texture and flavor. Try adding a tart apple to marinated salt herring. Or you may bake a layer of sliced apples under gingerbread.

Have you ever tried making applesauce in a bean pot? Peel and quarter the apples; lay them in layers, each sprinkled with brown sugar; stick in a clove or two and add just enough water so that the apples won't burn. Long, slow cooking in the oven completes the trick. It is excellent with roast duck.

Applesauce is such a homely dish that most of us don't consider it dessert for company. Yet it can easily be dressed up for unexpected guests by giving it a topping of meringue. There's a trick to this: spread the applesauce in an ovenproof pie dish and chill it well in the refrigerator. Flavor the meringue with vanilla and a few drops of almond essence, and when it is piled on the applesauce put the pan under the broiler for a browning so quick that the whole dessert remains chilled. Three or 4 minutes will do it, and the meringue bears watching lest it burn.

Have you tried sweetening applesauce with honey (about 2 tablespoons to the cup) and using a pinch of clove for spice?

BY THE WAY Do you know that a pound of apples gives 1½ cups of sauce? If you have a blender, don't pare the apples, just core them; when they're cooked down, a whirl in the blender gives you a fine sauce, with all the good of the apple left in.

LOUISE'S APPLE CHUTNEY

> 3 pounds tart apples
> 3½ cups cider vinegar
> 4 cups sugar
> 3 cups seedless raisins
> 1½ cups currants
> 1¾ cups chopped dates

2 tablespoons salt
½ teaspoon cayenne pepper
1 tablespoon ground ginger
1 clove garlic, minced

Pare and core the apples (there should now be 2 pounds, about 6 cups); put them through the medium-blade grinder, then cook them with the vinegar plus ½ cup of water until just under a rolling boil. Strain the vinegar into a large pan and put the apple pulp into a crock. To the hot vinegar add the remaining ingredients. Taste after adding the pepper, you may like another ½ or ¼ teaspoon; taste also after adding the ginger, you may want another ¼ teaspoon. Now boil the vinegar for 10 minutes. Pour it over the apples and cover the crock. Let it stand for 24 hours or more. Then boil up the chutney until it is as thick as you like it (20 minutes is about right for us). Seal in hot, sterilized jars.

Time required: roughly, 3 to 4 hours, over 2 days
Quantity produced: 5 to 6 pints

More tricks with apples: apple muffins are good—the apples taste surprisingly tart when you bite into them. Chop a cupful into your favorite muffin mix, and when the muffins are in their pans ready to bake, give them a topping of sugar mixed with cinnamon, nutmeg, and a dash of mace, all this moistened with melted butter. . . . And don't forget how good fried apples are of a Sunday morning with sausages or bacon . . . how warming hot spiced apple juice can be, served with doughnuts or gingerbread before a roaring fire. . . . And speaking of fireside snacks, what is better than a good raw red apple, a slab of Cheddar cheese, and a bowl of walnuts to crack?

THE SLOW-RIPENING PEAR If you get fed up on apples, dig into the storage bin for winter pears. These hard, grainy fruits are often quite unpalatable when eaten raw—I except, of course, the Royal Rivieras, so sweet and buttery that they are best halved, cored, and eaten with a spoon—but winter pears, when cooked, far outstrip their soft summer sisters, the Bartletts. They keep their shape, for one thing, and they lend themselves to experimenting with spices and flavorings. At the end of a hearty meal they come as welcome refreshment, spicy-sweet on the tongue. They'll be good to remember when the family palate gets jaded with the standard holiday desserts of pies, cakes, ice cream, and plum pudding.

Winter pears bake beautifully (allow at least 1 hour in a 300° oven), either plain in sugar syrup or fancy with raisins, nuts, and figs stuffed into the core. Another good pear dish is made with the small Seckel pear baked whole in a sugar syrup spiced with a dash of crystallized ginger and with a topping of whipped cream.

Or try this recipe, in which the fruity pear flavor is enhanced by the sophistication of wine and spice:

PEARS GLAZED IN WINE

> 4 winter pears
> 1½ cups claret
> ⅓ cup granulated sugar
> 1-inch stick cinnamon
> 20 cloves

Select perfect pears that are firm and slightly underripe. Measure the claret and sugar into an enameled saucepan; add the stick cinnamon and cook gently, stirring from time to time, until the sugar is dissolved and the wine hot. Meanwhile peel the pears, leaving them whole. Pull out the stems and remove the flower ends. Stick 5 cloves into each pear.

Lower the pears gently into the wine syrup and let them simmer until tender—about 20 minutes. Turn them occasionally so that they cook and take color evenly. Do this with a blunt wooden spoon to avoid nicking the surface. They are done when they can be easily pierced to the core with a toothpick.

Lift the pears to the bowl in which they are to be served. Let the syrup boil down to half quantity. Pour it over the pears, and as they cool, baste them occasionally with the wine sauce (a bulb baster is useful). Serve them chilled.

> *Time required: 45 minutes, exclusive of cooling*
> *Quantity produced: 4 servings*

For added glamor, a few Bing cherries (canned, at this season) or a dozen Tokay grapes, halved and seeded, may be added during the last 5 minutes of cooking. Chopped or slivered almonds sprinkled on the pears make a decorative touch, but don't use whipped cream with the wine sauce.

Pears Glazed in Wine borrow from the French, who have a flair for wine cookery. There are French touches with liqueurs, too, which are worth trying with stewed winter pears: Cointreau or curaçao, certainly (a spoonful per pear in the syrup after cooking); and for the experimenters: rum, brandy, crème de menthe, or Grand Marnier. For exotic decoration, crystallized ginger, candied orange and lemon peel, slivered into whipped cream to cap a pear baked in sugar syrup.

Perhaps you dislike fruit cooked in wine; cook pears in orange syrup. Parboil a sliced orange in a cup of water for 10 minutes, then use the orange water to make a heavy syrup (equal amount of sugar; boil 5 minutes). Return the orange to the syrup, add 4 pears, peeled and halved, and cook until tender. If the syrup hasn't thickened, cook it down, then pour it over the pears and orange. This dessert is good with the addition of a soft custard sauce and crushed macaroons sprinkled over all.

WATCH OUT FOR A CHINESE RED If you live in persimmon country, which I don't, and are a lover of this too-little-appreciated fruit, which I am, you're doubtless waiting for the frosts that will give an illusion of translucence to the persimmon, showing its readiness to adorn the festive board. For any board is festive when the satiny, Chinese lacquer-red persimmons are ushered in. They are best to be enjoyed, to my mind, when laid open like a flower, to be spooned, mouthful by delightful mouthful, from the tender skin. The taste, faintly sweet and cool, is ingratiating, and there's a ghost of the feel of pucker about eating persimmons, a sensation that adds to rather than detracts from the gustatory pleasure. The real pucker of the unripe fruit is unhappy—one does well to restrain impatience until the globes are very soft to the touch. Persimmons per se, sliced down to the stem base as described above, may be preamble to dinner or dessert.

They also make a pretty salad plate when cut in eighths, sliced from the skin, and laid out on curly endive with crescents of avocado and halved seedless grapes. French dressing made with lemon juice is de rigueur for such a salad.

NUTCRACKER SUITE As the month rolls its course, we begin to think of nuts. Expeditions to gather them—if there aren't "No Trespassing" signs—in the bright November sunshine, sessions of cracking them by the fireside or in the kitchen, hoarding them in special preparations against the feast days.

It's fair, isn't it, to count nuts as a produce of the home garden? In the South and West pecans are growing plump in their shells right in the back yard, and many a householder gathers a proud crop. And in the North pecans can either be bought on the market or begged from the bounty of friends in the pecan belt.

Pecans do indeed belong to the season of Thanksgiving, and so we make Pecan Balls, which look like sugared candy but are really miniature cookies, with a taste of pure pecan. They are a wonderful thing to have on hand at any season of the year—as glamor for afternoon tea, to dress up a simple dessert of fruit, or just for a delightful tidbit between meals. But especially right now, with Christmas crowding the heels of Thanksgiving, they are worth making in large batches. They make a fine addition to the usual list of Christmas cookies and are a lot easier to fabricate.

Pecan Balls as originally concocted in Austria should have the butter and sugar creamed together before the other ingredients are added. I have found it just as satisfactory, however, to throw all together and let the warmth of hand-kneading do the job of blending.

PECAN BALLS

> 1 cup pecans, grated or chopped fine
> 2 tablespoons granulated sugar
> ½ cup butter
> 1 teaspoon vanilla
> 1 cup pastry flour
> ⅛ teaspoon salt
> Powdered sugar (about ½ cup)

Measure all the above ingredients (except the powdered sugar) into a big bowl and hand-knead them until you can form a soft, well-blended ball. Pinch off small bits of the dough; roll them between your palms to make little balls about ½ inch in diameter. Lay these on a cooky sheet, allowing a little room for spreading. Bake them in a moderate oven (375°) until they are light brown— about 25 minutes. While they are still hot, roll them in powdered sugar, and spread them out, not touching each other, to cool. Then roll them in powdered sugar again. They may be kept for weeks if packed in a tin in layers separated by waxed paper.

Time required: 1 hour
Quantity produced: 50 to 60 balls

Southern cooks are prodigal with pecans. A handful, broken up, goes casually into chicken salad, into waffles, into sweet-potato fritters, into turkey stuffing. By the cupful they go into pralines and that pride of the South, pecan pie.

MRS. PAXTON'S PECAN PIE—from Mississippi

> 2 tablespoons butter
> 2 eggs
> ½ cup brown sugar
> ½ cup dark Karo molasses syrup
> ½ teaspoon vanilla
> 1 cup pecans
> Pie shell ready to bake

Have the butter very soft. Beat the eggs lightly—without separating —and add the sugar, Karo, butter, and vanilla. When well blended, stir in the pecans, unbroken so far as possible. Pour into the piecrust and bake for 40 minutes: first 10 minutes at 425°, the balance at 350°.

Time required: 1 hour
Quantity produced: 4 to 6 servings

Nuts make good sweetmeats: spiced pecans and walnuts, for one thing. Find yourself some perfect halves of these rich, meaty nuts and make enough so that you can hide some away, tin-boxed, for future reference.

SPICED PECANS AND WALNUTS

> 1 egg white
> ½ teaspoon salt
> ½ cup granulated sugar
> ¼ teaspoon each cinnamon, cloves, allspice, nutmeg
> 1 cup walnut halves
> 1 cup pecan halves

Beat the egg white and salt to a slight froth, adding 2 tablespoons of cold water. Sift the sugar and spices into this mixture and stir well. Roll the nuts around in the spicing, a few at a time, and spread them, flat side down, on an oiled cooky sheet. Bake them at 250°. It will take at least 1 hour to bring them to a nice golden brown. Cool them on wax paper, making sure they are not touching each other.

> *Time required: 1½ hours at the outside*
> *Quantity produced: 1 pint*

A slightly different treatment for walnuts sugar-coats them with a slight tinge of lemon flavor: grate 1 teaspoon of lemon rind into 1 cup of brown sugar and add ¼ teaspoon each of salt and ground cinnamon. Cook this mixture with 6 tablespoons of milk to just past the thread stage—236° on your candy thermometer—take it off the stove; add 1 teaspoon of vanilla and 2½ cups of walnut halves. Stir them around as they cool, and when they are sugary, turn them onto wax paper and separate them with two forks.

Nuts needn't always be sweetened. Salted almonds—they must be wholly dry before you roast them, and I prefer olive oil to butter for the process—are better than canapés with an apéritif of wine, and for the cocktail hour they can be salted with garlic or celery salt or a pinch of cayenne, saffron, or ginger.

There are other nuts and other uses for them.

Grandmother's Chestnut Stuffing was never soggy; no liquid was allowed in the mixture. She always baked a separate batch in a bread tin, basting it occasionally with drippings from the roasting turkey. To this day I do so too.

GRANDMOTHER'S CHESTNUT STUFFING

3 cups crumbled corn bread
3 cups stale bread crumbs (no crusts)
1 cup boiled chestnuts, broken up
½ pound sausage meat (optional)
1 cup butter, melted
¼ cup chopped onion
½ cup chopped celery
1 cup chopped mushrooms
¼ cup chopped parsley
2 teaspoons salt
⅓ teaspoon each pepper, thyme, marjoram, rosemary

Be sure the corn bread is not overly sweetened. Crumble it with the bread; add the chestnuts. Fry the sausage meat, stirring it frequently until it is lightly brown. Drain off the fat and use it for some other purpose. (You may use the turkey liver and giblets, previously cooked, but we like those in the gravy.) Add the butter, onion, celery, and mushrooms. Sauté for about 10 minutes, then pour all onto the crumbs. Add the parsley and seasonings and mix lightly with a fork.

Time required: 30 minutes
Quantity produced: dressing for a 15-pound turkey

And for the holiday season, too, here is a favorite of mine, Suppa di Castagne, a rich and subtle dinner soup. This is an old Italian recipe which dates back to the lordly days of Italian dining, a velvet purée whose delicacy of flavor requires careful planning of the course to follow. Duck or turkey or ham are too rich themselves to give contrast; something broiled—chops, squab, steak—are ideal accompaniments; or, if you like it, smoked tongue in a ring of spinach and mushrooms.

If the gardener's cook demurs at the nuisance of shelling the chestnuts, there is nothing to do but sympathize or offer to help. They are a nuisance to prepare, and I've tried many ways. The method I dislike least is the French: gash them crisscross, toss them with a little oil in a frying pan over a hot flame, and then dry them in the oven for a few minutes, hoping that the inner skin will detach itself easily. Don't forget that since the blight if you want to end up with 1 pound of edible chestnuts you must usually start with 1½ pounds.

SUPPA DI CASTAGNE

> 2 cups peeled chestnuts
> 1 large onion
> 2 carrots
> 2 leeks
> 2 stalks celery
> 1 tablespoon olive oil
> 2 quarts veal or chicken stock
> 6 sprigs parsley
> 3 cloves
> Salt and pepper
> ½ cup cream
> 2 tablespoons brandy
> Grated Parmesan cheese

Peel enough chestnuts to make 2 full cups. Chop coarsely the onion, carrots, leeks, and celery and brown them for 10 minutes in the olive oil in the bottom of the soup kettle. Then add the chestnuts, stock, parsley, cloves, a good dusting of pepper, and 1 tablespoonful of salt (less if the stock is already salted). Let the soup boil gently until the vegetables are soft—at least 1 hour.

Pick out a few whole chestnuts for the tureen and purée the soup in a food mill, blender, or fine strainer. Return the purée to the pot, add cream and brandy, and heat just to boiling. Serve from the tureen, with Parmesan cheese to be sprinkled (but sparingly!) in each bowl.

> Time required: 1½ hours, exclusive of
> preparing chestnuts
> Quantity produced: 2 quarts

Once the chestnuts are ready, the soup is little trouble to prepare and may be made a day ahead, leaving the cream and brandy as last-minute additions. We once did this to make a tasting party of Suppa di Castagne: the original recipe gave alternatives of brandy, marsala, and sherry, and we needed to know which was preferable. By unanimous vote brandy was approved, on the grounds that it unobtrusively smoothed the flavor and made it subtle, whereas the marsala was too sweet and the sherry intruded on the taste of the chestnuts.

CLEANUP FOR WINTER What about the garden these busy days? The wintering vegetables, are they hilled up with straw and earth for the heavy freezing to come? Are you keeping track of the kale? Are dead stalks and shriveled leaves cleared away? Did you cut out the fruited raspberry canes and cover the strawberries with straw? If you've been practicing garden sanitation as you go along, you've probably already seen to most of the winter cleanup; perhaps even sowed the vacant rows to winter rye to enrich it for spring. My garden doesn't get that, but we do give it a good layer of compost and manure and spade it over once, leaving the earth in rough clods.

What about the tools? Are they cleaned and oiled and properly stored in a dry place? Have you brought in a basket of good potting soil for the kitchen-window greenhouse and the house plants, and soaked out a gallon jugful of manure water, well labeled in letters of a size to be read without eyeglasses? Have you nailed a sunflower head to the tree for the birds and plenished the bird feeder and hung some suet cups nearby?

Fine. You may now take a dipper to the stone crock in the storage closet and we'll see how the tutti-frutti has fared.

CHAPTER XI

December

HOLIDAY COOKING FROM THE GARDEN'S BOUNTY

Let's do our Christmas thinking early. What do we give our cooking and gardening friends for Christmas? They're choosy folk, and well they may be; they practice exacting arts. They keep themselves pretty well supplied with the tools of their hobby, and it isn't always easy to discover what they will prize. They usually distrust gadgets, they abhor waste, they resent the clutter of useless objects on kitchen shelves or in the tool shed. On the other hand, they are childishly pleased with even the simplest gift that promotes their purposes and shows a perceptive appreciation of their activities.

You can't go wrong, of course, on a load of manure; it's the equivalent of a mink coat to gardening cooks. This rich and aromatic stuff calls forth cries of delight which scandalize the un-initiate—but whoever heard of a gardener who had too much? The only difficulty is that you can't put it under the Christmas tree. But the pleasure of sniffing its fragrance out beside the com-post, of anticipating the spring day when it can be spread, the suc-culent growth it will nourish, outweighs that deficiency. If you're not in the mink-coat money, don't hesitate to give a little fur piece of a bushel of manure.

You can't go wrong, either, on a favorite seed catalogue with a check made out to the company pinned to the order blank inside. This is a gift of more than money: it's a gift of the exquisite pleasure of reveling in indecision, of choosing first this, then that; a gift of dreams of the future that can be strung out over many a long winter evening.

Or you might select a gift that facilitates looking back instead of dreaming ahead. A garden log is really a must if one is to grow in the wisdom of the soil. Planting and harvest dates, crop yields and costs, experiments and how they fare, schedules for fertilizing and spraying that work for the particular terrain and climate, these are items the prudent gardener wants recorded, even if it's a chore to be methodical about jotting it all down. But it can be fun, especially as the journal grows, to look back over past seasons with their successes and, we hope, not too many failures. It's not just facts we recall to mind, either; we recapture the feel of a spring, the rhythm of the seasons and the weather; we assess our own patience or impatience, and our knowledge of our land and of ourselves deepens and widens. Maybe the perfect garden-journal gift would be a sturdy loose-leaf notebook to be kept individual-istically, with reference records all together and the log written long or short as inspiration dictates. Perhaps it would be the five-year-diary type for a sketchy few lines a day; these strike my fancy, because they allow such quick comparison from year to year.

Books, of course, and subscriptions to garden journals. Gardeners and cooks are always on the lookout for something new and interesting. If you know your man—or woman—there's sure to be something new along his specialty line or something rare and old to build the background of his lore.

Unless you have a gadgeteer on your hands, beware of gadget gifts. Too many of them are just excess baggage to the serious amateur. Sometimes gadgets do work out, though. I was given a pair of shocking-pink foam-rubber knee pads (very excess baggage) by a young friend who knew I liked to get right down to earth in my gardening. When I wore them, the neighborhood children were shocked out of their giggles. Besides, they were hot to wear. But they did spare my bones, and I finally figured that I could kneel in them without strapping them on, moving them from spot to spot as I progressed down the row. Now they are an integral part of the equipment in my basket of hand tools, more convenient than a flat pad, and easy to space at any comfortable distance apart. The same youngster another year, after laughing at my entanglement with string and stakes as I tried to mark out straight rows, made me a set of sharp-pointed, round-topped stakes and to one of them attached a wooden reel from which I could unwind and rewind any length of cord I needed.

Random thoughts on gifts for gardening cooks . . . A good pair of shears for cutting salad herbs—do they ever make them with sheaths, so that they're safe stuck in a pocket? . . . The good old French pepper mill whose whole top screws around. The one I brought back from France glows with a patina achieved only with years of handling. A couple of jars of whole peppercorns, Malabar Black and Lampong Black, for a suggestion, should go with the grinder so that it can immediately go to work at the Christmas breakfast table. . . . A salt grinder with a pound jar of salt crystals (try buttering brown-'n'-serve French bread loaves and sprinkling with ground salt and caraway seeds before you bake them) . . . They also make nutmeg grinders to match, although your purist may prefer to scorch her knuckles on one of the old-fashioned midget graters with the little compartment for the nutmegs in the top.

If she's known for her herb garden, why not give her dozens of screw-top matching jars (paint them black; darkness preserves the quality of the herbs) so she can make up sets for her own gifts— maybe she'll give you one! One-ounce jars are best for current use to conserve flavor; they can be replenished from a larger jar as required. . . . Some of your own kitchen prides—jellies, jams, conserves, fruit cakes, each with the recipe ribbon-tied to the jar . . . Why not a 2-quart jar of hearty soup (complete with recipe) for that day-after-Christmas slump? . . . Some herbs, potted up as seedlings in September (rosemary's for remembrance)? . . . Specialty cookbooks . . . A copper pipkin for melted butter . . .

And the "stocking" gifts: packets of newly developed strains of lettuce, say, if she's a salad enthusiast . . . chervil seeds sent for from France if she has an herb garden . . . sturdy plant labels, twist-'ems of various lengths . . . braided strands of leaf-green cotton cloth for tying up the tomatoes . . . jar labels. You could even hand-paint them with appropriate fruits and herbs. . . .

WHAT'S COOKING? In December "What are we going to eat?" follows hot on the heels of "What are we going to give?" especially with the young people home from college and the relatives gathering for the festivities. Standard fare for holiday eating we all know and prepare for lovingly, but what about the between times? What can we have that is different? These nippy days call for hearty fare, and skating parties and holiday entertaining send housewives scurrying to their files on casserole cookery for something that can be prepared ahead of time and left to its own devices in the baking.

You don't want to serve Boston baked beans all the time; there are other baking beans, including the cranberry beans you harvested last fall—or did you? The home drying of lima beans may be a thing of the past for many home gardeners in this day of the quick freeze, but baked dried limas should never be allowed to disappear from the home table. To prevent such a calamity, here are two recipes for baking limas.

Beans Bengal is an adaptation from Indian cookery, hot with curry (you may wish to start with 2 teaspoons instead of 3) and sweet with raisins. It is a wonderful dish to serve with ham or spiced corned beef, or it will give a party touch to the cold remnants of the Christmas turkey.

Beans Bengal makes a fine *pièce de résistance* for special occasions; you wouldn't want this every day, nor should you serve it with rich meats like pork or duck.

Our second recipe, however, is a trusty stand-by for good eating. It is all-American: in the excellence of Country-Baked Limas, Nebraska, Ohio, and California have had a hand. They go well with practically anything: ham, frankfurters, hamburgers, sausage (try baking link sausage on halved, cored apples), cheeses, cold cuts, Canadian bacon. Keep them in mind for summer picnics as well as winter feasts.

For both recipes the method is substantially the same, so I list the ingredients separately and give the cooking directions as one.

BEANS BENGAL

> 1 pound dried baby lima beans
> ½ pound sharp Cheddar cheese, broken up
> 3 teaspoons curry powder
> 4 tablespoons minced onion
> 4 tablespoons minced green pepper
> ½ cup olive or salad oil
> ¾ cup seedless raisins
> Salt

COUNTRY-BAKED LIMAS

> ½ pound dried large lima beans
> ½ pound bacon, cut small
> 1 big onion, chopped
> 1 teaspoon prepared mustard
> ½ cup (or more) dark molasses
> Salt and pepper
> ½ cup brown sugar

Soak the beans overnight, then drain and parboil them for 20 to 30 minutes (until semi-soft) in water with 1 teaspoon of salt. Butter a casserole and drain the beans into it, saving the bean water. Combine with the beans all the other ingredients (for Country-Baked Limas, the brown sugar comes later). Add 1 teaspoon of salt, stir well, and bake in a slow oven (300°) for 2 hours. Stir occasionally and add enough bean water to keep the beans moist but not runny. Beans Bengal are now ready to serve. For Country-Baked Limas, after 2 hours' baking, sprinkle on the brown sugar, leave uncovered, and bake another ½ hour.

Time required: 3½ hours, intermittently
Quantity produced: 4 to 6 servings

Don't forget that the remaining bean water makes a good addition to the soup pot. And a word to the wise: these baked limas are practically guaranteed to make a great hit with men.

Or take kidney beans—right from the can. In 20 minutes you can have a fine dish of Mexican Frijoles to fill out the menu for unexpected guests.

FRIJOLES

1 clove garlic, chopped
½ cup chopped onion
½ cup chopped green pepper
½ cup olive oil
5 cups cooked kidney beans
2 cups bean liquid
1½ teaspoons chili powder
½ teaspoon fresh-ground pepper
½ teaspoon salt

Cook the garlic, onion, and green pepper gently in the oil for 5 minutes. Thicken the sauce by mashing thoroughly into the skillet mixture 1 cup of the beans, then adding the 2 cups of bean liquid. Let it all boil up and then simmer until thick—about 15 minutes. Add the spices during the last 5 minutes. Pour this sauce upon the remaining 4 cups of beans, heat thoroughly, and serve.

Time required: 25 minutes
Quantity produced: 6 servings

Lentils, too, are at your command. In soup, in lamb stew, as a purée. The slightly peppery flavor of lentils is welcome as a change from the bland potato, and this legume may with profit to the palate replace potatoes or rice as accompaniment to meat. The cooking principle for lentils as a vegetable is the same as that for split peas or dried limas: soak them overnight, and they'll cook tender in less than ½ hour. The proportion is 2 cups of water to 1 cup of lentils. But spice them up a bit. Onion, parsley, a sliver of garlic, a couple of cloves, and a piece of bay leaf, tied in a bag, may be cooked with lentils. When done, they should have excess water poured off, be riced or mashed, and beaten up with 1 tablespoon of butter and 2 of cream. Or you may want to combine them with a sweet-sour sauce made with minced bacon and onion, sautéed, and moistened with red wine. Try a grating of nutmeg on this. A quarter teaspoon of ginger will spice a pint of lentils, and some like to add an equal amount of curry powder.

LAMB AND LENTIL STEW

> 2 pounds boned lamb shoulder
> 2 tablespoons olive oil
> 1½ cups lentils
> 1 onion, chopped
> 1 clove garlic, minced
> 1 bay leaf
> ½ teaspoon fresh (or ¼ teaspoon dried) thyme
> ½ teaspoon dried rosemary
> 2 teaspoons salt
> ½ teaspoon fresh-ground pepper
> 6 small onions, peeled
> 6 small carrots, cubed

Have the lamb cut in 2-inch cubes and brown it in the oil in a heavy kettle. Add 4 cups of water and the lentils (don't pre-soak them), together with the chopped onion and garlic and the seasonings. Cover the kettle and let it simmer for 2 hours. Now add the carrots and whole onions and resume cooking until they are just tender—about 30 minutes at a simmer. The lentils should thicken the stew properly; if not, use a little flour.

Time required: 3½ hours
Quantity produced: 6 servings

If you like these dishes and want to be enterprising, you can make them up early in December, store them in the deep freeze, and play the magician weeks later, whisking them out and into the oven without even donning an apron. One good trick for freezing casserole dishes of this sort is to line the casserole with aluminum foil, put in the Beans Bengal, for instance, lapping the foil tightly over the top. Quick-freeze the whole thing, then slip the foil-wrapped beans out of the casserole, package, and store. When you're ready to use them, remove the wrap and foil and slip them back into the same casserole for rebaking (which will take about 1½ hours).

IF YOU DIDN'T DRY THEM, BUY THEM It's not just the dry legumes that are the advance-preparation friends of the gardening cook at this busy season. The fruits she dried back in early fall repay the trouble now. Take apricots. If you didn't dry them, buy them.

Sometimes we forget how useful dried apricots are. Around holiday time, with a couple of pounds of them on the supply shelf, the imaginative hostess has the makings of desserts that can appear with a flourish that belies the ease of their preparation.

Stewed prunes, for one thing, sound humdrum but become a distinctive dessert when combined with apricots. The two kinds of fruit should be stewed separately, of course (the prunes with lemon slices); let 6 cloves cool in the prunes as they plump in their juice, and add ¼ cup of sherry to the apricots. The longer they stand, the better they taste; prunes and apricots can be combined at dessert time and served with macaroons or Pecan Balls.

Or you can make a fine compote of apricots alone: cook the grated rind of an orange with them and don't let them cook to pieces, but just to shapely tenderness. Sweeten them with ½ cup of sugar to 2 cups of apricots, cooking only enough to dissolve the sugar thoroughly. Lift out the apricots and pour over them

¼ cup of curaçao. Boil down the syrup, pour it over the fruit, chill it all, and serve with sugared almonds.

Make up a batch of apricot purée in some spare moment, and you can have apricot whip (½ cup of pulp to each egg white) in no time at all. You can fold apricot pulp into whipped cream as a sauce to dress up a pudding. Or you can transmute plain cupcakes into a party dessert.

The apricot pulp is a basic prerequisite: soak a pound of apricots in about 2 cups of water (just enough to cover them) for 2 hours. Simmer them in the same water, in an enameled pan, for 20 minutes or so, until they thicken and soften enough to mash. Press the mixture through a strainer or whirl it in a blender. Now measure the purée, and for each cup add ½ cup of sugar. After a quick boiling up, it can be stored in jars, cooled, and kept in the refrigerator for use as needed.

APRICOT-FILLED CUPCAKES

1½ cups apricot purée
1 teaspoon grated lemon rind
1 tablespoon lemon juice
1 teaspoon grated orange rind
½ teaspoon ground allspice
8 cupcakes, preferably lemon-flavored
½ cup cream, whipped stiff
¼ cup candied ginger, chopped

Mix the apricot purée with the lemon juice, the grated rind, and allspice. Slice the top off each cupcake and hollow out a small depression. Fill the holes generously with the apricot mixture and spread with whipped cream. Replace the cake tops, add a fluff of whipped cream, and sprinkle the chopped candied ginger over all.

Time required: 10 minutes
Quantity produced: 8 servings

. . . Ever try adding a sliced lime when you stew apricots?

If you need something to pinch-hit for candy, steam dried apricots in a sieve over boiling water until they are warm and beginning to be moist—5 minutes or so—then roll them in granulated sugar and let them dry on waxed paper.

HOW GOOD IT SMELLS! . . . Making fruit cake is a fine fragrant occupation that goes well with the smell of greens at Christmas time. Old hands at it, who prepare the fruits in great batches one day, dedicate the next to the mixing and baking, and perform the ritual of wrapping, tying, and storing on the third, string out the aromatic pleasure and make the kitchen an alluring spot for the whole family for three days.

Fruit cake is not difficult to make, provided you can plan time to take it leisurely; the three-day system is a good one even if you're making only once the recipe. Our recipe, and Merry Christmas to you, is for a white fruit cake, time-tested in the kitchens of many friends. It's not an economical cake to produce, but it's worth it, and it makes a wonderful gift for kitchenette friends.

WHITE FRUIT CAKE

The fruit: 3 pounds seedless raisins (or half and half raisins and currants)
½ pound citron
½ pound candied orange peel
½ pound candied lemon peel
½ pound candied cherries
½ pound candied pineapple
½ pound shelled, blanched Brazil nuts

The batter: 3 cups butter
3 cups sugar
12 eggs
1½ pounds (6 cups) all-purpose flour
¼ teaspoon mace
¼ teaspoon nutmeg
1 teaspoon salt
1 cup sherry or fruit juice

Chop the fruits and nuts fine. The batter is made in the usual way: soften the butter; add the sugar gradually until the blend is light and creamy. Beat the egg yolks and stir them in. Sift the flour, reserving 1 cup for dredging the fruit. Sift the spices and salt into the flour, and stir this into the batter alternately with the sherry. At the last, fold in the egg whites beaten stiff but not dry. Now dredge the fruits with the remaining flour and fold them into the batter. Use 4 middle-sized bread tins lined with heavy wax paper. Bake the cakes for 3 hours in a 300° oven.

Once baked, the loaves should be allowed to cool in the pans and should then have the wax paper removed. Rewrap in wax paper or aluminum foil and store in tin boxes.

Time required: about 5 hours minimum
Quantity produced: 4 loaves

Did you know, by the way, that when dark fruit cake gets dry it can be freshened by heating it over hot water in a tightly covered double boiler? You should then dribble into it warmed sherry or brandy until it is saturated. It can then be wrapped and stored again.

Dried raisins, essential to a proper fruit cake, provide a fillip to many dishes: in ham gravy . . . in a Waldorf salad . . . in waffles, with broken pecans and some coconut . . . in stuffing for duck, with walnut meats . . . in fruit cup, when plumped for some hours in fruit juice or brandy.

Christmas is a good time to have Scotch Fruit Squares on hand. These are really a cross between pie and cake. They are a spicy concoction of apples and currants baked in piecrust, but you bake them in a cake pan, cut them in squares, and serve them like cake.

SCOTCH FRUIT SQUARES

Pastry:	½ cup lard
	2½ cups flour
	½ teaspoon baking powder
	½ cup butter
	½ teaspoon salt
Filling:	4 apples
	1 pound black currants
	1 tablespoon butter
	1 cup granulated sugar
	1 teaspoon almond extract

            1 teaspoon ground cinnamon
            1 tablespoon cornstarch
            ½ teaspoon salt
Topping: ¼ cup powdered sugar

To make the pastry, chop the shortening into the flour sifted with the baking powder and salt. Add iced water (about ¼ cup) to make a stiff dough. Form into a ball and chill while you prepare the filling.

To prepare the filling, chop the apples fine; put them in a saucepan with the currants, butter, granulated sugar, spices, and salt. Add ½ cup of water and simmer until the apples are tender but not mushy—about 10 minutes. If the mixture is very watery, add the cornstarch and let it thicken. Now let it cool and add almond extract.

Roll out the dough and line a 15" x 11" pan, letting the dough come well up on the sides. Spread the filling and cover it with the remaining dough, wetting the edges and pinching them together. Prick the surface with a fork at 1-inch intervals. Bake in a 500° oven for 10 minutes; reduce the heat to 350° and continue baking for 25 minutes. Cool, sprinkle with the powdered sugar, and cut into 2-inch squares.

Time required: about 1½ hours
Quantity produced: 35 squares

A minor twist of Fruit Squares gives Minced Cranberry Pie. It can be baked in a rectangular pan and cut like the Squares or treated traditionally as a pie. Filling consists of 2 cups of cranberries and 1 cup of raisins put through a food grinder (add 1 cup of chopped apples for a really plump pie); for sweetening, 1 cup of sugar mixed with ½ cup of orange juice. Seasoning is 1 tablespoon of orange rind, plus 1 teaspoon of vanilla. You'll need to thicken the juice: mix 2 tablespoons of cornstarch with the sugar. Bake as a 2-crust pie.

For company to the noble bird, baked cranberries ring a welcome change on the usual sauce or jelly and are far easier to prepare. Spread washed cranberries in a baking dish, sprinkle them lavishly with sugar (to 2 cups of cranberries, 1¼ cups of sugar), cover the dish, and bake for 1 hour in a 350° oven. They can bake right along with the roast if you have room in the oven along with the extra pan of stuffing and the baked onions. The baked cranberries come out chewy, translucent, like candied cherries.

NIGHT RAID   A minor problem exists for those of us who during the holidays like to raid the icebox late at night for a glass of milk and a cold turkey sandwich with cranberry sauce. The cranberry is the problem. To spread the sandwich with cranberry sauce is unthinkable; to get out saucedish and spoon is not only a nuisance but out of key with the casual charm of operating with just one knife for the turkey platter, the butter dish, and the bread-board. Yet the cool tart taste of cranberry is gastronomically essential to a turkey sandwich. I think I've found the solution: cranberry juice.

Ruby red in its glass, ice-cold, cranberry juice gives an air to the midnight feast and zest to the sandwich. It's a good thing to stock during the holidays, anyhow; lends itself to many subtle variations, takes up little room in a refrigerator crowded with holiday supplies. You can make your own well ahead of time now that cranberries are plentiful in market—or have you a cranberry bog? Equal parts cranberries and water, boiled to bursting, strained and sweetened with an eighth part sugar, is the basis. Bottle it, and there it is, boon for the busy housewife.

It smooths the flavor to add a little orange juice and lemon juice as you sweeten the juice (2 tablespoons of each if you start with 2 cups of cranberries). This makes a distinguished preamble to the after-Christmas lunch of turkey, hash or à la king. If you're a Vermonter, you'll wish you had a sprig of fresh lemon balm to stick in the cranberry juice cocktail, or perhaps a sprig of mint.

You may want to experiment, as I've done, with fruit drinks based on cranberry juice. Two parts cranberry juice with one part orange juice and a dash of lemon juice is good; so is cranberry juice with half as much pineapple juice; so is cranberry juice with a touch of Hawaiian punch (use 1 teaspoon of punch to 1 pint of juice). Some people like grapefruit and cranberry mixed: to my mind, the grapefruit kills the clean flavor of the cranberry.

Spiced Cranberry Punch is an excellent holiday drink, either steaming hot in mugs (you can spike it with brandy) or chilled, with ginger ale or charged water.

SPICED CRANBERRY PUNCH

> 5 cups cranberries
> 2-inch stick cinnamon
> 6 cloves
> 6 allspice
> 2 cups sugar
> 1 cup orange juice
> 1½ tablespoons lemon juice

Boil cranberries and spices in 4 cups of water until the berries burst (about 10 minutes). Crush them through a strainer lined with cheesecloth. Meanwhile boil sugar with 2 cups of water for 5 minutes. Mix this with the cranberry, orange and lemon juices. To serve hot, boil up this spiced mixture (lace it with brandy if you like), and serve with a clove-stuck slice of orange in each mug. To serve cold, chill the punch, and when ready to serve add 1 quart of ginger ale or charged water.

> Time required: 30 minutes (hot)
> Quantity produced: about 2 quarts, exclusive of ginger
> ale or charged water

Tuck this recipe away in your mind, too, for next August!

On the same cranberry base—or you can use a quart of canned cranberry sauce—variations can be made. For instance, a fine hot punch to serve in mugs with, if you are that lavish, sticks of cinnamon for stirrers. Boil up ½ cup of sugar with 1 cup of water—5 minutes should see the sugar disappear. Now add a pinch of salt and spices to your liking: whole cloves (1 teaspoon), ground cinnamon and allspice (½ teaspoon each), and ¼-teaspoon grating of nutmeg. Four cups of cranberry sauce, 4 of pineapple juice, and 3 of water complete the spiced brew, except for a quick boil of 5 minutes.

DECK THE HALLS WITH BOUGHS OF HOLLY You may have your eggnogs and your Tom and Jerries. For New Year's

Day, if you must. But not at Christmastide. Christmas is to me a gentler feast best celebrated with the old-time wassails of mulled wine, hot spiced cider, *Glühwein*, negus—even spiced apple juice, as innocent of spiking as the hot cranberry punch. The principle of mulling and spicing is the same as that of cranberry punch. The spices, cloves, cinnamon, allspice, with a dash of nutmeg; the sweetening, sugar—white or brown; always lemon or orange peel or both. Your own palate must judge the exact combination, but you could follow the spiced cranberry combination for a start. Spices and sugar are boiled up with water, the usual proportion being ½ cup of sugar to 1 cup of water. Add a quart of your chosen liquid, which must be heated with the sweet spice, but never boil hard. Orange and lemon slices and shavings of pineapple may float handsomely in the bowl, and lucky the one who dips one out in his punch cup.

The thought of these hot, spicy punches brings to mind vivid dreams of fireside gaiety, dreams unmarred by any nightmare of the knockout count of calories. The gaiety is soft and muted as befits the season of the Christmas story; old songs stir memory and sweeten companionship while the heavy crock of hot punch warms at the edge of the fire. All the holiday goodies are there for nibbling, the cookies and fruit cake, the nuts and raisins and apples, the cheeses. For a snack before sleep, bring out the great wreck of the turkey, the loaf of bread, the bowl of softened butter, the bowl of celery and radishes. God rest you merry, gentlemen.

CHAPTER XII

January

THE PARADE OF WINTER FRUITS

Don't lose heart. Spring will come. The first mild day after January 15 I start cutting forsythia to force in the house. When it puts out its cheerful yellow, the back of my winter is broken. Although I well know we're likely to have snow into April, my confidence in the orderly pattern of Nature is restored. My conviction is reinforced by the catalogues which are beginning to dribble in. The upsurge is on for those of us in the fraternity of gardening cooks.

So I can look upon the fruits of winter that come from more favored climes with unjaundiced eye, enjoying them to the full, knowing that our own time will come, more cherished because so often long delayed. How abundant they are, the oranges, the grape-fruits, the bananas, the avocados, the pineapples, the limes, the coconuts! How they exhilarate the drab and sunless days! The oranges are little suns themselves, and I don't care if the color is synthetic, just so it be not hectic but aesthetically golden.

We all have our ways with oranges, and if we don't, there are long and tempting listings in the indexes of reference cookbooks. My ways are less those of cakes, icings, puddings, and creams, and more those of the fruit for itself or in combination with other fruits. What better than the bumper glass of breakfast orange juice or the halved orange that spurts golden liquid as the spoon cuts it? I do have one or two favorite orange confections, among them Orange Mousse, party dessert of my childhood, with its orange cap above and sweet white cream below; Greek Oranges, delectably chill and luscious; and their opposite, tongue-burning Flaming Oranges to brew for friends informally in the chafing dish by fire-light.

ORANGE MOUSSE

> 1 teaspoon gelatin
> Juice of 6 oranges
> Juice of 1 lemon
> 1 cup granulated sugar
> 1 teaspoon grated orange rind
> 1 pint whipping cream
> 1 tablespoon powdered sugar
> 1 teaspoon vanilla

Melt the gelatin in 2 tablespoons of cold water, then dissolve it in ¼ cup of boiling water. Add this to the orange and lemon juice, the granulated sugar and the rind. Pour into a melon mold, which should then be put in the refrigerator to start solidifying while you whip the cream with the powdered sugar and vanilla. Don't whip it stiff; let it be runny enough to spread all over the orange in the melon mold. Since there is no gelatin in the whipped cream, this mousse freezes best in a bucket packed in ice and salt for 4 to 5 hours. Be sure the mold is well sealed: coat the outside edge of the mold with lard, plaster wax paper over the top and well down the sides; lard the inner edge of the top and jam it into place over the wax paper. This will keep any salt liquid from seeping in.

Time required: 40 minutes, exclusive of freezing
Quantity produced: 6 servings

Greek Oranges, served with ginger cookies, make a fitting crown to top off any dinner party, but especially one that leads up to dessert with roast duck. Make it well ahead of time; two days ahead is even better than one, since it mellows and gains fragrance with time. The secret of success with Greek Oranges lies in two things, using thick-skinned navel oranges for the dish and having a shredder that will shave off very thin wafers of the rind. And your paring knife should be super-sharp for easy sectioning of the fruit. Greek Oranges must be icy-cold when served.

LYND WERNTZ'S GREEK ORANGES

> 10 oranges, thick-skinned navels
> 1½ cups sugar
> 4 tablespoons currant jelly

Shave very thin shreds of yellow outermost rind from the oranges; don't let any of the white part be taken off. You don't have to be scrupulous about getting every last bit of this rind, but have a generous amount of it. It shrinks, and you'll need at least 5 table-spoons of cooked rind. Shave the rind into a kettle and pour over it boiling water to cover it well; let it bubble rapidly for 10 minutes, then drain off the water and cover the rind again with freshly boiling water for another 10 minutes' boiling. Do this once again, three times in all, to remove any bitter tang from the rind. While this process is going on for ½ hour, peel the oranges, removing all the white membrane, and section them. Squeeze over them all juice from the residue of the sections. Also during this period make a syrup by boiling the sugar and currant jelly with ¾ cup of water, letting it boil rapidly for at least 5 minutes. Pour this boiling syrup over the orange sections and let stand for 15 minutes. Then pour the syrup off the oranges into a saucepan, bring it to a boil again, and add at least 5 tablespoons of the drained orange rind (you can use even more if you like). This mixture is now poured back boiling hot on the orange sections; the whole bowlful is cooled and then chilled. It must be as cold as possible when served.

Time required: 1 full hour
Quantity produced: 8 servings

You have to have a sweet tooth for Flaming Oranges, that perfumed Californian version of the French *cerises flambées*. You ought to have a chafing dish, and you can't be a teetotaler. And you mustn't use frozen juice. You may, if you like, prepare the fruit and sauce ahead of time, to be combined when you are ready to celebrate.

FLAMING ORANGES

> 7 oranges
> 2 tablespoons cornstarch
> ½ cup sugar
> 1 cup fresh orange juice
> 1 teaspoon grated lemon rind
> 2 tablespoons Cointreau
> ½ cup slivered blanched almonds
> ½ cup brandy

Use well-ripened, thickish-skinned juicy oranges; cut 6 of them into neat sections. The seventh orange is to provide 4 center-cut slices to decorate the chafing dish. Mix the cornstarch with the sugar, add gradually the orange juice plus 1 cup of water, then stir in the lemon rind. Bring this mixture to a boil and let it simmer for 10 minutes, stirring constantly as it thickens and becomes satiny. Lay the orange sections in a chafing dish; pour over them the hot sauce and the Cointreau; sprinkle with the almonds and float the orange slices. When smoking hot, pour on the brandy, warmed, and ignite it.

Time required: 40 minutes
Quantity produced: 4 generous servings

You can make flaming cherries in the same manner, using some of those big black ones you canned last summer, the juice from the can making the sauce. I like to add a little lemon juice and a whiff of cinnamon and clove.

Experimenting with fruit and liqueurs can have happy results: with oranges, curaçao, maraschino, kirsch, rum, white wine, as well as brandy and Cointreau. It's a good idea to try first one and then another to avoid the trap of monotony which I'm likely to fall into with my leaning toward brandy with fruits. Peeled oranges, sliced and arrayed in a glass dish, sprinkled with powdered sugar and one or another of the liqueurs, chilled and sprigged with mint: the sophistication of simplicity. Cherries naturally take to brandy or kirsch. Pitted Bing cherries or Tokay grapes split and seeded may be mixed half and half with fresh pineapple and served with a chilled strawberry sauce made by cooking down frozen berries with a little honey and a few spoonfuls of kirsch.

Pineapple does best with a sturdier liquor—rum. Make a fruit compote with whole strawberries and chunks of pineapple sweetened with honey. When these are well chilled, pour over them orange juice and a spoonful or two of rum. A sliced banana makes a bland addition to the cup and doesn't resent the rum. Another good blend is honey with curaçao and a few drops of lemon juice; this makes a felicitous sauce for pineapple, orange, and strawberries.

The gifted hostess combines winter fruits as judiciously as she does the fruits of summer. Where she stuffed a watermelon for a big buffet in August, in January to top off a rich and hearty meal she creates a stuffed pineapple in the manner of that agreeable concoction the French call *les fruits rafraîchis*.

STUFFED PINEAPPLE

> 1 large ripe pineapple
> 1 banana
> 1 teaspoon lemon juice
> 2 seedless oranges
> 1 cup perfect strawberries
> 3 tablespoons strained honey
> ½ cup kirsch

Cut the pineapple in half lengthwise (let the fronds stay on for decorative effect) and carve out the pulp in chunks, discarding the core. Put the chunks in a bowl and slice in the banana. Sprinkle the banana slices with lemon juice. Cover these with sections of orange free of white membrane, and lay the strawberries on top. Mix together the honey and kirsch (you may like it a little sweeter), adding any juice from the preparation of the oranges. Pour this over the bowlful of fruit and let all chill for several hours. When ready to serve, mix up the fruit very carefully so as not to bruise the berries or banana. Heap it in the pineapple shells and pour over it the liqueur sauce from the bottom of the bowl.

> Time required: 30 minutes
> Quantity produced: 6 servings

Those who don't care for kirsch may replace it with orange juice blended with 1 tablespoon of lime syrup, which gives an elusive freshness of flavor.

"AH, BUT WHEN I HAD THIS IN CUBA . . ." There's a vast difference between even the ripest, juiciest pineapple to be found in our eastern markets and the translucent, tropically sweet pineapple native to Hawaii or Cuba. If you can afford the luxury of a discriminating friend who will have flown to you one of these truly ambrosial pineapples, plus a couple of really milky coconuts, you may feast on that most exotic of delicacies, Cuban Pineapple. Even with a pineapple from the corner grocer's and frozen or canned coconut, you'll have a dessert to delight guests, but don't invite someone who can say, "Ah, but when I had this in Cuba . . ."

When it comes to grating coconut, I'm all thumbs. I can no more handle a coconut deftly than I can stretch strudel dough all over the kitchen table without tearing it. To watch an expert punch out the eyeholes, pour out the milk, tap round and round the shell and have it break open into neat halves—it looks so easy. I nearly always manage to smash mine, and then the trouble of the little brown flecks is upon me. Once in a while I'm lucky and the meat breaks out in chunks big enough for easy peeling and grating. One thing I've learned, not to score my fingers trying to grate the last little bits. They can go through the food grinder, be mixed with coconut milk, and frozen in small bags to use in curries.

For Cuban Pineapple, grated coconut and coconut milk are necessary. One large coconut should yield about 2 cups of grated coconut; 2 coconuts, therefore, will be needed for the recipe, and there'll be grated coconut enough for a cake besides. Coconut milk is made by pouring boiling water on grated fresh coconut, letting it steep for 20 minutes, then straining it through double cheesecloth, squeezing it to secure all liquid. If the coconut milk is allowed to settle for several hours in a pan in the refrigerator, a thick, creamy substance will rise to the surface and may be skimmed off. This is coconut cream, which makes a fine sauce for pudding. One cup of boiling water poured on 2 cups of coconut (for coconut milk, you can run it through the food grinder) yields milk enough for Cuban Pineapple. Start it a day ahead.

CUBAN PINEAPPLE

> 1 dead-ripe pineapple
> ½ cup rum
> 1 tablespoon cornstarch
> 1 cup coconut milk
> Few grains salt
> 2 tablespoons sugar
> 2 cups grated fresh coconut

Slice the pineapple into thick slices, discarding crust and core. Lay the slices in a shallow pan and soak them overnight in the rum. Turn them over in the morning.

Blend the cornstarch and sugar with a tiny pinch of salt; use a little of the coconut milk to make a smooth paste. Scald the rest of the milk, then add the paste and stir rapidly over very low heat until the mixture coats the spoon, about 5 minutes. Add the grated coconut and chill for several hours. Use this as sauce piled generously atop the rum-soaked pineapple. If the sauce separates, add ¼ cup of cream, whipped.

Lacking fresh coconut, a sauce for the pineapple is made by adding to 1 can (about 1⅓ cups) of moist coconut 2 tablespoons of honey and 3 drops of almond essence and blending this mixture with 1 cup of cream whipped just short of stiff.

> Time required: ½ hour, exclusive of chilling and
> preparing coconut
> Quantity produced: 6 servings

Really, though, for my taste, the best way to eat an ambrosial pineapple flown from Hawaii is in its complete native simplicity of perfumed flavor. Not, please, cut up in a saucer, but sliced lengthwise, fronds and all, into wedges. This is as pleasant a way as I know to eat pineapple when it is ripe, sweet, and juicy. The trick for graceful eating is to slice off the hard core at the top of each wedge and slip a sharp curved grapefruit knife between pulp and rind. The fruit is then sliced down to make mouth-sized triangles easy to lift with a fork. A sprinkling of red sugar is a festive touch for our pallid market pineapples, not to be thought of for the colossus from Hawaii.

I've found an adult use for the sticky delight of childhood, the marshmallow. It finds its way into this book by way of that culinary boon of wintertime, the grapefruit, in a dessert which for want of a better name our household calls "Grapefruit Suprême." This concoction, composed of seemingly incongruous elements, is worth serving to conclude that little dinner for friends on a snowy night. Its unusual flavor, blending the tang of grapefruit with the sweet of marshmallow, smoothed down with whipped cream, carries an unexpected air of sophistication; it is, moreover, disarmingly simple to prepare. The quantity of marshmallow given below is geared to my own not-too-sweet tooth; you may like to use more, but beware of getting the mixture too sweet, since it is the acid juiciness of the fruit that gives distinction to the flavor. For the same reason, don't try this recipe with canned sweetened grapefruit.

GRAPEFRUIT SUPRÊME

> 1 large grapefruit
> ½ cup marshmallows (about 6)
> ½ cup whipping cream

Separate the grapefruit into sections, removing all inner skin and veining, and cut these in half. Put them into a capacious bowl as you work, and pour off any juice that accumulates. (You can mix it with orange juice for breakfast.) Cut the marshmallows into quarters, mix them in among the grapefruit chunks, and set the bowl in the refrigerator to chill for at least 1 hour. The marshmallows will soften slightly and will faintly sweeten the fruit without drawing juice. Just before serving, whip the cream and fold it into the mixture. Pile it high in a serving bowl or individual sherbet cups. Serve at once.

Time required: 15 minutes' preparation
Quantity produced: 4 servings

By the way, how about saving the skins for candied peel?

WHAT'S YOUR STAND ON BROILED GRAPEFRUIT? Broiled grapefruit has become almost a controversial issue; the purist will have none of it. I'm for it once in a while and like to vary the flavoring of it. Brown sugar instead of granulated gives an elusive difference and sometimes crusts nicely; a minted cherry is a welcome change from maraschino. A spoonful of brandy and honey in each half is, for my taste, an improvement over the usual sherry. But better than either is a teaspoon of rum, and if you want to achieve a provocative smoothness, try a few drops of melted butter along with the rum. Grapefruit prepared for broiling should be at room temperature, and do let it broil until the edges are well flecked with brown.

And to clear the palate, so to speak, after considering these esoteric ways of treating grapefruit: have you tried sprinkling salt instead of sugar on your breakfast grapefruit? It brings out the fruit's own sweetness in a way that sugar never can.

VELVET, NOT CHIFFON . . . Let's not have lemon pie, let's have lime pie. And none of your chiffon, either. The true lime pie of southern connoisseurs is not puffed up with whipped egg whites, but velvet-smooth and creamy. You may put a meringue on it if you like, and I do like, but some claim this is heresy.

FRESH LIME PIE

> 5 tablespoons cornstarch
> 1¼ cups sugar
> 1½ cups milk
> 4 egg yolks
> ¼ cup lime juice
> 2 teaspoons grated lime rind
> 1 tablespoon butter
> 9-inch baked pie shell

Sift the cornstarch and sugar together and stir into it ½ cup of water. Put the milk in the top of a double boiler and scald it over direct heat. Add the cornstarch mixture, set over boiling water, and stir until it thickens—about 15 minutes. Now pour in the egg yolks beaten to a smooth lemon yellow and add the lime juice, rind, and butter. When all is smooth—about 2 minutes—cool the mixture and pour it into the pie shell. You may make a meringue of the egg whites—flavor it with vanilla and lime rind.

> Time required: 1 hour
> Quantity produced: 4 to 6 servings

Which is not to say I don't value lemons. I like lemon pie. I particularly like lemon ice with crème de menthe spooned over it. I like lemon in my bread pudding and in my rice pudding—the good poor man's pudding. At Christmas time I love the old-fashioned lemon icing on Christmas cakes, so simply made by flavoring confectioner's sugar with lemon rind and moistening it with lemon juice.

What I most prize lemons for is what they contribute to other foods. Lemon rind with its rich, tart oil deserves to be used more often as a flavoring agent, as I've suggested from time to time. You can even use it in piecrust (using half and half water and lemon juice for liquid) to give an apple or berry pie a surprise.

Lemon is useful, too, in cutting the oily taste of fat. The Dutch, for example, lay slices of lemon on pork chops when they braise them. After giving the chops a good browning in a skillet, the lemon slices are laid on top, a dusting of nutmeg is given and a little water added. The meat is covered and basted occasionally with the pan liquid as it cooks. If you cut the cooked lemon slices into the pan gravy and thicken it, the chops have a delicate and unusual flavor with no taste of grease. A duck benefits from being rubbed with a cut lemon before roasting, as does chicken and even steak. As for fish, lemon does more than garnish the platter. A few slices of lemon cooked with green shrimp in court bouillon adds to the savor of these shellfish; lemon juice blended with butter makes a fine spread for broiled fish.

THE BANANA IS A PLEASANT FRUIT   And, as usual, the pleasantest way to eat a just-right banana is the simplest way, in its skin. Only, for the sake of dignity at dessert, let's split the banana lengthwise in its skin, sprinkle it with lime or lemon juice and powdered sugar, and eat it as do the French, with fruit knife and fork. Any banana is at its best served in this manner, whether it be our familiar yellow banana, the rich red one, or the delicate pink miniature called strawberry banana.

Many cooks rely upon banana cake or banana cream pie as favorite ways with this delicate-flavored fruit, but there are other less usual recipes that come as welcome variations upon these themes. When you are baking pie, for example, how about making some extra tarts? Banana tarts are best made in the reverse of the French method, which is to put a spoonful of custard in the tart and top it with fruit glazed with jelly. For banana tarts, spread banana slices in the tart shell, then a dollop of strawberry or raspberry jam, and conceal this fruit layer under a covering of custard, which you may top with whipped cream if you like.

Banana fritters make good eating, especially if you soak the banana quarters in a mixture of rum, sugar, and grated lemon rind before dipping them in the batter. Or make banana bread—any basic cookbook will tell you how—which, when spread with softened cream cheese, gives distinction to teatime.

If you like baked bananas, try different flavor effects. Peel and halve them lengthwise, sprinkle them with lemon juice and coat them with a paste of brown sugar and butter, then pop them into a 400° oven for 8 or 10 minutes. You can even make a fancy dessert of baked bananas, again starting with bananas peeled and halved lengthwise. Roll them in melted butter, brush them with lemon juice, and sprinkle them with shredded coconut. Bake them for 15 to 20 minutes, or until the coconut is slightly browned. For the sweet-toothed, a sauce of thickened crushed pineapple may be served with these banana-coconut rolls, but to my mind it would be gilding the lily of flavor.

FRUIT FROM AN EVERGREEN TREE Avocado Mousse hardly ranks as salad, despite the fact that many people make the mistake of bedding it upon lettuce, which too soon wilts, losing that essential quality of a proper salad, crispness. It ranks rather as a bland and delicate accompaniment of considerable versatility. It requires some thought to provide the tang, the countertaste, to offset its smooth texture and elusive flavor. Make it in a ring, fill it with chicken, smoked tongue, shrimp, or crabmeat marinated in French dressing made with wine vinegar and touched up with a few drops of Worcestershire sauce. Surround the ring with crisp sprays of watercress and tips of French endive. Serve it with thin-cut toasted pumpernickel, and you need nothing but cheese, fruit, and coffee to round out a perfect lunch.

AVOCADO MOUSSE

> ½ tablespoon gelatin
> 2 cups ripe mashed avocado
> ¼ teaspoon onion juice
> ½ cup whipping cream
> ½ cup mayonnaise
> 1 tablespoon lemon juice
> 3 tablespoons minced parsley
> ½ teaspoon salt

Soak the gelatin in ¼ cup cold water, then dissolve in ¾ cup boiling water and set it in the refrigerator to chill. Meanwhile prepare the other ingredients, mashing the avocado, whipping the cream, and blending all to a smooth cream. When the gelatin begins to hold its shape, fold in the avocado mixture. Rinse a mold with cold water and spoon in the mousse. Let it chill until firm.

Time required: 40 minutes
Quantity produced: plenty for 4

This mousse may serve as the background for fruit salad. This time fill the center with watercress and surround the ring with fresh fruits: strawberries, pineapple, orange and grapefruit sections, for choice. This really needs no dressing, but if you wish one, use a French dressing made with lemon instead of vinegar.

A popular fancy is to cut avocados in half and fill them with creamed shellfish, crab, or shrimp, top the oval with buttered corn flakes, and heat to steaming. Or, for something different, you may want to work up an Avocado Dip for potato chips.

AVOCADO DIP

1 large ripe avocado
½ medium cucumber
1 package (3 ounces) cream cheese
1 teaspoon lemon juice
½ teaspoon Worcestershire sauce
6 to 8 drops onion juice
⅓ teaspoon salt

Scoop out the avocado meat; peel the cucumber and dice it very fine indeed. Mix all ingredients together.

Time required: 15 minutes
Quantity produced: about 1 pint.

Purists, however, have the best of it: avocados plain, split in half, dusted with salt and sprinkled with the juice of lime, and scooped out with a spoon. The cardinal sin with avocado is to serve it with mayonnaise.

SUMMER CAMP FOLLOWERS The brilliant parade of winter fruits has some camp followers: the strawberries we froze last June, the peaches we canned in August, all the stores of our freezers and shelves. They can't be left out of consideration of the pleasures of good eating in winter. They shouldn't be treated as nostalgic re-

minders of the delights of summer eating. Strawberry shortcake
in January? Perfectly feasible in our mechanical age, but how much
sounder gastronomically to let June have its shortcake and give
January Strawberries Romanoff. Let August keep its peaches and
cream, we'll have peaches and brandy topped with sour cream.
Blueberry pie? Any time of year, to be sure, but why not a cobbler
or a roly-poly? It's good sense palate-wise to take the rhythm of the
seasons into account as we plan our good eating. The rich, the
hearty, the festive belong to energetic winter months. So let's top
off January with a festival of strawberries, and the calories be
damned.

STRAWBERRIES ROMANOFF

> 1 quart strawberries (2 packages frozen whole)
> ¼ cup powdered sugar
> ½ pint vanilla ice cream
> ⅓ cup whipping cream
> 3 tablespoons lemon juice
> 1 tablespoon Bacardi rum
> 2 tablespoons Cointreau

The strawberries, if fresh, should be washed, hulled, sugared with
¼ cup of confectioner's sugar, then chilled. Have the ice cream soft
enough to stir but not melting. Work fast with cold bowls. Whip
the cream stiff, then fold it into the lightly whipped ice cream.
Sprinkle on this the lemon juice, rum, and liqueur, and when
well blended in, spoon the confection upon the sugared berries.

> Time required: 20 minutes
> Quantity produced: 4 servings

I CAN DREAM, CAN'T I? Another gardening year is ahead;
it's time for New Year's resolutions. What are yours? I have several
I make—and break—annually: to keep the garden log up to date
(this year I really will) . . . to have the lawn mower sharpened in
March, ready for April (that, too, I will) . . . to jot down recipes
on index cards instead of scraps of paper . . . never to put a
tomato in tossed salad (that's a resolution I do keep) . . . to try
something new (that's how I found out about Vichyssoise and how

easy it is to grow leeks; this year I'm going to try that new Matchless lettuce) . . . to experiment with combinations. Brown sugar in the rhubarb sauce, would that be any good? Is a sprig of marjoram cut up on a slice of tomato as good as my friend Win says it is?

. . . To wait until the soil is workable before planting seed—how self-defeating but how tempting to try to rush the season! . . . to go easy on herbs in vegetables and not mix too many kinds in a salad . . . to quit work in the garden earlier and take more time to enjoy it . . . not to cook something fancy when it's better plain: that's an easy resolution for the gardening cook to keep—who wants herbs in the succotash or sour cream on the first strawberries?

They'll be coming along before too long now, the strawberries; the crowns look thrifty under the mulch of straw and snow. New Year's resolutions may be broken, but there's no break in the satisfactions to be derived from cooking by the garden calendar. February will be a good month to adventure with soups.

IF YOU REALLY WANT TO KNOW. . . .

These books and pamphlets are suggested for the further edification of gardening cooks, to round out with specific and authoritative information ideas suggested in the body of this book. The list is purposely short and represents only a small sampling of what I myself have found helpful in my years with trowel and ladle. It is my hope that mention of these will lead gardening cooks to explore further the fascinating and provocative lore about the arts of gardening and cookery.

BOOKS

Grow Your Own Vegetables—Paul W. Dempsey, *Houghton Mifflin*
The Food Garden—Edna Blair, *Macmillan*
Fruits for the Home Garden—U. P. Hedrick, *Oxford University Press*
Herbs, Their Culture and Uses—Rosetta E. Clarkson, *Macmillan*
The Home Garden Book of Herbs and Spices—Milo Miloradovich, *Doubleday*
Herbs for the Kitchen—Irma Goodrich Mazza, *Little, Brown & Co.*
Pickling and Preserving—Flora Harris, *Abelard Press*, New York
Canning, Preserving and Jelly Making—Janet McKenzie Hill (revised by Sally Larkin), *Little, Brown & Co.*
Making the Most of Your Home Freezer—Marie Armstrong Essipoff, *Rinehart*
Your Home Freezer—Ann Seranne, *Doubleday*
Mary Meade's Magic Recipes for the Electric Blender—Ruth Ellen Church, *Bobbs-Merrill*

PAMPHLETS

Vegetable Garden Guide, *Better Homes & Gardens*, 1943
Growing Vegetables in Town and City, *U. S. Department of Agriculture, Home and Garden Bulletin No. 7*, April 1951
Growing Fruit for the Home, *Cornell Extension Bulletin 421*, February 1953
How to Grow Bush Fruits in the Home Garden, *Ohio State University Agricultural Extension Bulletin 323*, July 1951
Home Storage of Vegetables and Fruits, *Cornell Extension Bulletin 846*, October 1951
The Home Freezing of Farm Products, *Cornell Extension Bulletin 611*, revised August 1953
Home Freezing of Fruits and Vegetables, *U. S. Department of Agriculture, Home and Garden Bulletin No. 10*, July 1951
Blue Book, Home Canning and Freezing Recipes and Methods, *Ball Brothers Co.*, Muncie, Ind.
Marmalades, Preserves, Conserves and Butters, *Cornell Extension Bulletin 824*, June 1951

INDEX

NOTE: *Capital letters indicate formally presented recipes.*

acorn squash, 126
  baked whole, 188
almonds, 69, 214, 226
anise, 56, 89, 96
  substitute for, 47
appetizers (see also canapés; hors
  d'oeuvres): broiled grapefruit,
  242
  cranberry cup, 230
  fruits, 162
  herb-tomato cocktail, 154
  honeydew with ham, 162
  persimmon, 211
  pineapple wedges, 240
  raspberry cup, 118
apple: Chutney, 208
  Crunch, 207
  juice, 118, 165, 166, 232
  Pie, Sweet Potato and, 187
  sauce, 89, 181, 186, 208
apples, 120, 186-88, 192, 205-9, 228
  baking, 205-6
  growing, 158, 205
  in jellies, 199, 201-3
  in Maple Caramel, 206
  varieties of, 205-6
Apricot-Filled Cupcakes, 226
apricots, 161, 165, 225-26
  purée of, 226
artichokes, 48, 49-51
  Stuffed Italian, 50
asparagus, 77-81
  En Casserole, 80
  Loaf, 80
avocado, 19, 33, 234, 244-45
  Dip, 245
  Mousse, 244
  Soup, Cream of, 19

Baked: Limas, Country, 222
  Peaches, Brandywine, 68
  Potatoes with Herbs, Stuffed, 185
  Quince, 204
bananas, 162, 234, 237, 243-44

basil, 12, 17, 33, 56, 84-91, 95, 101,
  126, 154
  in Belgian Tomatoes, 85
  culture, 12, 82-84, 95, 198
  in herb butter, 86
  Jelly, 86
bay leaf, 89
Beach Plum Jelly, 169
Bean: and Lamb Stew, 43
  Soup, Black, 30
  salad, string, 129
beans, 20, 36-37, 40-43, 87, 96, 99,
  128-31, 170, 197, 221-23. See
  also green beans
  Bengal, 222
  black, 28-29
  Black Bean Soup, 30, 33
  Country-Baked Lima, 222
  cranberry, 147, 150, 221
  kidney, 16, 223
  lima, 99, 147, 222
  waterless cooking of, 99
beet greens, 37, 38, 57, 64-65, 109
beets, 20-22, 36-40, 59, 149, 192-93
  culture of, 37, 59
  in Orange Sauce, 38
  Polish, 37
  wintering, 192-93
Belgian Tomatoes, 85
black beans, 28-29
  Soup, 30, 33
blackberries, 121, 123-24, 163
blender, electric, 18, 28, 166, 208
blueberries, 115, 118-21
Blueberry: Jam, 118
  Pancakes, Seward's, 119
  Pudding, 120
borage, 90, 96
Bortsch: Polish, 20-21
  Russian, 20-22
Brandied Cherries, 124
Brandywine Baked Peaches, 68, 159
broccoli, 45, 126-28, 141, 156
  sauces for, 127

broccoli—(Cont'd)
  Soup, Iced, 127
  waterless cooking of, 99
brussels sprouts, 147, 149
burnet, 90, 96

cabbage, 59, 89, 127, 179–82, 191,
    192–93, 196
  Chinese (celery), 54, 58–59, 192
  Pickled, Mrs. Abrams', 196
  red, 59, 178–91
  Red, De Luxe, 178
  Red, with Chestnuts, 179
  slaw, 59, 179, 181
  wintering over, 191, 192–93
Caesar Salad, Romaine, 20, 59–60
Cake, White Fruit, 227
California Green Beans, 41–42
canapés (see also appetizers; hors
    d'oeuvres): Avocado Dip, 245
  chive balls, 86
  herb butter, 86
  orégano spread, 89
  parsley strips, 86
cantaloupe, 162–63
caraway, 13, 89, 127, 178
  sauce with sour cream, 127
carrots, 43–45, 59, 87, 103–7, 129,
    191–93
  in chunks, glazed, 44
  Dill-Spiced, 106, 107
  Flemish, 103, 104
  wintering, 191–93
casserole dishes
  Asparagus en, 80
  Beans Bengal, 222
  California Green Beans, 41–42
  Cauliflower, 141
  Corn-Tomato, 151
  Country-Baked Limas, 222
  Eggplant, 138
  Finocchio au Gratin, 47
  Greek Lamb and Bean Stew, 43
  Hemel en Aarde, 186
  Indian Corn Stew, 153
  Lamb and Lentil Stew, 224
  Poulet aux Lauriers, 148
casseroles, ideas for, 39, 42, 44, 79,

    108, 139, 140, 146, 177, 184,
    225
cauliflower, 26, 99, 129, 133, 140–41
  Casserole, 141
  Soup, Danish, 26
  waterless cooking of, 99
celeriac, 142–43
  in Ragoût aux Céleris, 143
  remoulade, 142
celery, 17, 18, 41–42, 105, 170, 192,
    197
  and Herb Soup, 17–18
chard, 57, 110
Charlotte's Maple Mousse, 67, 69
Cheese and Eggs, Green Pepper, 145
cherries, 122, 124–25, 161, 237
  Brandied, 124
cherry: bounce, 124–25
  salad, black, 125
Cherry Tomato Pickles, 194–95
chervil, 56, 87, 96, 126, 198, 221
  growing, 82, 198
Chestnut Stuffing, Grandmother's,
    214–15
chestnuts, 149, 170, 179, 214, 215,
    216–17
  Red Cabbage with, 179
  in Suppa di Castagne, 216
Chicken Pot, Hungarian, 23
Chicken with Herbs, Skillet, 93
Chinese cabbage, 54, 58–59, 192
chive: balls, 86
  butter, 86–87
chives, 53–56, 81, 82–87, 90, 95, 198
  growing, 14–15, 81, 82–86, 95, 198
  in salad, 53–56, 86, 87, 90
Chowder, Fish, 31–32
Chutney: Apple, 208
  Gooseberry, 123
  Plum, 167
Cobbler, Rhubarb, 74
coconut, 46, 238–39
  in Cuban Pineapple, 239
  grating, 238
  milk, 239
cole slaw, 59, 179, 181
collards, 57, 182
Conserve, Quince, 203
corn, 40, 129, 147, 149–53

corn—(Cont'd)
  Curry Soup, 28–29
  Custards with Fried Tomatoes, 152
  fried, 150
  fritters, 129, 150
  roasting ears, 150
  succotash, 40, 147, 150, 152
  Tomato Casserole, 151
  Stew, Indian, 153
corn beef hash, 193
corn salad (fetticus), 57, 58
Country-Baked Limas, 222
cranberries, 202, 229–32
cranberry: beans, 147, 150, 221
  juice, 165, 230
  pie, 229
  Punch, Spiced, 231–32
  sauce, 230–32
Cream Soup, Avocado, 19
Crème Vichyssoise, 14
cress (peppergrass, roquette), 63
Crunch, Apple, 207
Cuban Pineapple, 239
Cucumber Soup, Iced, 136
cucumbers, 83, 133–36, 194–95
  growing, 83, 136
  in pickles, 194–95
  Sautéed, 135
  Sour Cream, 134
Cupcakes, Apricot-Filled, 226
currant: jelly, 117
  juice, 118, 165
currants, 121–22

dandelion greens, 57, 63–65
  New England, 63, 64
  wine, 66–67
Danish Cauliflower Soup, 26
Deep-Dish Rhubarb and Strawberry
  Pie, 75, 77
desserts
  Apple Crunch, 207
  Apples in Maple Caramel, 206
  Apricot-Filled Cupcakes, 226
  Baked Quince, 204
  Blueberry Pudding, 120
  Brandywine Baked Peaches, 68
  Charlotte's Maple Mousse, 67
  Cuban Pineapple, 239

desserts—(Cont'd)
  Deep-Dish Rhubarb and Strawberry Pie, 75
  Flaming Oranges, 236
  Fresh Lime Pie, 242
  Gooseberry Fool, 122
  Grapefruit Suprême, 240
  Honeycream Strawberries, 111
  Lynd Werntz's Greek Oranges, 235
  Mrs. Paxton's Pecan Pie, 213
  Norwegian Rødgrøt, 117
  Orange Mousse, 234
  Peach Fritters, 160
  Pears Glazed in Wine, 210
  Rhubarb Cobbler, 74
  Rhubarb Jelly, 74
  Rhubarb Sherbet, 73
  Scotch Fruit Squares, 228
  Strawberries Romanoff, 247
  Stuffed Pineapple, 237
  Sweet Potato and Apple Pie, 187
  White Fruit Cake, 227
  White Grape Dessert, 164
dill, 40, 56, 85, 87–89, 96, 107, 185, 198
  growing, 82, 96, 198
  -Spiced Carrots, 107
dressings, salad, 55–56, 126, 135, 142

Eau de Melon, 166
eggplant, 45, 126, 129, 137–40
  baked, 137
  Casserole, 138
  freezing, 140
  Stuffed, 139
  and tomatoes, 139
elderberries, 115
elderblossom fritters, 115

fennel (finocchio), 46–48, 56, 96
fetticus (corn salad), 57, 58
fiddleheads, 63
figs, 77, 182, 184
Finocchio au Gratin, 47
Fish: Chowder, 31–32
  Fillets with Herbs, 91, 92
Flaming Oranges, 236
Flemish Carrots, 103, 104

freezing: casseroles, 225
fruit, 76, 77, 116
juices, in ice cubes, 156, 165
vegetables, 15, 38, 104, 140, 156
French Onion Soup, 25
Fresh Lime Pie, 242
Frijoles, 223
Frittata, Italian, 108–9
fritters: elderblossom, 115
Peach, 160
fruit (see also fruits), 62, 76, 77,
116, 118, 125, 158–59, 162,
164–65, 166, 188–89, 211, 230–
32, 237–38, 242, 245–46
cake, 227–28
Cake, White, 227
drinks, 76, 118, 125, 165–67, 230–
32
freezing, 76–77, 116, 156, 165
honey with, 158–59, 164–65, 166,
237, 241
liqueurs with, 158–59, 162, 188–
89, 211, 225, 228, 237–38, 241
salad, 162, 212, 244–45
Squares, Scotch, 228
fruits (see also fruit, and under names
of fruits), 75, 76–77, 110–25,
156–69, 185–86, 199–212, 225–
32, 234–38
combinations of, 75, 118, 122–23,
162–64, 201–3, 211, 225, 228,
237–38, 244–45
freezing of, 76–77, 116, 156, 165
for the garden, 113, 115–16, 121,
157–58, 204–5
preserved (see also by name), 118,
122, 123, 167–69, 199–204
in tutti-frutti, 112

garden: crops, winter care, 81, 177,
191–93, 198, 217
fruits for the, 113, 115–16, 121,
157–58, 204–5
greens to try, 57–59, 62–63
herb, the (see also herbs), 59, 81–
84, 90, 221
information, 34–35, 248
jigsaw puzzle, 83–84
planning, 33–35, 37, 45–46

garden—(Cont'd)
salad, the, 57–59, 81–84
Soup, 155
thinnings, 38, 82–83, 109
vegetables to try, 15, 45–46, 103,
146, 170, 182, 191–92
gardening aids, 72, 113, 219–21
gardening ideas: fruits, 113, 115, 116,
157–58
herbs, 15, 62, 71–72, 87, 89, 109
vegetable, 77, 83–84, 97–98
vegetables, 110, 130, 146
garlic, 17, 45, 53–56, 109, 156, 184
Minced Kale with, 184
to retrieve, 109
geraniums, 90, 96
gooseberries, 121–24
Spiced, 123
Gooseberry: Chutney, 123
Fool, 122
Grandmother's Chestnut Stuffing,
214–15
grape (see also grapes)
Butter, Spiced, 194
Dessert, White, 164
juice, 165–66
grapefruit, 113, 165, 240–41
Suprême, 240–41
grapes (see also grape), 158, 162,
164–66, 178, 237
Greek: Lamb and Bean Stew, 43
Oranges, Lynd Werntz's, 235
Green: onions (scallions), 44, 83, 98
Pepper, Cheese and Eggs, 145
peppers, 57, 83, 137, 143–47, 197
tomatoes, fried, 193
green beans (snap, string), 37, 40–43,
126–31
California, 41–42
in casserole, 42
dressings for, 40, 127–29, 170
with herbs, 40, 82, 87, 88
à la Niçoise, 130
Poulette, 131
slicing of, 128–29
with Sour Cream Sauce, 41
greens, 37, 38, 53–55, 57–59, 63–67,
109–10, 182–84
beet, 37, 38, 57, 64–65, 109

greens—(Cont'd)
  dandelion, 57, 63–67
  drying, 54
  in Gumbo Z'Herbes, 65
  salad, varieties, 53–56, 57–59
  washing, 64, 110
  wild, varieties, 63–65
  wilted, 64–65
Gumbo Z'Herbes, 65

Hemel en Aarde, 186
herb (see also herbs, and under names
  of herbs)
  butter, 86–87
  and Celery Soup, 18
  culture, 81–84, 87, 93–96, 198
  garden, the, 59, 81–84, 90
  information, 34, 94, 248
  Omelet, 91
  tasting, 82, 88–89
herbs (see also herb, and under name
  of herbs)
  as annuals, 81–84
  the Big Five, 83–87, 95
  the Big Ten, 83–89, 95–96
  Fish Fillets with, 92
  in fruit drinks, 89–90
  in meat, fish, egg dishes, 47, 84,
    85, 87–94
  in salads, 56–57, 84, 88, 106–7,
    126, 134, 142
  Skillet Chicken with, 93
  in soups, 13, 32–33, 84, 85, 87–89,
    154–55
  storing, 94, 221
  Stuffed Baked Potato with, 185
  in sweets, 47, 89, 90
  in vegetables, 40, 84–85, 87–89, 99–
    101, 106–7, 126, 129, 134
honey with fruits, 158–59, 164–66,
  237, 242
Honeycream Strawberries, 111
honeydew: melon, 146, 162–63, 166
  Surprise, 163
hors d'oeuvres (see also appetizers;
  canapés): beets, 38
  cauliflower, raw, 141
  celeriac, 142
  cherry tomatoes, raw, 193

hors d'oeuvres—(Cont'd)
  Chinese cabbage, raw, 59
  fennel, raw, 47
  fetticus, raw, 58–59
  kohlrabi, raw, 175
  leeks, 15
  mushrooms, raw, stuffed, 173
  Mushrooms, Stuffed, 171
  radishes, 98
  relish bowl, 133
  turnips, raw, 175
  watercress, 62
Hot Potato Soup, 13
Hungarian Chicken Pot, 23

Iced: Broccoli Soup, 127
  Cream of Cucumber Soup, 136
Indian Corn Stew, 153
Italian: Frittata, 108–9
  Stuffed Artichokes, 50

jam: blackberry, 121
  Blueberry, 118
  four fruit, 122
  Quince Honey, 200
jelly: Basil, 86
  Beach Plum, 169
  ideas for, 115, 118, 122
  paradise, 202
  quince in, 199–203
  Rhubarb, 74
juices (see by names), freezing, 156,
  165
Julia's Stuffed Eggplant, 139

kale, 109, 182–84, 192
  Minced with Garlic Dressing, 184
  Pot Pourri of, 183
kidney beans: in Frijoles, 223
  in Minestra, 16
kitchen aids, 18, 28, 108, 166, 200,
  202, 208
  blender, 18, 28, 166, 208
  scales, 202
  spinach cutter, 108
  thermometer, 202
  vegetable scraper, 200
kitchen-window greenhouse, 198
kohlrabi, 176, 177

Lamb: and Bean Stew, Greek, 42–43
  and Lentil Stew, 224
leeks, 11, 13–16, 83, 156, 192
  as appetizer, 15
  freezing, 15, 156
  growing, 11, 15, 83, 192
lemon, 55–56, 201, 242–43
  juice in pie crust, 243
  juice in salad, 55–56
  with pork chops, 243
lemonade, 118, 156, 165
Lentil: and Lamb Stew, 224
  Soup, 27
lentils, 20, 224–25
lettuce, 39, 53–59, 83, 99–100, 248
  drying, 54
  growing, 59, 83
  lamb's, 57, 63, 65
  in tossed salad, 53–56
  varieties of, 54, 58–59
  in waterless cooking, 39, 99–100
lima beans, 99, 147, 222
  in Beans Bengal, 222
  cooking unshelled, 147
  in Country-Baked Limas, 222
lime, 33, 162, 241–42
  Pie, Fresh, 242
liqueurs with fruit, 158–59, 162, 188–
    89, 211, 228, 237–38, 241, 242
Loaf, Asparagus, 80
Lynd Werntz's Greek Oranges, 235

maple sugar, 69–70
maple syrup, 67–70, 159, 206
  in Baked Peaches, 68
  in Caramel, Apples in, 206
  keeping, 70
  in Mousse, Charlotte's, 67, 69
  in Sugar-on-Snow, 69
marjoram, 13, 17, 33, 40, 56, 82–84,
    87–89, 95, 170, 198
  growing, 81, 82, 95, 198
  in herb butter, 87
  in salad, 56, 84
  in soup, 13, 17, 33, 84
  in vegetables, 40, 84, 88, 89, 170
meat dishes
  corn beef hash, 193

meat dishes—(Cont'd)
  Greek Lamb and Bean Stew, 43
  Indian Corn Stew, 153
  Julia's Stuffed Eggplant, 139
  Lamb and Lentil Stew, 224
  meat and vegetable salad, 148–49
  Ragoût aux Céleris, 143
  Sarma, 181
melon, 161–64, 166
  cantaloupe, 162, 163
  Eau de, 166
  honeydew, 146, 162–63, 166
  selection, 161
  varieties of, 161
  watermelon, 162–63
menu suggestions, 19, 20, 27, 43, 60,
    69, 80, 92, 101, 104, 106, 125,
    137, 138, 144, 145, 149, 151,
    154, 155, 164, 175–76, 179,
    183, 186, 193, 209, 222
milkweed shoots, 63
Minced Kale with Garlic Dressing,
    184
Minestra, 16
mint, 89, 96, 166, 198
Miz D's Mustard Mix, 195
Mont St. Michel Omelet, 91
Mousse: Avocado, 244
  Charlotte's Maple, 67
  Orange, 234
Mrs. Abrams' Pickled Cabbage, 196
Mrs. Paxton's Pecan Pie, 61–62
mushrooms, 42, 58, 100–1, 106, 169–
    73, 189
  Preserved, 172–73
  raw, 173
  Stuffed, 170, 171
mustard: butter sauce, 180
  greens, 63
  Pickles, Miz D's, 195

nasturtiums, 90, 96
nectarines, 161
New England Black Bean Soup, 30,
    33
New England Dandelion Greens, 64
Norwegian Rödgröt, 117
nuts (see also by names), 212–17

okra, 46, 140, 145, 152
Omelet Mont St. Michel, 91
onions, 12–14, 26, 42, 44, 83, 98,
    156, 184, 188–91, 196
    green (scallions), 44, 83, 98
    quick pickled, 196
    varieties, 26
    winter care, 191–92
Onion Soup, French, 25
orange juice in drinks, 165
orange sauce, 38, 111, 211
oranges, 234–37
    Flaming, 236
    Greek, 235
orchard, back yard, 115, 157–58
orégano, 89, 146
    canapé, 89

Pancakes, Seward's Blueberry, 119
paradise jelly, 202
parsley, 81, 82–83, 86, 90, 95, 105,
    148, 198
    canapés, 86
    growing, 82–83, 198
parsnips, 177, 191
Peapod Soup, 101–2
peach: desserts, 68, 158–62
    drinks, 166
    Fritters, 160
    trees, 157–58
peaches, 68, 157–61, 246
    Brandywine Baked, 68, 159
    broiled, 159
    with liqueurs, 158
pears, 158, 203, 209–11
    baked, 210
    Glazed in Wine, 210
    with liqueurs, 211
    in orange syrup, 211
peas, 98–103, 126, 170, 189
    All' Italiano, 100
    Continental, 101
    sugar, 103
    waterless cooking of, 99
Pecan: Balls, 212
    Pie, 213
pecans, 127, 188, 212–14
    and Walnuts, Spiced, 214
pepper, green, 83, 143–46

pepper, green—(Cont'd)
    Cheese and Eggs, 145
    Sauté, 144
peppergrass (cress, roquette), 63
peppers, 46, 83, 143–46
persimmons, 211–12
pickled: beets, 40
    Cabbage, Mrs. Abrams', 196
    onions, quick, 196
pickles: Cherry Tomato, 193–94
    Mustard, 195
    tail end of the garden, 197
pies: Cranberry, 229
    Fresh Lime, 242
    Fruit Squares, 228
    Pecan, 213
    pumpkin, 188
    Deep-Dish Rhubarb and Straw-
        berry, 75
    Sweet Potato and Apple, 187
pineapple, 72, 75, 165, 203, 231,
    237–40, 244
    Cuban, 239
    Stuffed, 237
    wedges, 240
Piselli All' Italiano, 100
planning, garden—see garden
Plum Chutney, 167
plums, 161, 167, 169
Polish: Beets, 37
    Bortsch, 20–22
potato: balls, sweet, 187
    Pie, Sweet Potato and Apple, 187
    Soup, Hot, 13
potatoes, 12–14, 31, 87, 184–85, 191,
    192
    Baked with Herbs, Stuffed, 87, 185
    scalloped, 184–85
    sweet, 186–88, 191, 192
Pot Pourri of Kale, 183
Poulet aux Lauriers, 148
Preserved Mushrooms, 172–73
prunes, 225
Pudding, Blueberry, 120
puffballs, 173
pumpkin: 188–89
    Purée, 189
Punch: Cranberry, Spiced, 231
    Rhubarb, 76

punchettes, 165–67
Purée: Pumpkin, 189
　Turnip, 176

quince, 199–205
　Baked, 204
　Conserve, 203
　Honey, 200

radishes, 57, 83, 98, 109, 198
Ragoût aux Céleris, 143
raisins, 75, 122, 227–28
raspberries, 73, 75, 116–18, 122, 156,
　　165
　freezing, 116, 156
　Norwegian Rödgröt, 117
red cabbage, 178–80
　with Chestnuts, 179
　De Luxe, 178
rhubarb, 71–77
　Cobbler, 74
　Jelly, 74
　Punch, 76
　Sherbet, 73
　and Strawberry Pie, 75
Rice Ring, Savory, 105–6
Rödgröt, Norwegian, 117
Romaine Salad, Caesar, 60
roquette (cress, peppergrass), 63, 65
rosemary, 40, 56, 82, 87–88, 96
Rumanian Stuffed Mushrooms, 170,
　　171
Russian Bortsch, 22
rutabagas, 175–76

sage, 89, 96
salad: dressings, 55–56, 126, 135, 142
　garden, the, 57–59, 81–84
　greens, varieties, 53–55, 57–59, 65
　herbs in, 56–57, 84, 88, 106–7,
　　126, 134, 142
　ingredients for, 26, 58, 62, 105,
　　109, 126, 129, 134, 135, 179,
　　228
　making, 52–58
　NATIS, 58
　tossed green, 54–58
salads: Avocado Mousse, 244
　Belgian Tomatoes, 154

salads—(Cont'd)
　black cherry, 125
　Caesar, 59–60
　celery remoulade, 142
　cole slaw, 179, 181
　cucumber, 135
　fruit, 162, 212, 245
　meat and vegetable, 148–49
　persimmon, 212
　Sour Cream Cucumbers, 134
　string bean, 129
　tomato aspic, 154
salsify, 191
Sarma, 181
sauces: Brandied Cherries, 124
　canapé, 142, 245
　mustard butter, 180
　preserved mushrooms for, 172
　raspberry rum, 116
　sour cream, 127, 134
　strawberry-orange glaze, 111
　for vegetables, 38, 127, 129, 135,
　　142, 180
sauerkraut, 89, 181, 189
Sautéed Cucumbers, 135
Savory Rice Ring, 105–6
savory (summer), 56, 81, 87–89, 96
scallions, 44, 83, 98
Scotch Fruit Squares, 228
shallots, 26
shell beans, 28–29, 130, 221, 222
Sherbet, Rhubarb, 73
Skillet Chicken with Herbs, 93
snap beans. See green beans
sorrel, 13, 57, 63
soup, 11–33, 46, 126, 142, 154, 221
　canned, tricks with, 32–33
　herbs in, 13, 32–33, 84, 85, 87–89,
　　154–55
soups: Avocado Cream, 19
　Corn-Curry, 29
　Crème Vichyssoise, 14
　Danish Cauliflower, 26
　Fish Chowder, 31
　French Onion, 25
　Garden, 155
　Gumbo Z'Herbes, 65
　Herb and Celery, 18
　Hot Potato, 13

soups—(Cont'd)
  Hungarian Chicken Pot, 23
  Iced Broccoli, 127
  Iced Cream of Cucumber, 136
  Lentil, 27
  Minestra, 16
  New England Black Bean, 30
  Peapod, 102
  Polish Bortsch, 20
  Russian Bortsch, 22
  Suppa di Castagne, 216
  Watercress, 61
sour cream: Green Beans with, 41
  with caraway, 127
  Cucumbers, 134
  with fruits, 110, 111, 164
  with soups, 21, 22, 155
  with vegetables, 37, 38, 41, 107, 127, 134
Spiced: Carrots, Dill-, 106-7
  Cranberry Punch, 231-32
  Gooseberries, 123
  Grape Butter, 194
  Pecans and Walnuts, 214
  strawberry jam, 112
spinach, 82-83, 109-10
  in Italian Frittata, 108-9
squash, 126, 146, 188, 191
  acorn, 126, 188
Stew: Greek Lamb and Bean, 43
  Indian Corn, 153
  Lamb and Lentil, 224
strawberries, 73, 110-13, 163, 237, 246
  growing, 112-13
  Honeycream, 111
  with liqueurs, 237
  with other fruits, 73, 112, 163
  Romanoff, 246
strawberry: jam, 111-12
  and Rhubarb Pie, 75
string beans in salad, 129. See also green beans
Stuffed: Artichokes, 50
  Eggplant, 139
  Mushrooms, Rumanian, 171
  Pineapple, 237
  Potatoes with Herbs, 185

Stuffing, Grandmother's Chestnut, 215
succotash, 40, 147, 152
Sugar-on-Snow, 69
Suppa di Castagne, 216
Sweet Pepper Sauté, 144
Sweet Potato and Apple Pie, 187
sweet potatoes, 186-88, 191, 192

tail end of the garden pickles, 197
tarragon, 33, 39-40, 56, 79, 82, 88, 90, 96, 126, 134, 142
thinnings, garden, 38, 82-83, 109
thyme, 56, 81-83, 87, 88, 95
  in herb butter, 87
tomato: aspic, 154
  Corn Casserole, 151
  juice, 152-53, 156
  NATIS, 58
  Pickle, Cherry, 194-95
  rarebit, quick, 154
  soup, 17, 33, 155
tomatoes, 58, 62, 83, 85, 139, 152-56, 193
  baked, 85, 152
  Belgian, 85
  broiled, 85
  Corn Custards and Fried, 152
  and eggplant, 139
  in Garden Soup, 155
  green, fried, 193
  NATIS, 58
  in salad, 58, 62
tossed salad, 54-58
Turnip Purée, 176
turnips, 57, 64-65, 109, 174-76, 191-93
tutti-frutti, 112

vegetable dishes
  Asparagus en Casserole, 80
  Asparagus Loaf, 80
  Beans Bengal, 222
  Beets in Orange Sauce, 38
  California Green Beans, 41
  Cauliflower Casserole, 141
  Corn Custards with Fried Tomatoes, 152
  Corn-Tomato Casserole, 151

vegetable dishes—(Cont'd)
Country-Baked Limas, 222
Dill-Spiced Carrots, 107
Eggplant Casserole, 138
Finocchio au Gratin, 47
Flemish Carrots, 104
Frijoles, 223
Green Beans à la Niçoise, 130
Green Beans Poulette, 131
Green Beans with Sour Cream
    Sauce, 41
Hemel en Aarde, 186
Julia's Stuffed Eggplant, 138
Minced Kale with Garlic Dressing,
    184
New England Dandelion Greens,
    64
Peas Continental, 101
Piselli All' Italiano, 100
Polish Beets, 37
Pot Pourri of Kale, 183
Pumpkin Purée, 184
Red Cabbage de Luxe, 178
Red Cabbage with Chestnuts, 179
Sautéed Cucumbers, 139
Savory Rice Ring, 105
Stuffed Baked Potatoes with Herbs,
    185
Stuffed Italian Artichokes, 50
Sweet Pepper Sauté, 144
Turnip Purée, 176
vegetable gardening, 77, 83–84, 97–
    98
    ideas, 110, 130, 146

vegetable and meat salad, 148–49
vegetables (see also vegetable dishes,
    and names of vegetables): freez-
    ing, 15, 38, 104, 140, 146, 156,
    173
    herbs in, 40, 84–85, 87–89, 154–
    55
    sauces for, 38, 127, 129, 135, 142,
    180
    to try, 15, 45–46, 103, 146, 170,
    180, 191–92
    waterless cooking of, 39, 99
    winter care of, 81, 177, 191–93,
    198, 217
Vichyssoise, Crème, 14

walnuts, 186–88
    Spiced Pecans and, 214
watercress, 53, 57, 61–63
    Soup, 61
waterless cooking of vegetables, 39,
    99
watermelon: boat, 162–63
    spiked with champagne, 162
White: Fruit Cake, 227
    Grape Dessert, 164
window greenhouse, kitchen, 198
wine: dandelion, 66–67
    Pears Glazed in, 210
winter care of crops, 81, 177, 191–93,
    198, 217

zucchini, 17, 45, 99, 146
zwetschenkuchen, 161